Blairsville Junior High School

Blairsville, Pennsylvania

920
S

Sullivañ, George 5520 Sul

Pro football's
all-time greats

DATE			
DEC 23	MAR 2 6		
FEB 1 0	OCT 1 74		
FEB 2 8			
MAR 1 4			
MAY 8 1	OCT 31 84		
Oct. 4			
NOV 2 2			
DEC 6			
DEC 1 9			
JAN 2			
JAN 23			
APR 6			

920
Sul

5520
Sul

Blairsville Junior High School

Blairsville, Pennsylvania

√

PRO FOOTBALL'S ALL-TIME GREATS

PRO FOOTBALL'S ALL-TIME GREATS

THE IMMORTALS IN PRO FOOTBALL'S
HALL OF FAME

by George Sullivan

G. P. PUTNAM'S SONS
NEW YORK

Acknowledgments

I am very grateful to the countless people who helped to make this book possible—to the Hall of Fame members themselves, and to various league and team officials. Special thanks are due Don Weiss, Public Relations Director, National Football League, and Peter Hadhazy of the NFL office; Earl Schreiber, President, Hall of Fame Board of Trustees, and Jim Lucas, Acting Director.

I am also grateful for the opportunity to consult the following source material: the files of *Sport* magazine and *Sports Illustrated; The Chicago Bears* by Howard Roberts (Putnam); *The Green Bay Packers* by Arch Ward (Putnam); *Return to Glory, The Story of the Cleveland Browns* by Bill Levy (World); *Always on Sunday* by Bobby Layne with Bob Drum (Prentice-Hall); *Great Teams of Pro Football* by Robert Smith (Dell); *Pro Football's Hall of Fame* by Arthur Daley (Quadrangle); *The Story of Pro Football* by Howard Roberts (Rand McNally); *Pro Football: The History of the Game and the Great Players* by Robert Smith (Doubleday); *The Giants of New York* by Barry Gottehrer (Putnam); *Footsteps of a Giant* by Emlen Tunnell with William Gleason (Doubleday); *The Official Encyclopedia of Football* edited by Roger Treat (A. S. Barnes).

G. S.

Foreword

What the Pro Football Hall of Fame is today—and what it will be tomorrow—is a tribute to many people but especially to Richard Paul McCann.

Dick McCann left his job as general manager of the Washington Redskins in 1962 to become the director of the Hall of Fame at a time when it was little more than a hole in the ground. He set up an office consisting of two small rooms in the Onesto Hotel in Canton and began the job of sorting out the memorabilia of the fastest growing game in American sports.

He called it "going from the Redskins to Jim Thorpe," but it was more than that. It was going from an organization that represented a part of professional football's history and tradition to an institution that today and tomorrow represents it all.

When he died suddenly in November, 1967, the Hall of Fame building that is located on the hillside in the park in Canton had been host to more than 250,000 visitors.

Each summer the annual renewal of "Football's Greatest Weekend" is attended by upward of 50,000 persons for the enshrinement of new Hall of Fame members and the playing of the annual Hall of Fame preseason game.

As this is being written, the museum houses some 18,000 artifacts of all kinds, including helmets, shoes, books, programs, films, sound tapes, and other mementos.

From creation on April 27, 1961, through groundbreaking on August 11, 1962, from dedication on September 7, 1963, to the present, the Hall of Fame has been the result of the hard work of many.

But most of all Dick McCann.

PETE ROZELLE
Commissioner

Members of Pro Football's Hall of Fame
(in alphabetical order)

236 Elroy (Crazylegs) Hirsch
55 Robert (Cal) Hubbard
58 Don Hutson
171 Walt Kiesling
66 Earl (Curly) Lambeau
202 Bobby Layne
142 Sid Luckman
113 Roy (Link) Lyman
173 George McAfee
80 Johnny "Blood" McNally
70 Tim Mara
75 George Marshall
114 August (Mike) Michalske
240 Wayne Millner
243 Marion Motley
84 Bronko Nagurski
89 Ernie Nevers
176 Steve Owen
183 Hugh (Shorty) Ray
209 Dan Reeves
117 Art Rooney
213 Ken Strong
217 Joe Stydahar
95 Jim Thorpe
121 George Trafton
246 Charley Trippi
222 Emlen Tunnell
184 Clyde (Bulldog) Turner
147 Steve Van Buren
153 Bob Waterfield
249 Alex Wojciechowicz

Introduction

Pro Football's Hall of Fame

Mementos of Jim Thorpe's career are here, the blanket he used in his days with the Canton Bulldogs, and his Carlisle sweater. Here can be found the much-traveled equipment trunk used by Ernie Nevers in his career with the Duluth Eskimos, a bronze casting of Sammy Baugh's right hand, a goalpost fragment from the 1958 NFL championship game, and a helmet of Knute Rockne's. These are just a small sampling of the items on display at Pro Football's Hall of Fame, mementos that trace the history of the sport from its raffish days just after the turn of the century to its present eminence. Although the structure may not yet rival Disneyland or the Statue of Liberty as a tourist attraction, hundreds of thousands of people now call upon the Hall of Fame each year.

The National Professional Football Hall of Fame—to use its official title—was especially built to serve as a showcase of the sport. Dedicated in 1963, it is a unique and elaborate structure, dominated by a 52-foot dome, an architectural suggestion of a football pointing skyward. The structure is located on a fourteen-acre slice of wooded parkland a few miles west of downtown Canton, Ohio.

Why Canton?

First of all, Canton had a valid historical claim. The first national professional championships were decided in Canton not long after the turn of the century. Further, it was in Canton in 1915 that Jim Thorpe, as a member of a local team known as the Bulldogs, first drew national attention to the pro game. Five years later, on September 17, 1920, Ralph Hays' automobile showroom in Canton was the site of the organizational meeting from which the National Football League sprouted.

Other cities had claims just as meritorious, however. For instance, Latrobe, Pennsylvania, is generally recognized as the site of the first professional football game. (It was played on August 31, 1895. The Latrobe YMCA defeated a team representing Jeannette, Pennsylvania, and the score was 12–0.) Latrobe bid for the Hall of Fame, and so did Green Bay, Los Angeles and Detroit.

Germane Swanson, a sportswriter (and now city editor) for the Canton *Repository*, the city's football-minded newspaper, was the first to champion the idea of a Pro Football Hall of Fame for the city. He discussed his plans with Harold Sauerbrei, general manager of the Cleveland Browns, who gave him encouragement. Swanson next went to see Clayton Horn, editor of the *Repository*. Horn thought so well of the plan that he responded with a feature story that carried the challenging headline: PRO FOOTBALL NEEDS A HALL OF FAME. . . . AND LOGICAL SITE IS HERE.

Canton reacted enthusiastically. Business, industry, labor and civic groups pitched in. Volunteers signed up to do the legwork. There were pledges of financial support. Public land was made available. At the NFL owners meeting on January 25, 1961, the city of Canton, represented by William E. Umstattd, Chairman of the Executive Committee of the Timken Roller Bearing Company, made its formal bid. Approval was granted a few months later.

In the months that followed, a fund-raising committee received $406,000 in pledges. On August 11, 1962, ground-breaking ceremonies were held and the structure was completed less than a year later.

In 1962, an affable Irisher named Dick McCann was appointed director of the Hall of Fame. Immensely knowledgeable about football by virtue of having been a sports columnist in Washington, D.C., and, later, general manager of the Washington Redskins, McCann awakened national interest in the Hall of

Fame. It was he who set the selection policies for Hall of Fame membership, enlisting the cooperation of press, television and radio representatives. Much of what is now displayed in the Hall of Fame was gathered through McCann's efforts. It was McCann who transformed the raw structure built in Canton into an exciting exhibition chamber. His death in 1967 was a deep loss to professional football.

Actually, the Hall of Fame is two buildings, one circular, the other tongue-shaped. They are connected by a glass-enclosed passageway. From the entrance of the main building, a spiral ramp leads the visitor from ground level to a magnificent rotunda where a wide variety of exhibits are presented. Besides the memorabilia, there is audio and video equipment which enable the visitor to see and hear his favorite Hall of Fame personalities.

The Hall of Fame boasts a 125-seat theater and offers a collection of films dating to 1924. They include annual league and team highlights, world championship games, and historic documentary films.

The Hall of Fame library boasts much more than just books (although an effort is being made to collect at least one copy of every publication concerning football). It offers the most comprehensive collection of pro football information available anywhere in the country. It is made up of programs from more than two thousand games that date to the sport's earliest days; rulebooks from as far back as the 1890's, and thousands of photographs of players, coaches and officials. The Hall of Fame also houses an art gallery and a gift shop.

Each of the members of the Hall of Fame is depicted in both a bronze bust and a lifelike mural. These are displayed along dramatically lighted corriders, with an identical amount of space devoted to each member.

Each year a National Board of Selectors meets to choose new members for the Hall of Fame. Seventeen persons were selected as charter members in 1963, and seven or eight additional members have been chosen each year since.

At present there are sixteen selectors, one from each city with a team in the National League. Sometime in the future representatives from American League cities will be added to the roster. The selectors are:

Lewis Atchison, the Washington Evening *Star*
James Conzelman, speaker and author, St. Louis
Art Daley, the Green Bay *Press Gazette*
Arthur Daley, the New York *Times*
Buddy Diliberto, WVUE-TV, New Orleans
Herb Good, the Philadelphia *Bulletin*
Chuck Heaton, the Cleveland *Plain Dealer*
Charles Johnston, the Minneapolis *Star*
Bob Oates, the Los Angeles *Examiner*
George Puscas, the Detroit *Free Press*
Jack Sell, the Pittsburgh *Post-Gazette*
Blackie Sherrod, Dallas *Times-Herald*
John Steadman, the Baltimore *News Post*
George Strickler, the Chicago *Tribune*
Al Thomy, the Atlanta *Constitution*
Roger Williams, the San Francisco *Examiner*

At their annual meeting, the selectors decide how many new members are to be chosen and by a unanimous vote. Nominations can come from anyone—fans, players, or officials. A player must be retired for five years in order to be considered.

This book profiles each member of the Hall of Fame and presents the career statistics for some of the players. During pro football's early days few records were kept, and therefore statistics are not available for such players as Red Grange or even Bronko Nagurski, whose career began in 1930. In addition, no statistics are compiled for linemen, with the exception of pass receivers.

A final word about the Hall of Fame. In the years since it has been instituted, it has achieved remarkable eminence, and has come to be regarded as much more than a repository for the relics of the sport. It is both a tribute to the foresighted citizens of Canton who brought their idea to reality and a striking monument to pro football's gridiron heroes and visionary pioneers as well.

PRO FOOTBALL'S ALL-TIME GREATS

1963

Sammy Baugh

The year was 1936, and the Washington Redskins had just been trounced in the NFL championship game by the Green Bay Packers. Head coach Ray Flaherty tried to console his team with the statement that all they needed to win the championship next year was a forward passer. Flaherty promised to find one. There were a number of fine passers among the graduating collegians, and the most notable of them all was a tall, lean, rubber-armed young man from Texas Christian University named Sammy Baugh. But Baugh was so spare and skinny that most pro clubs weren't interested in him.

"Take my advice," sportswriter Grantland Rice told George Marshall, owner of the Redskins. "If you sign him, you'd better insure his right arm for a million dollars, because the tough guys in this league are going to tear it off him."

Poor fragile-looking Sammy Baugh. All he did was set an all-time record for durability in the National Football League, playing an incredible sixteen seasons. Through many of the years he was a double- or single-wing halfback and defensive safety, and in more than a few games he was a sixty-minute offensive-defensive performer.

It was as a passer, however, that Sam was supreme. Dick Mc-Cann, Director of the Pro Football Hall of Fame until his death in 1967, put it this way: "Never mind what other fellows have written about other quarterbacks. Sammy Baugh was the best . . . and is the best . . . and will still be the best, long after the long pass has been thrown by some as yet unborn boy in some distant decade."

Statistics can be dull, but in Baugh's case they are anything but. During his career, he completed an amazing 1,709 passes for a total of 22,085 yards, approximately thirteen miles. He was the most efficient passer of all time. In a game in 1945 against the Pittsburgh Steelers, Baugh completed a fantastic 18 of 21 passes, for an 85.7 percentage. That season he boasted a 70.3 percentage. His career mark was 56.5. Sid Luckman, Otto Graham, Johnny Unitas—no one has done as well. When Baugh retired in 1952, he left more than a page of passing records for quarterbacks of the future to shoot at.

Baugh's importance to professional football transcends what has been set down in the official records. When Sam came on the scene, the forward pass was regarded as a wild piece of strategy, a weapon to be used to surprise or out of desperation. But Sam threw so often and with such success that when he left professional football, the pass was accepted by every team as an offensive staple.

Baugh is significant for another reason. He was Mr. Meal Ticket for the Washington franchise. Crowds flocked to see him perform, and he made the turnstiles whirl season after season. Over one period, the Redskins registered forty consecutive sellouts, and this in a day when pro football's status was scarcely what it is now. "Sammy took the Redskins out of the red, and put them in the black," owner Marshall said.

Baugh was born on March 17, 1914, near Temple, Texas. His father was a checker for the railroad. Sam took part in many sports, and played his first football in the fourth grade. Because of his height, he played end. In high school he started out as a receiver, but was switched to the back field when the coach noticed that he returned the ball better than the passers who were serving him.

The coach recommended that Sam practice to improve his accuracy. He hung an old automobile tire from two ropes attached to a tree branch, and had a brother push it so that it swung like a pendulum. Then Sam fired at it. He got so good that he could thread passes through the opening on the run. Sam's high school team—Sweetwater—almost won the state championship twice.

They reached the quarterfinals in his junior year and the semifinals when he was a senior.

Sam also excelled in baseball. He played third base for Sweetwater High as well as for the Abilene town team. He had quick hands and a whiplike arm. It was from baseball that he got his nickname, not football. Amos Melton, a writer for the Fort Worth *Star Telegram,* watched Baugh rifle the ball from third base to first and immediately dubbed him "Slingin' Sam."

Dutch Meyer, the baseball coach at Texas Christian University, persuaded Sam to come there to play baseball. When Meyer, also the freshman football coach, saw Sam fling a forward pass, he convinced him to play football, too. Meyer became the varsity coach just before Sam's sophomore year. It was from Meyer that Sam gained most of his football knowledge. In the Meyer system, the quarterback did not pass to a spot, as he does now. He threw to a man in the open, and he had to help him get them—with body fakes, head fakes, anything.

Sam developed slowly. As a sophomore he made few headlines, but in his junior year he pitched TCU into the Sugar Bowl, guiding his team to a grueling 3–2 win over Louisiana State University in the driving rain. After his senior year, Baugh was hailed as the most valuable player in the history of the Southwest Conference, and he won a multitude of All America honors.

George Marshall knew almost all there was to know about Baugh, and when the draft choices were made—Washington had second pick—the Redskins grabbed the Texas Tornado, as some newspapers called him. Professional baseball was also interested in Baugh, the St. Louis Cardinals in particular. Should he sign with the Redskins or the Cardinals? Baugh spared himself the agony of a decision; he simply signed with both.

Sam joined the Cardinals in spring training and they assigned him to a triple-A farm. Since he naturally had been picked to perform in the Chicago *Tribune* College All Star football game, he interrupted his baseball career to appear at Soldiers' Field. Playing third base had not done him the slightest harm. The pro champion Packers were the opposition, and Baugh's pass to Gaynell Tinsely toppled Green Bay, 6–0, and gave the college squad its first victory in All Star competition.

Baugh was an immediate sensation at the Redskin training

camp. Coach Flaherty diagramed a play on the blackboard. "You," he said to end Wayne Millner, "take ten steps downfield, then hook back." Flaherty drew an X on the board.

"When he reaches here, Sam, I want you to hit him in the eye."

"Sure, Coach," Sam said. "Which eye?"

In his debut as a Redskin, Sam threw sixteen passes and completed eleven. He played the full sixty minutes. Washington won, 13–3. Sam wasn't the star, however. Cliff Battles and Riley Smith were; Sam did not hit his stride until mid-season. By that time his receivers had learned to hold his bullet tosses, and the offense had geared itself to mixing Baugh's passes with Battles' rushes—with dramatic results.

Washington blazed to a 7-3-0 record, challenged only by the New York Giants who were 6-2-2. The showdown game was played in New York, and more than ten thousand Redskin fans made the trek North. They marched up Broadway before the game behind a loud brass band and a vanguard of lavishly costumed Indians.

In the dressing room before the game, Flaherty reminded the team how they could have won the year before if they had had a passer. "Well, now we've got one," he said, "and he's the best in the world.

"I don't know whether the Giants are out to get Baugh or not," he continued. "All I do know is that I'm holding you guys responsible for Sam's safety. If anything happens to him, you'll hear from me."

Nothing happened to Baugh; it was the Giants who were struck by disaster. When the New Yorkers got set for a run, Baugh passed. When they braced for a pass, Battles ran. Baugh threw fifteen passes and completed eleven, and twice he delivered key blocks on touchdown runs by Battles. It was a rout, the Redskins winning, 49–14.

With the division title theirs, the Redskins went to Chicago to meet the Bears for the NFL championship. The team arrived on the heels of a blizzard. The temperature plunged to below zero, and the field was frozen and slippery.

Baugh was unmindful of conditions, however. The Redskins got possession of the ball for the first time on their own nine-yard line. The Bears thought that Washington would kick, and the Redskins seemed to confirm this strategy by lining up in punt formation. But the kick never came. Baugh crossed up Chicago with a short pass to Battles, the play covering 42 yards. In the 1930's, quarterbacks seldom passed from inside their 30-yard line. To pass from one's end zone was practically unheard of. The play shocked Chicago. Shortly afterward Battles went seven yards on a reverse for the touchdown.

But Baugh was just getting started. Twice he passed to Millner for touchdowns; one play was good for 55 yards, the other for 78. The Bears managed to keep the game close, however. In the final stages Baugh delivered again. This time he connected with Ed Justice for 35 yards and the winning touchdown. The final score was 28–21. For the day, Baugh completed 17 passes in 34 attempts, good for 347 yards. Quite a day for a rookie.

Early the next spring, Baugh returned to the baseball wars. He played for Rochester, and one day when the team was in Baltimore, Baugh visited George Marshall in Washington and signed a three-year contract with the Redskins. Not long after he quit baseball for good.

The pass was only one of Baugh's weapons. He was a brilliant punter, and the kicking records he set still stand. In the 1940 season, he averaged 51.4 yards per punt, and his lifetime average is 44.9 yards.

The quick kick was a big gun in Baugh's arsenal. It developed easily out of the single-wing formation. In the 1942 championship against the Bears, which pitted Baugh against Sid Luckman, another premier passer, the Bears buried the Redskin kickoff receiver on the 12-yard line. The Bears, a bit used to Sam by now, expected him to start throwing. He took the first pass from center and started back, the ball held high, his eyes fixed down field, seemingly to spot a receiver. But then, with just one stride, he put his foot into the ball, and shot a low line drive over the head of the unprepared safetyman. It rolled and rolled. When the Bears finally got to the ball, it rested on the Chicago five-yard line.

It was in the same game, with the Bears anticipating a pass every time Baugh got his hands on the ball, that Sam sent twelve consecutive plays into the center of the line. On the twelfth one,

Andy Farkas scored. Baugh threw for the Redskins' other touchdown, and Washington won, 14–6.

In Baugh's first ten years with the team, the Redskins did not have a single losing season, and never finished worse than second in the standings. They won their division title five times and took the NFL championship twice.

By today's standards Baugh was woefully underpaid, but even by the standards of his day he was no more than adequately compensated. George Marshall was not a person inclined toward extravagance. He paid Baugh an $8,000 salary as a rookie, and in the years that followed, Baugh was able to nudge the figure upward to $15,000. Sam added to this with a number of commercial enterprises and endorsements. These included a sojourn in Hollywood where in eight weeks he made a twelve-chapter serial called *King of the Texas Rangers*. Neither Sam's performance nor the film in general was quite of Academy Award caliber.

Baugh's mode of living did not demand a high income. He did not drink; he lived by the clock. When a practice session was set for two o'clock, Sam would be there at two o'clock, or perhaps before. He owned his own home and a Texas ranch, and the future did not worry him. His major vice was a passion for pinball machines; he could not pass one by.

In 1943, the Redskins won their division title and met their perennial playoff game rivals, the Bears. Sid Luckman, operating from the T formation, threw five touchdown passes, while Baugh accounted for only two. He did suffer a concussion that kept him on the sidelines through the final stages of the game. The Bears won, 41–21.

For the next season Marshall brought in Dud De Groot and Clark Shaughnessy to install the vaunted T. At first it bewildered Baugh. He had to learn to fake and bootleg, but more important, he had to change his passing style. No longer could he take a direct snap from center, simply survey the field, and fire. Now he had to fade back and learn to stay in the protective pocket.

Sam had some trying moments with the T. In one game he announced in the huddle, "Let's get back into the old single wing. We'll use the old formations and the old assignments."

The team did, and Sam passed the opposition into oblivion.

By 1945, however, Sam had the T working smoothly, and even sang its praises. He ridiculed the idea that he had ever thought ill of it.

"The easiest position in football to play is quarterback in the T formation," he said. "All you do is hand the ball off or pass. If they had had the T when I started to play pro ball, I could play until I was forty years old.

"There are a lot of T formations an eight-year-old boy could learn. But the ones Shaughnessy taught us are very complicated. Why, we had over twenty plays to get around one end. The only trouble was we couldn't find anybody that could do it."

In 1945, the Redskins under Baugh made their final appearance in NFL championship playoff competition. This time their opponents were the Cleveland Rams. The game was played at Municipal Stadium. It was freezing cold and a fierce wind blew. Baugh was the game's goat. He attempted a bold pass from behind his goal line, but the ball hit the goalpost and rebounded into the end zone for an automatic safety. The two points were the margin of victory as the Rams won, 15–14.

Many dark days followed, and the Redskins were seldom regarded as serious title contenders. A rare bright moment came in the 1947 season. The Redskins faced the Chicago Cardinals who were headed for the NFL championship. Before the game the fans were to give Baugh an automobile. While Sam was out on the field for the presentation ceremonies, Joe Tereshinski, a Redskin end, said to his teammates, "Baugh's the greatest football player who ever lived. Let's show him what we think of him. Let's see to it that he doesn't get any dirt on his pants today!"

Sam got as much protection as if he were playing behind the Great Wall of China. Not a Cardinal laid a hand on him. He responded by completing 25 of 33 passes for 355 yards and 6 touchdowns. The Redskins won, 45–21; it rated as one of the year's major upsets.

Through the late 1940's, there were constant rumors that Baugh would retire. Yet week after week, season after season, he was in there, rearing back on spindly legs, his rubber arm firing to the bull's-eye. In 1952, Baugh broke his hand shortly before the season opened. He knew this signaled the end. His appearances that year were mainly as a ball holder on place-kicks and field goal attempts, another facet of the game in which he excelled. The next year he was gone.

In 1960, Sam was lured back into professional football by the late Harry Wismer, onetime associate of George Marshall and owner of the New York Titans in the American Football League. As Titan head coach, Baugh endowed the team with an explosive passing attack; unfortunately, there was little regard for defense, and in Baugh's two-year tenure with the club the Titans lost as many games as they won. Following the Titans, Baugh saw brief service with the Detroit Lions as an assistant coach.

As for the Redskins, after Baugh's departure they fell on evil times. They reached their all-time low in 1961, showing only one victory for the entire season. The fans missed Baugh, too. But it's easy to reminisce. All one has to do to call the past to mind is flip through the record book. Baugh's name will always be there.

Sammy Baugh Career Passing Record

Year	Attempts	Completions	Pct.	Yards	Touchdowns	Interceptions
1937	171	81	47.3	1,127	7	14
1938	128	63	49.2	853	5	11
1939	96	53	55.2	518	6	9
1940	177	111	62.7	1,367	12	10
1941	193	106	54.9	1,236	10	19
1942	225	132	54.1	1,524	16	11
1943**	260	149	57.3	1,953	24	21
1944	146	82	56.2	849	4	8
1945	182	128	70.3*	1,669	11	4
1946	161	87	54.0	1,163	8	17
1947	354	210*	59.3	2,938*	25	15
1948	315	185	58.7	2,599	22	23
1948	255	145	56.9	1,903	18	14
1950	166	90	54.2	1,130	10	11
1951	154	67	43.5	1,104	7	17
1952	33	20	60.6	152	2	1
Total	3,016*	1,708*	56.5*	22,085*	187*	205*

* *League Record.*
** *Includes Divisional Playoff.*

Bert Bell

Bert Bell's first contact with professional football came in the early 1920's. One day, when strolling down Broad Street in Philadelphia, he happened to meet Lou Little, Heinie Miller, and Lud Wray, all former teammates of his at the University of Pennsylvania. The three were in town to promote a game against the Canton Bulldogs at Baker Bowl. Pro football of the day being what it was, the trio was short of cash. An immediate and pressing problem was how and where to feed and house the players.

Bell came to the rescue. "What am I in the hotel business for," he said, "if I can't help out some old friends? Bring the fellas over—as my guests."

This was the first time that pro football cost Bell money. It was not to be the last—not by any means. In 1933, Bell and Wray bought the Frankford Yellowjackets for $2,500 and immediately established new records for losing games and money. In 1940, Bell, with Art Rooney, acquired the Pittsburgh Steelers, and they had the misfortune to operate them during the war years, a time when both players and gate receipts were very hard to come by. Seldom was football ever a winning proposition for Bell, right up until the time he was named NFL commissioner in 1946. Ironically, it was under his command that the pro game skyrocketed to new heights of popularity and financial stability.

Bell was born to a Philadelphia Main Line family, the son of John Cromwell Bell, Attorney General for the State of Pennsylvania. His mother was Fleurette de Benneville Myers Bell. When Bell was born, he was named de Benneville after his mother. As soon as he could, he rejected the name in preference to Bert; then turned his back on the Main Line "swells," spurning a bright career in politics.

"For me there was never anything but football," he once said.

In 1914, young Bell captained the football, basketball and baseball teams at Haverford School. People were curious about his plans for college. They asked Bert's father, a onetime Penn football player, head of the athletic association and a Penn trustee, what school the young man was going to.

"Bert will go to Penn or he'll go to hell!" his father answered. Bert went to Penn.

Bert spent thirteen months as a first sergeant in the Army in France, and returned to captain the 1919 Penn football team. Afterward he became associated with his father in the hotel business and also began a long sojourn as backfield coach at Penn and later at Temple.

Football was not Bert's principal interest, however; the good life was. He drank too much, and he gambled too much. Two things led him to reform: the stock market crash of 1929, which thrust him into overwhelming debt, and his marriage to Frances Upton, a Broadway musical comedy star. Miss Upton elicited a promise from Bert that he would not drink, and he kept it.

After Wray and Bell were awarded the franchise to operate the Frankford Yellowjackets, Bell moved the club from the suburbs into Philadelphia proper and renamed it the Philadelphia Eagles, after the blue eagle symbol of the National Recovery Administration, the American "thunderbird," which was meant to symbolize the nation's industrial rebirth.

In 1935 the courts invalidated the NRA and the emblem was abolished. Sometimes Bell must have wished for the same kind of treatment for his team.

The Eagles got off to a good start, attracting 20,000 fans to Baker Bowl to see them whip the Portsmouth Spartans on October 23, 1933. But after that it was a downhill slide. The team lost game after game, and there was no "name" to pull in customers. In three seasons the Eagles lost $80,000, a significant amount of money in the early 1930's, and won only nine of thirty games. The other investors fled, leaving Bell as the sole owner.

Bert did everything possible to keep the Eagles aloft. He was the general manager, ticket manager, press agent and auditor. He once hawked tickets on a Philadelphia street corner. To bolster the gate, he hired Alabama Pitts, a noted player of the day, who had been the mainstay of the Sing Sing prison team. Pitts proved of little value.

These were football's scruffy, ragtag days, and the Eagles were among the scruffiest of teams. There were no sleek jets for intercity travel, no luxury hotels. Players traveled in ramshackle buses, stopping for practice when they spotted an open field. They carried their lunches in brown paper bags and bedded down overnight in run-down hotels or boardinghouses. Bell never lost heart, however.

In 1936, Bell took over the coaching reins, and the team finished with a 1-11 record. The next year they won only twice. The year 1938 was Bert's best season, the Eagles finishing with five wins against six losses. This "success" so emboldened him that he offered $12,000 a season to Davey O'Brien, a unanimous All American from Texas Christian University, and the most renowned star of the day.

Often called the mighty mite, O'Brien was one of the smallest players ever to attempt pro ball. Worried that O'Brien might be torn limb from limb by some football behemoth, Bell had him insured by Lloyds of London. If O'Brien were to be injured, the Eagles would receive $1,500 for each game he was sidelined. But O'Brien never missed a game.

O'Brien's career was brief and brilliant. He did pick up the gate, but was never successful in getting the team to win. For the 1939 and 1940 seasons, the Eagles' victory total was two.

In 1940, Bell sold one-half of his interest in the Eagles to his friend Art Rooney, who then sold his Pittsburgh Steelers to Alexis Thompson. Then the franchises were switched, Thompson taking Philadelphia, and Rooney and Bell moving to Pittsburgh.

The Steelers had a good season in 1942, winning seven and losing only four. But World War II brought dismal days. The Pittsburgh and Philadelphia franchises were merged into one in 1943, and Pittsburgh and the Cardinals combined in 1944. The last-named combination went winless in eleven tries.

It was during this period that Bell proposed that just-graduated collegians be drafted by clubs according to the league standings; last place meant first choice, next to last place, second choice, and so on. Adopted in 1945, and in use today, the policy helped to even out competition, eliminating perennial "weak sisters" and powerhouses. The policy has been a sturdy building block upon which the pro sport has grown.

In 1946, the NFL became deeply involved in a costly war with a rival league, the All America Conference. The NFL owners were disenchanted with the way their commissioner, Elmer Layden, was handling hostilities and forced his resignation. Bell was appointed his successor.

It was a happy choice, indeed. Bell, then fifty-one, a little, round man with a gravelly voice, proved to be a leader of great skill and incessant devotion.

The first thing to hit Bell was a potential scandal of sizable proportions. On the morning of the 1946 championship game between the Bears and the Giants, the story of an attempted bribe was revealed. Two New York players, Frankie Filchock and Merle Hapes, had been offered money to juggle the point spread. Neither player had accepted money, but they were guilty of not reporting the offer to team officials or the police.

Bell swung into action. He permitted Filchock to play because there was no evidence against him, but Hapes was suspended. Bell made no attempt to cover up proceedings; the press was kept fully informed. Later, after new evidence was brought to light, Filchock was also suspended. Both players were reinstated several years later.

The Filchock-Hapes tangle was a valuable lesson for Bell, and throughout his tenure as commissioner he regarded gambling as a serious menace. He knew he could do nothing to stop people from betting on pro football, but he was determined that gambling would never in any way taint the sport. Players were warned to steer clear of professional gamblers. He employed investigators to ferret out the slightest hint of a fix. He watched game odds himself, and if they fluctuated crazily, his suspicions increased and he sought an explanation.

In his first years as commissioner, Bell's greatest problem was the matter of schedule making. Powerful teams and well-to-do owners preferred to play the weaker and less appealing teams early in the year to bolster their won-lost records, and to make late-in-the-season sellouts more possible. Bell opposed this.

"Weak clubs should play weak clubs, and strong clubs should play strong clubs early in the season," he said. "It's the only way to balance competition." Reluctantly, the owners went along. In time they were glad that they did. Bell's policy helped to prevent weak teams from being eliminated early in the year. It kept fan interest alive throughout the season.

Once asked to cite what he considered the most difficult part of his job, Bell answered, "To be able to say 'yes' or 'no' at the snap of an owner's finger." It is a matter of fact that he said "no" much more than he said "yes." Yet Bell did not rule by brute force. He had the respect, even the deep affection, of every owner. They knew that everything he did was for the good of the NFL and football in general.

The television policy that Bell enunciated was perhaps the most farsighted piece of wisdom to come out of his administration. Many credit this policy with creating the lofty status that pro football attained during the 1960's.

Bell had seen television wreck baseball's minor leagues and all but devour the sport of boxing. Yet he did not fear television; he knew it could be of great benefit. What Bell did was control TV. He did this by "blacking out" sets in home cities when the local team played there. "You can't give a game to the public for free and expect them to go to the ball park," he once said.

Bell was often under enormous pressure to lift the ban. The 1957 NFL title game between the Lions and the Browns, played in Detroit, is a case in point. A sellout, the contest had generated intense interest, and fans, as well as state and federal legislators, pleaded with Bell to relax his policy. But he would not budge. "It's not honest," he said, "to sell tickets to thousands of people on the basis of no television, and then, afterward, when all the tickets are gone, to give the game away on television."

Eventually Bell's policy was tested in the courts—and upheld. On November 12, 1953, Federal Judge Alan K. Grim handed down a decision stating that clubs were entitled to reasonably restrain telecasts of their games.

Late in 1949 it became apparent that the rival AAC was ready to capitulate, and early the next year Bell set down the terms of surrender. The Cleveland, Baltimore and San Francisco teams were taken into the NFL. Bell also negotiated a peace treaty with the Canadian football leagues which sharply restricted the raiding of players.

Year after year the owners kept rehiring Bell. Originally he signed a three-year contract calling for a salary of $20,000 a year. But the year after he signed it, the owners tore it up and gave him a new contract for five years with a 50 percent boost in salary. Two years later, he got another new contract, this one for ten years. In 1954 this was extended for twelve years. Each time he received a healthy salary increase.

Newspapermen, club owners, and legislators, anyone who had dealings with him, regarded Bell as a completely forthright figure. "We know him to be square," said one owner. "He will fight and argue, but he doesn't hold a grudge. And no matter how friendly you are with him, if he thinks you're wrong, he'll tell you."

It is significant that when Lamar Hunt was quarterbacking his American Football League into existence in 1959, he made Bert fully aware of his plans. "I always felt Bell would give us a fair shake," Hunt says.

Bell never became involved in the hot NFL-AFL war. One bright October day in 1959, as he watched his two old teams, the Eagles and the Steelers, battling at Franklin Field, where it had all begun a half century before, Bell succumbed to a heart attack. "It was," wrote Red Smith, "almost as though he were allowed to choose the time and place."

Joe Carr

The National Football League has had six presidents or commissioners since 1920, the year of its founding. Jim Thorpe, the great Indian player, was the first. Then came Joe Carr, Carl Storck, Elmer Layden and Bert Bell. The commissioner today is Pete Rozelle.

Thorpe was named president largely because of his name value. He served only one year. Joe Carr, the man who succeeded Thorpe, was NFL president from 1921 until his death in 1939. It was Carr, a dedicated and indefatigable little man, who endowed the league with stability and integrity, and in so doing provided a foundation upon which those who followed could build. Carr, perhaps more than any other individual, made the NFL successful.

Carr was born in Columbus, Ohio, in 1880, and worked as assistant sports editor of the *Ohio State Journal*. Columbus was a hotbed of sports activity and Carr was always in the thick of things. He organized a baseball team among the employees of the Panhandle Division of the Pennsylvania Railroad, and later a football team. They were called the Columbus Panhandles, too.

The Panhandles featured the Nesser brothers, the most famous group of brothers ever to play pro football. There were seven in all, plus the son of the oldest brother. They were big, rugged men, all of them boilermakers for the Pennsy. The club was able to challenge teams everywhere since the players, as employees of the railroad, could ride far and wide on passes, thus saving the cost of travel.

Players of the day often jumped from team to team, going to the highest bidder. The Panhandles once faced Knute Rockne six times in a single season, and each time he represented a different team. The Nesser brothers, too, switched teams during the season. Carr and Jerry Corcoran, one of his associates, abhorred this practice, and this was a factor in the founding of the National Football League.

Professional football's first organizational meeting of record was held in Akron, Ohio, on August 20, 1920. It was agreed that no club could negotiate with any player attached to another professional team, and a ban was put on the signing of college players. A few weeks later, on September 17, a larger group of team representatives met in the automobile showroom of Ralph Hay in Canton and organized a league to be called the American Football Association. Thorpe was named its president. Early the next year, on April 30, in a meeting at Canton's Cortland Hotel, the league went through a reorganization and Carr supplanted Thorpe as president. He was voted a salary of $1,000 a year. The following year, 1922, the name of the organization was changed to National Football League.

Carr had served as president of the Ohio State Baseball League and he now put this experience to use. One of his first moves was to introduce a standard playing contract, modeled after the type used in organized baseball.

Carr established himself as a no-nonsense executive early in his reign. In 1922, he cracked down on the winked-at practice of hiring college players under assumed names. When he was given evidence that Green Bay was guilty of such mischief, he ordered the Green Bay franchise returned to the league. It was.

Carr handled his first major crisis with exceptional skill. In November 1925 the Chicago Bears plucked Red Grange off the campus of the University of Illinois, and a great furor resulted. In December of the same year, Ernie Nevers, who attended Stanford, traded in his school books for a spot in the backfield of the Duluth Eskimos. Now the colleges were positively enraged.

Carr quickly restored peace. He did it by having the owners adopt a resolution that read:

The National Football League places itself on record as unalterably opposed to any encroachment upon college football and hereby pledges its hearty support to college authorities in maintaining and advancing interest in college football and in preserving the amateur standing of all college athletes.

We believe there is a public demand for professional football . . . and to the end that this league may not jeopardize the amateur standing of any college player, it is the unanimous decision of this meeting that every member of the National Football League be positively prohibited from inducing or attempting to induce any college player to engage in professional football until his class at college shall have graduated, and any member violating this rule be fined not less than one thousand dollars or loss of its franchise, or both.

The rule proved a tremendous boon to pro football. It was adopted in February 1926 and it has remained in effect to this day. Carr enforced the rule to the letter. In 1931, when it was discovered that Chicago, Green Bay and Portsmouth had players on their rosters whose college classes had not graduated, each club was fined the prescribed $1,000.

Carr worked tirelessly to bring financially independent businessmen into pro football. He secured a firm Eastern anchor for the league when he sold Tim Mara on the merits of pro ball in 1925. Mara, of course, founded the New York Giants. Carr talked George Marshall into starting a team in Boston, and Art Rooney of the Steelers acquired his franchise by virtue of a friendship with Carr.

It was during Carr's tenure that professional football took on much of its present-day character. Ideas presented by Tim Mara, George Marshall, George Halas, and Curly Lambeau were put into force by virtue of Carr's power and persuasiveness. He presided over the streamlining of pro football's playing rules, the division of the league into conferences with an annual championship playoff, and the institution of scores of new operating procedures, like the player draft and the waiver rule.

Carr was also very active in other sports. From his office in Columbus he served simultaneously as president of the NFL and the American Basketball League, a forerunner of the National Basketball Association. It was Carr who sold officials of Madison Square Garden in New York and the Arena in Philadelphia on the fiscal benefits of basketball.

Carr held administrative posts in baseball, too. In 1926 he became president of the Columbus team in the American Association, a position he held until 1932. Professional baseball owes Carr a great debt of gratitude for what he accomplished in organizing its minor league setup. In 1938, of the thirty-seven minor leagues in operation, twenty-six owed their existence to Carr's efforts.

After Carr had succeeded in making the minor leagues prosper, Branch Rickey approached him and asked if he would be interested in devoting himself to baseball exclusively. "If you give up football," Rickey told Carr. "I'll make you the biggest man in baseball."

Carr shook his head. "If that's the price I'd have to pay," he answered, "I want no part of it."

Carr never saw the results of his industry and devotion. He died in 1939, an era when a gate of 25,000 customers was considered excellent, and a player whose salary was $10,000 a year felt amply rewarded. But Carr endowed the league with the strength to weather the lean years of World War II, and the tenacity to fight off the encroachments of the All America Conference. Professional football's days of glory soon followed. Joe Carr had done his work well.

Earl Harry (Dutch) Clark

Dutch Clark holds no records for points scored, passes caught, yards gained rushing, field goals or anything like that. Only once in his five-year career with Detroit did the Lions win the Western Division championship and the NFL title. Yet Clark definitely belongs in the Hall of Fame. Significantly, he is a charter member.

A quarterback, Dutch had extraordinary skills. As a ballcarrier he had good speed and remarkable feints. He passed with the best and was one of the best dropkickers of all time. Furthermore, he was one of the brainiest players ever. Clark Shaughnessy, the great coach, said of him, "If Clark stepped on the field with Grange, Thorpe and Gipp, Dutch would be the general." Unfortunately, the record book does not rate players according to intelligence or the ability to think quickly. If it did, Clark's name would lead the list.

Clark was born in Fowler, Colorado, in 1906, and grew up in Pueblo. At Central High School he starred in baseball, football and basketball. No less a figure than Amos Alonzo Stagg, who at the time conducted an annual national interscholastic tournament, called young Dutch "the finest schoolboy basketball player I ever saw."

Clark enrolled at tiny Colorado College in 1926. He won varsity status as soon as he was eligible and was named to the All Rocky Mountain team as quarterback for three consecutive years. He first won national attention when Alan Gould, sports editor for the Associated Press, chose Clark for the AP's All America squad in 1929. Gould was widely criticized for this because Dutch was relatively unknown. It was not until 1931, the first year that Clark won All Pro honors, that Gould's choice was justified in the public's mind.

Dutch's first years in the NFL were spent with the Portsmouth Spartans, a perennial contender for the championship, but never a winner. In 1934 the Portsmouth franchise was switched to Detroit, and that's where Clark achieved his most glittering days.

G. A. (Dick) Richards, the enthusiastic and imaginative owner of the Detroit club, was determined to make the Lions the league's best. He garbed the team in brightly colored uniforms—silver and Honolulu blue. He staged half-time entertainment and arranged for radio broadcasts of the games.

Richards hired Steve Hannegan, the renowned publicist, and assigned him to make Dutch Clark the No. 1 name in football. But Clark, a retiring type, would have none of this. He scuttled his press agent's efforts with the announcement that his own skills were second to those of Bronko Nagurski and perhaps to those of the Green Bay's Clarke Hinkle, too.

Richards, in his determination to mold a new image for the Lions, did not overlook the team itself. He built the Lions' backfield into a thing of beauty. Clark was called the quarterback because he was the field general. But, operating out of the tailback spot in the single wing, he was a full-fledged running back. Rugged Leroy (Ace) Gutowsky, a specialist at barreling into the line, was at fullback. Ernie Caddel, a nonpareil on the reverse, and Frank Christiansen, a standout blocker, were the halfbacks.

In their first year in Detroit, the Lions lost only three of thirteen games, two of them to the Chicago Bears, who, unfortunately for Detroit, did not lose at all. But even though they did not win the championship, the Lions of 1934 were one great team of professional football. They recorded a remarkable string of seven consecutive shutouts to open the season and won three more in a row before they lost. In the seven shutouts, the Lions' opponents did not penetrate deeper than Detroit's 20-yard line. The next year, however, the Lions did win the Western Division crown.

Detroit had a supercharged ground attack, and although Clark was a splendid passer, the team invariably ran the ball. The 1935 championship playoff between the Lions and the Giants is a case in point. Ace Gutowsky scored first for Detroit on a short plunge. Then Clark found the end zone on a 40-yard sprint. In the final quarter the Lions scored two more times, once on a blocked punt, once on an interception. Only five times that afternoon did Dutch attempt to pass, a record low for playoff competition. Nobody thought to criticize the Lions' board of strategy, perhaps because they overwhelmed the Giants, 26–7.

Dutch was named All League quarterback four times in his career with the Lions—in 1934, 1935, 1936 and 1937. He became as popular in Detroit as Henry Ford.

At the end of the 1937 season, Potsy Clark (he and Dutch were not related) resigned as the Lions' coach. Richards asked Dutch to take over. He brought the Lions to two second-place finishes, then left Detroit to coach the Cleveland Rams. He stayed with Cleveland four years until 1942 when the war forced the Rams to suspend operations. Dutch's record there was not outstanding.

Dutch Clark will be remembered not as coach, but as fleet quarterback. Potsy Clark once described him in these terms: "He is like a rabbit in the brush heap when he gets in the secondary; he has no plan but only instinct and the ability to cut, pivot, slant and run in any direction equally well. He gets out of more holes than any player I ever saw. Just when you expect him to be smothered, he's free of tacklers."

Despite praise like this, Dutch remained wholly modest. Once the Detroit club staged a Dutch Clark Day in his honor. It was arranged that he would be removed from the game and then be replaced on the playing field in the fourth quarter so he could receive an ovation from the fans. When the time came for him to return to the field, he refused to leave the bench.

"Why should I take all the bows?" he explained. "The guys on the field have been doing the rough work all afternoon."

He entered the auto business in Detroit and slipped into relative obscurity. Then in 1963 the selection board of the Hall of Fame thrust him into the limelight once more by naming him for membership along with such members of football's elite as Red Grange, Sammy Baugh, Bronko Nagurski and Jim Thorpe.

Dutch Clark never needed a Steve Hannegan. He became the best and he did it on the playing field.

Earl Harry (Dutch) Clark Career Rushing Record

Year	Carries	Yards Gained	Average Gain	Touchdowns
1932	111	461	4.2	2
1934	123	763	6.2	6
1935	120	412	3.4	4
1936	123	628	5.1	6
1937	96	468	4.9	5
1938	7	25	3.6	0
Total	580	2757	4.8	23

Red Grange

The appearance of Red Grange in the backfield of the Chicago Bears in 1925 marked a significant turning point for professional football. Everywhere crowds stormed the gates to see him. For the Bears he made a booming success out of what had loomed as a dismal season, and he rescued the New York Giants from drowning in red ink. But perhaps more important than anything else, he gave respectability to professional football at a time it desperately needed it. Red Grange is one of the original members of the Hall of Fame. It would have been improper had his admission been delayed a single moment.

Grantland Rice, the dean of American sportswriters, wrote about Grange in these terms: "Grange runs as Nurmi runs and Dempsey moves, with almost no effort, as a shadow flits and drifts and darts. There is no gathering of muscles for an extra lunge. There is only the effortless, ghostlike weave and glide upon effortless legs with a body that can detach itself from the hips, with a change of pace that come to a dead stop and pick up instant speed, so perfect is the coordination of brain and sinew." Indeed, it was for his magnificence as a runner that Grange was hailed. But he had one other outstanding talent: he could fill ball parks. In the former art he was merely greatly skilled; in the latter, he has had no peer.

Harold Edward Grange was born June 13, 1903, in Forksville, Pennsylvania, the son of a lumberjack. His mother died when he was five, and after her death the father moved the family—two boys and two girls—to Wheaton, Illinois. At Wheaton High, Red starred in every sport. For four consecutive years, he won letters in football, basketball, baseball and track. The last-named was probably his best sport. He didn't compete in just one or two events, but in six of them. He ran the 100- and 220-yard dashes, the low and high hurdles, and competed in the broad jump and high jump. He participated in the state championships in his last three years at Wheaton and each year he won a different event. Later, Grantland Rice nicknamed him "the

Galloping Ghost." The word "galloping" was indeed proper; from the first, speed was one of his great assets.

Because of his speed and agility, Red played end his freshman year. The next season he was switched to halfback. His record for three years at Wheaton High showed 75 touchdowns and 82 conversions, a total of 532 points.

In the early 1920's, college scholarships for superior skill in athletics were unknown. Red might easily have passed college by if it hadn't been for his father. "He was set on my going," Red once recalled. "He wouldn't hear of anything else." George Dawson, a neighbor of the Grange family, and a junior at the University of Illinois, talked Red into going there. He earned the money to pay for his education by working summers as a deliveryman on an ice truck.

As early as his sophomore year Red was a standout on the gridiron. In his first varsity game he broke loose for touchdown runs of 35, 65 and 72 yards. For the season, he scored twelve touchdowns, and Walter Camp, the then unchallenged All America selector, named Red to his first team.

Red's greatest day as a collegian was October 18, 1924. More than 67,000 fans, the largest crowd ever to have watched football in the Midwest up to that time, jammed Memorial Stadium to see Illinois and Michigan renew their bitter rivalry. Red took the opening kickoff on his five-yard line and headed for the right sideline, a horde of Michigan tacklers after him. Streaking down a sideline was a Grange trademark, but this time, using a piece of strategy cooked up by Bob Zuppke, the Illinois coach, Grange cut abruptly to his left and sprinted directly across the field. When he got to the other sideline, he ran a straight course for about twenty yards, then veered sharply back again, and finally angled into the end zone. Within the next ten minutes, Red scored three more times. That was not all. In the second half, Zuppke had Red do some passing, and he threw twice for touchdowns. Illinois won, 39–14, Red accounting for all six of his team's touchdowns. He earned his name the Galloping Ghost that day.

In 1925, Red's senior year, he captained an inexperienced Illinois team that managed to win only one victory in its first four games. Then came a key contest against mighty Pennsylvania at Franklin Field, a game that marked Red's first appearance in the East. Many Eastern sportswriters, never having seen him play, were dubious of his achievements. But when the game was over, there was not a single doubter in the press box.

On the first play from scrimmage, Red raced 55 yards for a touchdown on a muddy field. He scored two more times that day, and piled up 363 yards in rushing. Underdog Illinois buried Pennsylvania, 24–2. Wrote Damon Runyon: "This man Red Grange is three or four men and a horse rolled into one. He is Jack Dempsey, Babe Ruth, Al Jolson, Paavo Nurmi and Man O'War."

Often this period is referred to as the Golden Age in Sports, but somehow professional football managed to escape the gilding. The National Football League, in existence for only four years, was a loosely knit organization of twenty teams confined solely to cities of the East and Midwest. New York, Cleveland, Chicago and Detroit were represented, but so were cities like Canton, Ohio, Rock Island, Illinois, and Pottsville, Pennsylvania. Pottsville was a powerhouse, winning the league championship in 1925. (The league owners, however, in some mysterious fashion, judged the Chicago Cardinals to be the titleholders.)

Players of the day were paid $50 to $75 a game, and they often played with two different teams under different names on the same weekend. The league schedule was a haphazard affair; rival teams arranged games whenever it was mutually convenient. All in all, it was a dismal period.

George Halas, owner of the Bears, saw his team's salvation in Grange. He began negotiations with Red's agent, Charles C. "Cash and Carry" Pyle, a man who owned a chain of movie theaters in Central Illinois. Red's decision to sign with the pros was an extremely difficult one to make. The newspapers aired various sides of the argument on their editorial pages. Some said that he should pass up the "tainted" money offered by pro ball, that to be paid for playing was somehow unclean. Others agreed with C. C. Pyle, who was urging Red to cash in on the value of his name while he had the opportunity.

Red's last appearance as a collegian was against Ohio State, and before 85,200 spectators, the largest crowd ever to see an American sports event to that time. They had gathered, said Grantland Rice, "to hear for the last time the thudding hoofbeats of the redhead's march. . . ." Rice said it was all "like a tremendous circus, multiplied ten or twenty times. And every tongue was spinning but one name—Grange."

After the game, which Illinois won, it was announced that Red would join the Bears. He was to be guaranteed $3,000 a game against a hefty percentage of the gate receipts.

"I'm going into professional football to make money out of it," Red announced with characteristic candor. "I see nothing wrong in playing pro football. It's the same as playing professional baseball, it seems to me. I have to get the money now because people will forget all about me in a few years." Halas and Pyle immediately began lining up a barnstorming tour for Grange and the Bears.

Grange's debut as a professional came against the Cardinals at Wrigley Field in Chicago on Thanksgiving Day, 1925. It was not a triumphant beginning. Paddy Driscoll, a kicking star from Northwestern University, refused to kick the ball anywhere near Grange. He punted twenty-five times and on only three occasions did the redhead get his hands on the ball. "Kicking to Grange," Driscoll said, "is like grooving one to Babe Ruth." Red's longest run was a seven-yard gain off right tackle. He threw six times and didn't complete a pass.

From an attendance standpoint it was a different story, however. A capacity crowd of 36,000 filled the park, something that had never happened before for a Bears-Cardinals meeting. It was the shape of things to come.

After the game in Chicago, the Bears and Grange set off on a frantic exhibition that had them playing nine games—more than half a season's schedule by present-day standards—in nine days. It was a brutal grind for every player, but particularly for Grange whose contract dictated that he had to play at least thirty minutes of every game.

The Sunday following Thanksgiving Day the Bears were in action again at Wrigley Field. This time they faced the Columbus Tigers. Again Red had a frustrating day, but again the gate was sensational, with 28,000 fans on hand to cheer Grange's every move. On Wednesday, the team played in St. Louis. This was followed by a train trip east, and on Saturday the merry-go-round stopped at Philadelphia. Here 35,000 people turned out despite a cold drizzle. Red lived up to his press notices, scoring both touchdowns as the Bears turned back the Frankford Yellow-jackets, 14–0.

Then the show moved into New York. With just one night's rest, the Bears took on the New York Giants at the Polo Grounds. The Bears did not have time to have their uniforms cleaned and they were still wet and mud-stained from the game in Philadelphia. (It was unheard of for a team to have more than one set of uniforms.) They were a sorry and bedraggled sight compared to the Giants, all clean and polished.

The stop in New York was the high point of the Eastern tour. The crowd began gathering late in the morning and by game time every seat in the Polo Grounds was filled and standing-room space was put on sale. More than 65,000 people roared when the kickoff arced into the air. It was the biggest crowd ever to see a pro game up to that time.

Red thrilled the gathering in the fourth quarter by intercepting a Giant pass and streaking 30 yards for a touchdown. Thousands in the huge throng knew little about football; they had been attracted by the magic name of Grange. By his interception, he sent them home happy. Very few were grieved that the hometown team lost.

It was a bruising afternoon for the redhead. Late in the second quarter, Red was slugged in the back of the headgear by Joe Williams of the Giants. Westbrook Pegler, covering the game for the Chicago *Tribune,* described the incident this way: "Williams . . . wound up like an old barroom fighter throwing the 15-pound cuspidor and let Grange have it. Red stumbled unsteadily but did nothing about it, and neither did the officials who were about as hostile to fistfighting as Tex Rickard is." Another Giant kicked Red during the game, and a third grabbed him around the neck in an apparent effort to twist his head from his shoulders.

But the money Red received was balm for these indignities. It was spectacular. A Chicago newspaper even published a box score of his earnings, and computed that he made an average of $300 an hour, twenty-four hours a day, over the first eleven days of the tour. In New York he hit the jackpot, with a share of the gate that came to approximately $30,000. Red also signed to make a movie, an enterprise that enriched him by another $50,000. He endorsed shoes and sportswear, soft drinks and health drinks, and a Red Grange doll. At games vendors hawked the redhead's picture and even Red Grange peanuts.

Grange's appearance in New York was a badly needed shot in the arm for the New York franchise. Fans seldom showed much interest in the team, and owner Tim Mara was in the red for $250,000. "I felt sure pro football ought to go," Mara told Grantland Rice, "but it wasn't going fast enough, not as fast as my money was.

"Then we met the Bears—with Grange. I would have been glad to have seen 25,000 people in the stands. Instead, the house was swamped. I knew my worries were over."

The New York game was on a Sunday. The following Tuesday the Bears played in Washington, and on Wednesday, the coldest day of the year, they were in Boston to face the Providence Steamrollers. The murderous schedule was beginning to take its toll. Red was haggard and drawn; on the field he moved listlessly. The crowd booed him heartily. Once he picked up the ball to toss it back to the referee and the fans let out a derisive cheer to see him "complete" a pass. The next day in Pittsburgh things got worse. Red tore a muscle in his left arm. He had to be benched, and he was unable to play in Detroit the next day, a merciful reprieve. The Bears had to refund thousands of dollars to ticket holders. Grange did manage to get into the lineup for the final game of the tour, a homecoming date against the Giants at Wrigley Field.

Red rested his black-and-blue and aching body, but only briefly. The frantic caravan resumed in January, this time beginning in Florida and ending in Oregon. Jacksonville, Miami, Tampa, New Orleans, San Diego, Los Angeles (where 70,000 people turned out), San Francisco, Seattle and Portland were the stopovers. This string of exhibitions brought Red's personal earnings to over $100,000.

For the 1926 pro season Pyle demanded that Halas give Grange a share of the Bears. The Chicago owner refused, and then Pyle tried to get an NFL franchise in New York. Rebuked again, he started a league of his own, with Red and himself the owners of the New York franchise, the Yankees. Despite its drawing card, the league was a financial disaster and both Pyle and Grange lost heavily. Pyle had no choice but to seek an armistice. Out of the peace settlement, he was awarded an NFL franchise in New York. Red played for this team, which retained the name Yankees.

In the third game of the 1927 season, the New Yorkers were in Chicago for a contest with the Bears at Wrigley Field. The stands were jammed. Late in the game, Red collided with George Trafton, the huge center for the Bears; his cleats caught in the turf and his knee twisted as he fell. Trafton landed on top of him. Red was on crutches for four months as doctors pondered how to repair the damage. Their efforts were in vain. The injury robbed Red forever of his great speed and elusiveness. "After it happened, I was just another halfback," Grange once said.

Red didn't play football at all in 1928. He made some vaudiville appearances and filmed a movie.

In 1929, George Halas invited Red to return to the Bears. Red knew that his talents as an explosive runner were gone, and he had misgivings. But he gave it a try, and developed into a fine pass receiver and blocker. His career stretched six more seasons.

In 1931 he made the NFL All Star team as a left halfback. In the 1932 title game, he caught a short jump pass from Bronko Nagurski and scored the winning touchdown. Grange's final moment of glory came in the 1933 championship game between the Bears and the Giants. The scene was the Polo Grounds. The Bears had a slim lead, 23–21. In the last seconds of play, Harry Newman, the New York quarterback, completed a 28-yard pass to Dale Burnett.

As Burnett streaked for the end zone, he found teammate Mel Hein at his side, and only Red Grange blocking their path to a touchdown. Burnett's plan was clear. He would wait until Grange tackled him, then toss a lateral to Hein. But Grange was equal to the moment. He grabbed Burnett high, clasping his arms to his sides so he could not throw the ball. He wrestled Burnett to the ground as the gun went off.

Red retired in January 1935 after a post-season exhibition game. He started an insurance business which flourished, and for a time he was active in football as a television broadcaster.

Throughout his career, Red shrugged off the headlines. After his premiere appearance at the Polo Grounds in 1925, he told the New York *Journal*, "People say I'm commercial. I am, for

I realize that ten years from now no one will know or care what Red Gange did or who he was." He was wrong, of course. More than any other figure, Red Grange helped to put pro football on the map. Because of that, it is not likely he will ever be forgotten.

George Halas

George Halas really didn't invent professional football but he might as well have. For more than half a century he has been as vital to the sport as cleats and goalposts.

Yet George Halas began as a baseball player. In 1919, fresh out of the Navy, Halas was skillful enough to win a tryout with the New York Yankees. In spring training he quickly nailed down a starting assignment, and Yankee manager Miller Huggins called him "one of the best outfield prospects I've ever seen."

The Yankees faced Brooklyn in an exhibition game, and Halas bristled at the taunts of Rube Marquard, the Dodger pitcher. In his first time at bat, Halas laced one of Marquard's throws between two outfielders, and he tore around the bases, sliding into third inches ahead of the ball.

It was a momentous slide. Halas seriously injured his hip.

"The Yankees said I should be treated by a Youngstown, Ohio, steel puddler named Bonesetter Reese, and they sent me to see him," Halas recalls. "Bonesetter dug into my thigh with his superhuman hands and gave a twist. I was cured."

But when Halas returned to the Yankees, his position had been taken by someone else. "And this guy could hit curve balls," Halas says.

Halas finished the season with St. Paul in the American Association. The next year pro football beckoned.

Halas recently completed his fiftieth year in pro ball. His mark upon the sport is conspicuous at every level. He was one of the first to cry out for the rule changes that transformed the game from a wrestling match between opposing linemen to the wide-open brand of play familiar today. It was Halas, along with Ralph Jones and Clark Shaughnessy, who developed the T formation, with the man-in-motion concept, to such a high degree of sophistication that it was eventually adopted by every pro club.

Halas was the first coach to hold daily practice sessions, and the first to utilize films of opponents' games for study. His team was the first to use a major league baseball park as home grounds, the first to make a barnstorming tour, and the first to broadcast games via radio. He was the first to use a tarpaulin to protect the playing field from adverse weather.

A band to entertain spectators, a team song (entitled, "Bear Down, Chicago Bears"), and a public address announcer to cite the ballcarrier and call out the amount of yardage gained—all these are innovations of George Halas!

Halas has more than a plaque in the Hall of Fame to immortalize his attainments. He has an imperishable monument called the Chicago Bears. He organized the team in football's mean and miserable days and saw it develop into a gridiron powerhouse, and a profitable one. With Halas at the helm, the Bears have won twelve Western Division titles and seven NFL championships. Twice Halas-coached teams have gone unbeaten and untied through an entire season; twice he achieved winning streaks of eighteen consecutive games. Only eight times in 48 years have the Bears lost more games than they have won. If you're going to build a monument, you might as well build a successful one.

George Stanley Halas was born in Chicago on February 2, 1895, the youngest child in a family of seven. George's father and mother were born in Prague, and, like most immigrant parents, they did not take kindly to their sons' interest in sports. But George was persistent and, besides, his older brothers paved the way for him. Their athletic accomplishments broke down most of the barriers.

George, physically, was never any Bronko Nagurski. In his senior year at Chicago's Crane Tech, he weighed only 140 pounds, yet his aggressiveness was such that he became a starter at right tackle.

When he enrolled at the University of Illinois in 1915, his athletic skills were scarcely noticed. He tried out for a post at halfback, making up in eagerness what he lacked in muscle and bulk. After watching his breakneck style of play in a practice session, Bob Zuppke, the Illinois coach, turned to an assistant and said, "He runs so hard he'll kill himself; make him an end." An end he became.

Halas also played basketball at Illinois and was the team captain during his senior year. His skill on the baseball diamond has already been mentioned.

After graduation in 1918, with the United States in the throes of World War I, Halas entered the Navy as an ensign. He was assigned to the Great Lakes Naval Training Station, which just happened to have the best football team of the day. Jimmy Conzelman and Paddy Driscoll were among its stars, and both were to win high praise as professionals within a few years.

The high point of the year for the sailors came on New Year's Day, 1919, when they defeated the favored Mare Island Marines in the Rose Bowl. "That was the only game I ever really starred in," Halas remembers. He caught two passes from Paddy Driscoll for touchdowns, and he intercepted another and ran it back to the Marines' three-yard line. "It was a good day," he observes.

Once discharged from the Navy, and following his brief sojourn with the Yankees, Halas' lifelong career in pro football took root. A. E. Staley, owner of the Staley Starch Company of Decatur, Illinois, hired George to head his company's athletic program. Organizing a football team was high on the agenda. Halas loaded the team with top talent, bringing together such notables as Ed "Dutch" Sternaman, Guy Chamberlin, George Trafton and Charley Dressen, who was to win fame in baseball as manager of the Dodgers and later the Tigers.

After the team came the league. On a humid September night in 1920, in the automobile agency of Ralph Hay in Canton, Ohio, a handful of coaches and owners, Halas among them, doled out franchises in an organization they called the American Professional Football Association. An era was beginning. The next year, at Halas' suggestion, the name of the organization was changed to the National Football League. Halas' team was a splendid on-the-field success, winning all but one of its thirteen games. And the players did well financially, each pocketing about $1,900 for the season. But Halas' days in Decatur were numbered. Staley had adjudged the football team was too great an investment for him to support. One day he suggested to Halas that he move the team to Chicago. He gave George a check for

$5,000 to help with expenses, but with the understanding that the name Staleys be retained for a year.

Twenty-six-year-old George Halas had no easy road of it in Chicago. By present standards of professional football, these were primitive times. Halas' office was whatever suit he happened to be wearing. The league schedule was a hodgepodge, with individual teams playing whenever and wherever a match could be arranged. Games were frequently canceled because of rain or snow or any spell of bad weather that might adversely affect the gate.

As a coach, Halas maintained tight control. His word was law. Disobedience or insubordination were not tolerated. "He'd fine himself if he was late," one player remarked.

Halas established daily morning practice sessions not long after the club was shifted to Chicago. But they weren't primarily meant to increase the players' proficiency. "A big city is filled with varied attractions for a young athlete," Halas once remarked. "If a player has to report for a morning practice, he won't do too much playing of a different sort at night."

Halas took in Dutch Sternaman as a partner, and the pair negotiated a lease arrangement with William Veeck, Sr., then president of the Chicago Cubs, for the use of Wrigley Field. Early in 1922, Halas changed the name of the club to the Bears. He was a devoted follower of baseball's Cubs, and, since he shared Wrigley Field with them, the new name was natural.

The Staleys won the imaginary league championship in 1921 with a 10-1-1 record, but as the Bears the team was not nearly so successful—at first. It was 1932 before they came in first again.

In 1925, Halas made a bold move that rocketed pro football out of the doldrums. He signed Red Grange off the University of Illinois campus. A swivel-hipped halfback, Grange was to football of the day what Babe Ruth was to baseball. The ink was hardly dry on Grange's signature when Halas and C. C. Pyle, the redhead's manager, booked the Bears on a frantic barnstorming tour that took them through the major cities of the East, then south into Florida, and, finally, to the Pacific Coast. The tour was a wondrous success, and not only because it set box-office records almost everywhere. It established pro football in the public mind as both a respectable profession and legitimate business enterprise.

This does not mean that there were no more bleak days. Even Red Grange came to cause Halas some grim moments. For Grange's sophomore season, Pyle demanded a one-third interest in the Bears. When Halas refused, Pyle attempted to gain control of the New York Giants. Again he was rebuffed. His next play was to organize a league of his own, the American League, he called it, and he took the New York franchise for himself and Grange.

This was not Halas' only headache. Joe Sternaman, his partner's brother, left the Bears' organization to start a competing team in Chicago—the Bulls. In the struggle for patronage in Chicago, Halas lured Paddy Driscoll, the star halfback of the Chicago Cardinals, into the Bear camp. But attendance still dropped. One Sunday that season the Bears drew only 12,000, while on the other side of town almost twice that number turned out to watch Grange and his Yankee teammates play the Bulls.

The next year Pyle's American League folded. The Bears began to prosper. In 1932, Halas bought out Sternaman's interest in the club. Today Halas is said to hold approximately 90 percent of the Bears' stock. The balance is in the hands of relatives and friends.

Halas retired as a player in 1929, although in the decades that followed, his participation in the games was only slightly less intense than in the days when he held down right end. He invariably stalks the sidelines, a familiar figure in dark-tinted glasses, a slouch hat and a buttoned-up overcoat. In recent years he has been bothered by a slight limp. He has been known to storm out onto the playing field to impress a point upon an official. Even the most casual observer at any Bear game knows who is in charge.

In 1933 the NFL split into Eastern and Western divisions. The Bears took part in the first two playoffs, winning one and losing one. Many experts say that the 1934 Bear team was the best ever. It featured Beattie Feathers, a sleek halfback, who galloped behind the infallible blocking of Bronko Nagurski. The team roared through the entire league season of thirteen games without suffering a single defeat.

Halas assembled another memorable Bear team in 1940. Sid Luckman, a shrewd and daring T-formation quarterback, was the team's standout performer. Chicago took the Western Division title, and then crushed the Washington Redskins for the NFL championship by the incredible score of 73–0.

Halas has said that this game marked a turning point in pro football. "It converted everyone to the T," he states. "All of today's formations—the man-in-motion, the split end, the flanker —evolved from this game."

Clark Shaughnessy is generally credited with having fathered the T formation. But Halas says that Ralph Jones, who coached the Bears from 1930 to 1932, deserves the lion's share of credit. Jones, who came to the Bears from Lake Forest Academy, widened the spacing in the backfield and split the end, and it was Jones who introduced the idea of the man-in-motion.

In 1946 the Bears took the league crown again, but a full decade passed before they were contenders once more. In 1956, led by a fearless fullback named Rick Casares, the Bears were supreme in the Western Division, but they lost to the Giants in the title playoff. Then a number of cheerless seasons followed. The critics began to howl. They said Papa Bear was too old, that he had not been able to keep pace with the sophisticated offense and defense of the day.

Halas silenced those who were crying for his scalp the best way he knew how. In 1963 he again brought the Bears into the championship playoff; again they faced the Giants. The Bears' defense, which had allowed only 144 points all season, rose to the occasion. They bottled up the Giant runners and made five interceptions, two of which led to touchdowns. It ended with the Bears on top, 14–10. Halas was the happiest man on the field, bestowing handshakes and hugs on anyone who came close. He was named the NFL's Coach of the Year. Not a word was heard from the critics—for a while.

Looking back over half a century in professional football, Halas said his biggest thrill came the day his magnificent Bear machine whipped the Washington Redskins, 73–0. His biggest disappointment was losing to the New York Giants in the 1934 championship playoff. This was the famous "sneakers" game, in which the Giants used basketball shoes to cope with the frozen field.

Halas said that the greatest performance he ever saw came in 1965, the day that Gale Sayers, then a Bear rookie, scored six touchdowns against the San Francisco 49ers. Halas is reluctant to name his all-time All Star team, but he once compiled a "dream" backfield for a reporter. It consisted of Sid Luckman, quarterback; George McAfee and Steve Van Buren, halfbacks; and Bronko Nagurski, fullback.

In his final years as the Bears' field general, Halas was urged to retire as coach many times, to replace himself with a younger man.

Actually, he had relinquished the coaching reins of the team three times. The first time he quit was in 1930. He hired Ralph Jones, but Jones lasted only two seasons. Halas next left the Bears in 1942 for duty with the U. S. Navy. Then in 1956 Halas appointed Paddy Driscoll as head coach, but Driscoll had been Halas' assistant for fifteen years. It was no secret who was really running the club.

Halas made two concessions to time. He rode about in a golf cart during the Bears' practice sessions, and he napped each afternoon for about two hours. "He used to promise he'd retire when he was fifty-five," his wife once said, "but when he got there, he changed it to sixty. Later it became seventy."

During 1967 pre-season play, the Bears were severely manhandled by the Kansas City Chiefs of the American Football League. The score was 66–24. The Chiefs tallied nine touchdowns, seven extra points, one two-point conversion and one field goal. Never before in the history of the Bears had so many points been scored against them. One writer called the shambles the "Stupor Bowl."

A new wave of criticism descended upon Halas' shoulders. "Are you going to retire now?" he was asked.

"After a defeat like that?" he answered. "Don't be silly. I've got a lot of work to do."

The 1967 season, however, did prove to be Halas' last as a coach. In May, 1968, he announced he was calling it quits. The news was carried in streamer headlines on page one of the Chicago daily newspapers.

At a news conference announcing his retirement, Halas disclosed that he realized his coaching days must end when he discovered he could no longer run up and down the sidelines upbraiding officials, one of his favorite pastimes. He recalled that during the final game of the season he had tried to chase an official who was pacing off a penalty against the Bears. Said Halas: "I suddenly realized I wasn't gaining on him."

Mel Hein

If you name Mel Hein of the New York Giants as the greatest center in pro football history, you will get very, very few arguments.

One of the first notable college players to sign with the pros, Hein joined the Giants in 1931, and he stayed a long, long time —fifteen years. Arthur Daley, the New York *Times'* columnist, once estimated that Mel played more minutes of more games than any other man in pro football history. Hein himself does not disagree with this statement.

Hein played both ways. On the offense he had no peer in snapping the ball back. And in those days it went way back, to a tailback. He was huge—6 feet 3, 235 pounds—but mobile. He would often pull out of the line to lead a run, or drop back to protect the passer. In Hein's early days with the Giants, both of these maneuvers were wholly unique, at least for centers.

If it hadn't been for the quick thinking of a Pullman, Washington, postmaster, Hein might never have been a Giant. He was All America at Washington State, and member of their Rose Bowl team in his senior year, 1931. After graduation Mel received offers from two pro teams—the Providence Steamrollers and the Portsmouth Spartans. Mel would have preferred to sign with the New York Giants, but they never contacted him.

Providence had made Hein the better offer so he signed their contract and mailed it at the campus post office. Then he left with the basketball team for a game against Gonzaga University at Spokane. Gonzaga's coach was Ray Flaherty, an end for the Giants. After the game, Flaherty sought out Hein.

"Did you get your contract yet?" Flaherty asked.

"What contract?" said Hein. "I never heard from them. I signed with the Steamrollers."

"Oh, no," said Flaherty. "How much did they offer you?"

"One hundred and thirty-five dollars a game," Hein replied. Flaherty shook his head. "The Giants will give you at least a hundred and fifty," he said. "I'll get in touch with the club tomorrow and see if I can get them to send you a contract right away. But you have to get the other one back and tear it up."

When Hein returned to Pullman, he went to see the postmaster. "The letter's already left," he said. "About all you can do is wire the Providence postmaster, describe the letter, and ask him to return it."

It was good advice. Ten days later the letter was returned. Mel signed with the Giants soon after.

At the Giants' training camp Mel quickly established himself as a crashing tackler and a fearsome blocker. However, the club already had a dependable center in George Murtaugh, and Rookie Hein saw little action during pre-season exhibitions and in the Giants' first game of the regular season. In the second game, against Portsmouth, Murtaugh was injured and Steve Owen sent Hein in as his replacement.

On the first play, Mel flattened a Portsmouth back who tried to sweep left end. The Spartans lost ground on the next play. It was third down and 13 yards to go, and, according to the custom of the day, a punt was in order. As the ball was snapped, Hein started downfield to cover. As he was running he felt a sharp thud against the back of his neck. It was the ball. The Portsmouth quarterback had called a pass play, but his aim was poor and he had hit Hein. "It was then that I learned the difference between college and pro ball," said Hein. "They didn't always go by the book in the pros. You had to be ready for anything."

Although Hein was thoroughly aggressive, indeed he was coldly ferocious when it came to tackling and blocking; he was a gentleman player. Gouging, kneeing, piling on, and other similar misdeeds of the day were not in his repertoire. The flare-ups he had were few. One exception involved George Musso, the mammoth guard of the Chicago Bears.

As Mel, his head down, snapped the ball back, Musso clobbered him. "Don't do that again," Mel warned. Musso laughed. Again Mel centered; again he got belted. The next time Mel bent over the ball, he passed it back with one hand and walloped

Musso with the other. All Musso said was, "Nice going, Mel." Later the two became close friends.

During Hein's twenty-five years as a football player—two years in grammar school, four in high school, four in college, and fifteen with the Giants—he scored only two touchdowns, one in college, one while with New York. It happened during the 1938 season. Mel intercepted a Green Bay pass and galloped 50 yards for the score.

The same year the Giants met the Packers for the NFL championship. Early in the game the Packers were grinding out small but consistent yardage against Hein. Coach Owen began to fret and called Hein to the sidelines, for an explanation.

"Don't worry," Hein said. "I'm letting them commit themselves before I commit myself. Sure they're getting some short yardage, but Hutson's not able to get behind me for a touchdown."

Hein's theory worked. Hutson was stopped cold. The Giants won, 23–17.

Late in Hein's career the Giants held Mel Hein Day at the Polo Grounds to honor their indestructible center. Mayor LaGuardia made a speech and Hein received a car loaded with gifts. Then the Giants took the field and lost to the Dodgers, 14–6. "We're sorry we didn't win for Mel," said Giant halfback Hank Soar after the game. "But, hell, every day the Giants have played in the last ten years has been Mel Hein Day."

Hein was born in Redding, California, on August 22, 1909, and brought up in Glacier, Washington. A 145-pound center, he captained the football team in his last two years in grammar school. He was a tall, trim 175 pounds when he entered high school in Bellingham, Washington. He played center but also, in succession, guard, tackle and even halfback. Coach Babe Hollingberry lured him to Washington State. Hein patrolled rugged mountain trails for the U. S. Forest Service during the summer to build his legs, then won the starting center's spot during his sophomore year. He was an All Coast selection as junior, and an All American as a senior.

Hein was a member of seven Eastern Division champion teams and two NFL champion teams in his years with the Giants. "The

Giants were a team of great pride when I was with them," he once recalled. "There were no cliques and very little dissension. We were just one big, happy family."

Hein retired after the 1942 season. He accepted an offer to coach football at Union College in Schenectady, New York. Because of the World War II manpower requirements, Union was forced to drop football, but Mel stayed on to help train Navy officer candidates.

In 1943, Steve Owen prevailed upon Hein to rejoin the Giants as a "weekend center." He played with New York on Sunday, then returned to Union on Monday for the balance of the week.

It was not easy. Hein recalls the season opener in 1944. It was played in Boston on a blazing-hot September Sunday. Hein was then thirty-five, and not in the very best of shape. He played the entire sixty minutes. "But I thought I was going to die," he recalls. In 1945, with the war over and young talent available again, Mel quit for keeps.

The year after Hein retired, the All America Conference was formed and the new league began to bid wildly with the NFL for playing talent. The going rate for linemen was $10,000; some veterans received more. The situation gave Mel cause to lament. In his last year with the Giants he was paid $5,000, and he was the highest-salaried lineman in the league.

In 1951, after brief stopovers as a coach with the Los Angeles Dons, the New York Yankees and the Los Angeles Rams, Hein joined the coaching staff of the University of Southern California. A colleague of his was Al Davis. Later Davis became general manager of the Oakland Raiders and, in 1966, commissioner of the American Football League. During this time Davis appointed Mel to be supervisor of officials for the AFL. He holds that post today.

Hein was an All Pro center for eight consecutive years, an achievement no player in any position has ever matched. He was elected the Giants' team captain year after year—ten in all. The players addressed him as "Cappy," a name which implied both their affection and respect. When Hein left the Giants following the 1945 season, the club retired his No. 7 jersey. Surely it was the luckiest 7 in Giant history.

Wilbur (Pete) Henry

Linemen are often the forgotten men of football but Pete Henry, a tackle, was a noteworthy exception. He entered the pro ranks in 1920, joining the Canton Bulldogs. The day he signed his pro contract the news earned front-page headlines in the Canton *Repository*, with the editor using the size of type usually reserved for wars or armistices.

The day that Henry signed it was also announced that a group of franchise holders had met and formed a professional football league. This organization was a forerunner of the NFL. But this story was strictly secondary in importance. The news about Henry overshadowed everything.

Henry did not look like a football player. He was 6 feet tall, but round, a roly-poly 250 pounds. They called him "Fats." But it was an inappropriate nickname, for his flesh was concrete-solid.

Although Henry may not have moved with gazellelike grace, he had plenty of speed. He was fast enough afoot to be a constant menace on offense. "Watch out for Henry!" opposing players would warn one another when Canton had the ball. Henry, on a "tackle over tackle" play, was one of the foremost ground gainers for the Bulldogs.

But it was on defense that Henry shone the brightest. George Halas, who played end for the Chicago Bears, faced Henry on hundreds of plays. "Only once," Halas said, "was I able to block him out."

Halas had no need to feel chagrined over his ineptitude. One man was seldom enough to handle Pete and sometimes several of them could not do the job. Once in a game against the Buffalo All Americans, their coach, Tommy Hughitt, decided to run every play straight at Henry. "Everyone rack him up at once," Hughitt instructed his players. "We'll show him who's boss."

The first time Buffalo got possession of the ball, Hughitt put his plan into action. The result was carnage. Henry flattened the entire side of the Buffalo line, and then rocketed into the backfield to spill the ballcarrier for a substantial loss.

One of Buffalo's fallen linemen was Lou Little, their end. "Damn you, Pete," Little moaned as he staggered to his feet.

"You don't mean that, do you?" Pete asked.

Buffalo's Swede Youngstrom heard the exchange and turned on Little. "Keep your mouth shut, Lou," he ordered. "Just get up like a gentleman. Let's not get Pete mad and have him stomping us."

When the All Americans huddled, Hughitt hurriedly changed his strategy. No more plays were run at Henry that day.

Henry was born in Mansfield, Ohio, in 1897. He played fullback on his high school team, but when he tried out for the squad at Washington and Jefferson College, Bob Folwell, the W & J coach, switched the 215-pound youngster to tackle. Henry's heroics at that position were to win him plaudits from every quarter. Said Grantland Rice, "The best tackle I ever saw was Fats Henry." Walter Camp, the No. 1 football authority of the day, called Henry "one of the most remarkable performers I ever saw on the gridiron." Camp named Henry to his All American team in 1919.

Henry was one of the most spectacular tackles college football has ever known. In one game Washington and Jefferson faced West Virginia Wesleyan, one of the powerhouses of the day. Henry blocked a punt (a specialty of his), grabbed up the ball and raced for a touchdown. He booted the extra point. He also kicked two field goals that day. W & J won, 13–6. Every one of the team's points had been scored by Henry.

Henry kept a careful chronicle of his days at Washington and Jefferson. His diary is now a part of the extensive collection of Henry memorabilia at the Pro Football Hall of Fame. One poignant entry sums up his feelings about the game he loved. "Now that football's over," Henry wrote, "I don't know what to do."

In his professional career, Henry played six seasons with the Bulldogs. In two of those seasons—1922 and 1923—the team was undefeated. Henry won All Pro honors in 1921, 1922 and 1923. He played part of the 1927 season with the New York Giants, and ended his career with the Pottsville Maroons in 1928.

In the later stages of his career, Henry became noted for his prowess as a kicker, both on place-kicks and punts. He and Jim

Thorpe would practice punting by standing on opposite goal lines and kicking to one another. A 90-yard punt by either one was not considered extraordinary.

The NFL record manual attests to Henry's greatness as a kicker. It contains this entry: "Longest Punt, 94 yards, Wilbur (Pete) Henry, Canton vs. Akron, October 28, 1923."

And this one: "Longest Drop Kick Field Goal, 50 Yards, Wilbur (Pete) Henry, Canton vs. Toledo, November 13, 1922."

Pete Henry died in 1952 while serving as athletic director at Washington and Jefferson. He was already a legendary figure. He had been elected to the College Hall of Fame and to both College and Professional Halls of Fame sponsored by the Helms Foundation. He was a tackle on the mid-century All American team selected by *Collier's* magazine.

The Canton *Repository* summed up Henry's extraordinary career the best. In his account of a game during the 1922 season, a correspondent for the paper wrote: "Tackles will come and tackles will go but never will pro football enthusiasts see the peer of Wilbur Henry."

Robert (Cal) Hubbard

In the days before the pros adopted the unlimited substitution rule, each team carried a "policeman," a big, rawboned player who was possessed of sound judgment and an even temper. When an opposing player was guilty of dirty play, it was the policeman's duty to convince the wrongdoer of the error of his ways. Cal Hubbard, a mammoth tackle, was the policeman for the Green Bay Packers during the 1930's. He was so respected by the teams of the league, by fans and officials, that when he meted out punishment he was never questioned. It was recognized that the victim had merited it.

It must be said at once that Hubbard was much more than simply an efficient law-enforcement official. Many authorities consider him the greatest tackle ever to play professional football. And more than a few rate Hubbard as the sport's best lineman, bar none.

Hubbard had all the necessary physical requirements. He was

big; indeed, gigantic by standards of the day—6 feet 5, 250 pounds. The late Russ Winnie, who broadcast the Packers' games, used to say, "Cal Hubbard weighs between 265 and 280, depending upon what he had for breakfast." But Cal himself protests that he never exceeded 255. He was extremely agile for his size, and he hit like a ton of bricks. His attitude was another important factor in his success. He gloried in the game; he played it to the hilt.

A farm boy, Cal was born in Keytesville, Missouri, on October 31, 1900. His boyhood idol was Bo McMillin, quarterback of the Praying Colonels of Centre College in Kentucky, an unheralded team from the backwoods that defeated mighty Harvard in 1921. When McMillin became coach of tiny Centenary College in Shreveport, Louisiana, Hubbard enrolled at the school. The "Southern Gentlemen," as McMillin called the team, won the Louisiana Intercollegiate Association championship in 1922. In intersectional competition in 1923 and 1924, Centenary seldom lost, and Hubbard was the outstanding player on the team. The school was too small to be noticed by most football experts, and as a result Hubbard failed to win All America designation. When McMillin moved to Geneva College in Beaver Falls, Pennsylvania, Hubbard went along. In 1926 he played right end for Geneva and showed such skill that Grantland Rice named Cal to his All America team that year.

Several pro teams bid for Hubbard's services. McMillin advised him to sign with the New York Giants. "At least they'll be sure to pay you," he said.

The Giants made efficient use of Hubbard's speed and menacing power. On defense he became a prototype for the modern-day linebacker, often pulling out of the line in the pursuit of a ballcarrier. On offense he was equally valuable. The Giants installed him as an offensive end on a screen pass play. He would take two steps, then turn slightly to be ready for a bullet pass. The play was often good for five or six yards.

Hubbard played 34 games with the Giants, and only once was he anything less than a sixty-minute performer. In one game he cracked a bone in his foot. This sidelined him for the last two minutes of play.

In 1929, Hubbard moved on to the Green Bay Packers, switching teams in an offhand manner typical of the time. Cal, a small-town boy, got little pleasure from the hustle and bustle of New York. The Giants went to Green Bay for a game with the Packers and, since they were playing the Bears in Chicago the following Sunday, remained in Green Bay for a full week of practice. Hubbard got to like the town so much that he asked the Giants to trade him to the Packers. They obliged.

At Green Bay, Hubbard reached his glittering best. Three times—in 1931, 1932 and 1933—he was named All League tackle.

Joining the Packers with Hubbard were Johnny Blood from Pottsville, and Mike Michalske from the New York Yankees. This trio was the driving force that brought three consecutive world championships to Green Bay—in 1929, 1930 and 1931.

"We really won four in a row," Hubbard protests, "but they didn't give it to us. In 1932, we had a 10-3-1 record. The Bears won only seven, tied six and lost one. But ties didn't count in those days, so they gave the title to the Bears. We beat them once that year and we tied them once."

Lon Evans, a guard for Green Bay from 1933 to 1937, once recalled what it was like playing alongside Hubbard: "In my first game, the guy on the other side of the line slugged me in the mouth and knocked out a handful of my teeth. Then he started to go to work on me.

" 'That guy is killing me,' I said to Hubbard. I told him I was going to tell the referee.

"Hubbard was shocked," Evans remembers. " 'Lord, no, don't do that,' he declared. 'Don't get the ref excited. On the next play we'll be on defense; then we can take care of him.' "

Throughout his career as a pro football player, Hubbard also served as a baseball umpire, and a distinguished one. His size precluded any arguments or back talk. He started out in the Piedmont League in 1928, and worked his way up to the American League by 1933. Eventually his baseball duties forced him to postpone his arrival at football training camp each fall, a factor in the Packers' decision to place him on the inactive list in 1935.

The New York Giants secured him that year and he played in several games. Not long before the end of the season he saw a player break a leg. He suddenly realized that should he become the victim of such an injury, it would ruin not one career, but two. Except for a brief appearance in the lineup of the Pittsburgh Steelers in one game the next season, Hubbard never played football again.

No one can say that it was not a wise decision. In 1952, Cal was appointed umpire-in-chief of the American League, a post he holds today. He also owns and operates a 300-acre cattle farm near Milan, Missouri.

Hubbard hesitates to single out his most memorable game in the National Football League. "They were all great for me," says Cal. "I just loved to play."

During Hubbard's career, perhaps his most noted opponent was Bronko Nagurski, the battering-ram fullback of the Chicago Bears. The two were involved in many violent collisions.

Hubbard happened to meet Nagurski and his wife at a dinner in 1965. "You know," he said to Mrs. Nagurski, "your husband and I experienced some pretty violent times together. It still makes me shudder to think of them."

"Mr. Hubbard," Mrs. Nagurski replied, "he says the very same thing about you."

Don Hutson

The record book can be dull reading, but not when one comes to the name of Don Hutson. He put drama and excitement into its pages.

When Hutson retired in 1945, his exploits were so numerous and so varied that he required a full page. Even today, after a whole new generation of specialists have whittled away at the records he set, Hutson's name still gets featured billing.

Though Don himself is philosophical about it, and feels that one day all of the records he established will probably be eclipsed, some of them look completely out of reach. Among the marks he holds are these:

Pass Receptions

Most Seasons Leading League—8
Most Consecutive Seasons Leading League—5
Most Consecutive Games—95

Most Touchdown Passes Caught, Lifetime—100
Most Yards Gained Catching Passes—8,010

Scoring

Most Seasons Leading League, Touchdowns—8
Most Points, One Quarter—29
Most Seasons Leading League, Scoring—5

Further proof of Hutson's matchless talents is scarcely needed, but a quick glance through newspaper stories of the day also gives testimony to his greatness. Typical headlines read: DON PACES PACKERS TO WORLD TITLE; AMAZING HUTSON CAN'T BE STOPPED; and HUTSON NFL's MOST VALUABLE—NATURALLY! To put it simply, Don Hutson was the best end who ever played professional football.

Besides his ability as a pass receiver, Hutson was a skilled place-kicker. In 1943, he led the league in field goals. Hutson's accomplishments are all the more impressive when one realizes that he played "both ways," as a defensive as well as an offensive end. Tall and stringbean-slim, he was hardly a "block of granite" on defense, but he had a solid build and runners respected him. Eventually he became a defensive halfback; he could cover the swiftest ends and was a dependable tackler.

Hutson first began to draw attention during his junior year at the University of Alabama. Sportswriters called him the best end in the South. In 1934, as a senior, he won a raft of All America honors as the receiver in one of the best two-man combinations in football—Howell to Hutson, the Howell being Dixie Howell, Alabama's big and strong-armed quarterback. The two took Alabama all the way to the Rose Bowl.

Enter Curly Lambeau!

One of the founders of the Green Bay team, Lambeau made an annual trip to the Pacific Coast to scout the Rose Bowl teams for prospective Packers. On a late December day in 1934 he arrived at Brookside Park in Pasadena to watch the Alabama team work out, but the drills were secret and Lambeau was barred from entering. Undaunted, Lambeau scaled the wall, tearing his trousers in the process. But what he saw was worth the travail. Hutson's speed and grace astonished him.

"He would glide downfield," Lambeau said, "leaning forward

as if to steady himself close to the ground. Then, as suddenly as you gulp or blink an eye, he'd feint one way and go to the other, reach up like a dancer, gracefully squeeze the ball, and leave the scene of the accident—the accident being the defensive backs who tangled their feet up and fell trying to cover him." One day before the Rose Bowl game, Lambeau met Hutson and told the young man that Green Bay would be glad to offer him a job after graduation.

The Rose Bowl game itself increased Lambeau's anxiety to sign the sleek speedster he had scouted. Howell threw seven passes to Hutson that day, and Joe Riley threw one. Seven of the eight were completed and two went for touchdowns, as underdog Alabama upset Stanford, 29–13.

This was one year before the National Football League adopted the player draft, which enables each club to approach players without competition from other teams. A number of clubs wanted Hutson. Shipwreck Kelly, who operated the Brooklyn team in the NFL, managed to talk to Don in the wild clubhouse after the Rose Bowl, and told him that his team was going to offer him a contract.

When Don returned to Alabama, the jousting began in earnest. Lambeau ran up fat telephone bills calling the young star. "We have a passing team," he told Hutson. "Brooklyn relies on power. We have Arnie Herber, the greatest passer in football. Our attack is built around passing. You belong with Green Bay."

Hutson agreed to sign with the Packers, but said that he wanted to notify Kelly. He did, and heard nothing. So he signed with the Packers. When Kelly heard the news, he took a plane to Alabama and convinced Hutson he should sign a Brooklyn contract, too.

When the two contracts, each properly signed, reached the office of Joe Carr, the league president, he exercised Solomon-like wisdom, letting the date stamps decide the issue. The contract mailed in by Lambeau was postmarked 8:30 A.M.; Kelly's was postmarked 8:47 A.M. Carr judged Hutson to be a Packer—by seventeen minutes.

Don Hutson was born on January 31, 1913, in Pine Bluff, Arkansas, a railroad town in the southeastern corner of the state. He was skinny and shy as a youngster, and, in athletics, often overshadowed by his younger twin brothers, Raymond and Robert.

Hutson showed little interest in football in high school, but Bob Seawall, a boyhood chum and the star of the team, talked him into trying out. Don developed into a fine player, although he never became a star of Seawall's caliber. After graduation, many colleges sought Seawall's services. He said he would go to Alabama, but only if the college would take Don Hutson, too. Grudgingly, Alabama agreed. What happened is ironic. Seawall dropped out of college after two years, while Hutson became the South's leading pass receiver.

Hutson was not only fast, he had blinding speed. He could run the 100-yard dash in 9.7, and the 220 in 21.3.

He put his speed to good use in his debut as a professional, which came in Green Bay's second game of the 1935 season.

Arnie Herber took the kickoff and was piled up on the 17-yard line. On the first play from scrimmage, Herber dropped back to pass. The Bear defense swung to the right to cover the Packers' Johnny Blood, one of the surest receivers in the NFL. Hutson, almost ignored, broke from his left-end position like a startled colt. Herber hit him at the 45-yard line. Only the Bears' Beattie Feathers, with a good reputation for speed himself, barred Hutson's way. The fleet rookie shifted into high gear. Feathers made a desperate lunge, missed, and Hutson streaked into the end zone for the game's only touchdown. So began the fabulous scoring career of Don Hutson.

Don quickly became a Green Bay hero, and local sportswriters nicknamed the long-legged youngster the "Alabama Antelope." He could outrace and outmaneuver virtually every defenseman in the league.

The Packers finished second in Don's rookie year, but in 1936 they won the Western Division championship, and then met the Boston Redskins (they moved to Washington the next season) for the league crown. In the opening minutes of play, Don took a 43-yard touchdown pass from Arnie Herber, and Green Bay breezed to a 21–6 win. The Packers would win three world titles and four Western championships with Don in the lineup. Not until his final season did they fail to finish either first or second, and then they were third.

Rival coaches devised all manner of special defensive tactics in an effort to keep Hutson in check. Frequently he had as many as three men guarding him.

Even the strongest defenses were often inadequate. Steve Owen, the defensive genius who guided the New York Giants, was content to force Hutson to break toward the sideline after he had caught the ball. He knew he couldn't keep Hutson from catching passes, but he could try to prevent him from scoring touchdowns after he caught them.

George Halas, the Papa Bear, despaired of Hutson's skills. "I just concede him two touchdowns a game," Halas said, "and I hope we can score more."

Brooklyn coach Jock Sutherland took a dim view of Hutson's ability at first. For the Dodgers' initial meeting with Green Bay, he arranged his defenses so that only one man was covering Don. An assistant coach told Sutherland that other teams in the league put two or three men on him.

"Nonsense," Sutherland snapped. "No man could be that good."

Before the game Sutherland told the press, "We aren't worried about Hutson particularly; what worries us is the Green Bay defense."

Hutson was close to being perfect that day. He caught six passes, two of them for touchdowns, kicked four extra points, served as a decoy, and played a splendid game on defense, and the Packers trounced the Dodgers, 38–7.

After the game Sutherland wore a dazed look. "That man can run three ways at once," he said. "He's incredible, just incredible."

In 1939 and again in 1944, Green Bay won the NFL championship. The 1944 title game demonstrated Hutson's great value as a decoy. The Giants were the Packers' rivals; the game was played at the Polo Grounds. Late in the second quarter, Irv Comp passed to Hutson who was driven out of bounds on the Giant 30-yard line. Two pass plays went incomplete. On third down, Hutson broke to his right, three New York defensemen trailing him. Too late they realized their great mistake. Comp faked to Hutson, then pivoted and fired to Ted Fritsch, speeding down the opposite side of the field in the clear. Fritsch grabbed the ball on the 13-yard line and waltzed into the end zone unmolested. The touchdown was the margin of victory in the Packers' 14–7 win.

Hutson was not colorful like Nagurski or Johnny Blood. Instead, he was quiet and subdued; some players called him a loner. His mother once said, "Don wouldn't say two words in an A-bomb attack. He doesn't talk unless he has something to say." Apparently, Don was content to let the record book speak for him.

Throughout his career, Hutson attracted superlative passers. In college there was Dixie Howell. In his early years at Green Bay, Hutson had Arnie Herber to do the throwing. After Herber came Cecil Isbell, a college star at Purdue. Often there were rumors that Hutson and Isbell didn't get along, but Don has often named Isbell as "the greatest passer Green Bay ever had."

In the Pro Bowl game of 1939, the Isbell-to-Hutson combination clicked for one of the longest scoring plays in the history of football. Hutson's team had the ball on their own two-yard line. As the team huddled in their own end zone, Isbell said to Hutson, "Let's shoot the moon!"

Hutson knew exactly what he meant. With the snap of the ball, he turned on the speed. There was no faking, no twisting, just straightaway speed. Isbell got off a tremendous floater. It traveled 69 yards in the air. When it came down, Hutson was there. But no one else was. Hutson strolled into the end zone. From where Isbell had thrown, to the goal line was a distance of 108 yards.

When asked to name the most thrilling moment of his career, Hutson invariably cites the first play of his first pro game, the one in which he took a Herber pass to score a touchdown that beat the Bears. Another big thrill was the time he *threw* a touchdown pass.

It happened in 1943 in a game against the Giants. With the ball on the New York 38-yard line, Tony Canadeo took the pass from center, handed off to Tony Falkenstein who, in turn, handed to Hutson. Don tucked the ball to his chest and headed toward the right sideline on what appeared to be an end-around play. But suddenly he straightened up and tossed to Harry Jacunski in the end zone. When Jacunski wrapped his arms around the ball, Don's usual poker face broke into a wide grin.

In the late stages of his career Hutson, increasingly weary

from the rigors of the game, would announce his retirement at the end of each season. But the lure of the game was great, and the next fall he would be back. After the 1944 season, which saw the Packers take the NFL title, Hutson said again that he would not return. Just two days before the season opened, however, he reversed himself. Fans of the Detroit Lions will be forever sorry that he did. One afternoon that season Hutson and his teammates went on the wildest one-quarter scoring spree until that time in pro football history. The Lions were the unfortunate victims.

Detroit fielded a solid team that year, and no one was surprised when Chuck Fenebock blazed into the Green Bay end zone on the first play of the second period to put Detroit ahead, 7–0.

From that moment until the end of the first half, the Packers went berserk, and no player was more touchdown-crazed than Hutson. Four times he crossed the Detroit goal and he booted four conversions, a total of 29 points for the quarter, a record that still stands. Clyde Goodnight and Ted Fritsch also scored for the Packers to give Green Bay a total of 41 points for the quarter. That's a record, too (although it was equaled in a Los Angeles-Detroit game in 1950). At the end of the turbulent day, the Packers were on top, 57–21.

Don booted two more extra points later in the game to give him a total of 31 for the day, and left him only nine shy of Ernie Nevers' all-time mark of 40.

Hutson said afterward that it was "just one of those days when everything fell in place. The passes were accurate and the defenses that Detroit had set for us made it possible."

At the end of the season, Don made his perennial retirement announcement. This time he made it stick.

He was an assistant coach for the Packers for two seasons, and then left the team to devote full time to his business enterprises. Today he lives in Racine, Wisconsin, but he follows the pro scene closely. He says that if he were playing today, he would be a flanker. "That would be fun."

Don feels that football is different today. "The defensive backs are better," he says, "and the main reason is that they play only defense. This makes a tremendous difference. They're specialists, just as much as kickers are, and they're good.

"However, a real good defensive back can't cover a real good receiver man for man. If the receiver has time to maneuver, it's impossible to cover him."

How good was Don Hutson? Jimmy Breslin tells this story. Paul Hornung and Jesse Whittenton, a fine defensive back for the Packers, were sitting in the dressing room at Green Bay, screening some old Packer game films.

"Look at this," Hornung said. He pointed to Hutson who came out of the huddle and got down in a stance that Whittenton said "looked like a duck waddlin'."

Then the ball was snapped and Hutson broke downfield. Three Chicago Bears picked him up. Then Hutson turned on his great speed. The three Bear players were left behind. But the pass never came because Whittendon had put the film in reverse to run the play over again.

"I gotta see that again," he said. "No one player could cover that man."

Hornung nodded in agreement. "I'm a believer," he said. "Lord, am I a believer! You know what he would do if he were in this league today? The same things he did when he played."

Don Hutson Career Pass Receiving Record

Year	Passes Received	Yards	Average	Touchdowns
1935	18	420	23.3	6*
1936	34*	536*	15.8	9*
1937	41*	552	13.5	7*
1938	32	548*	17.1	9*
1939	34*	846*	24.9	6
1940	45	664	14.8	7*
1941	58*	738*	12.7	10*
1942	74*	1,211*	16.4	17*
1943	47*	776*	16.5	11*
1944	58*	866*	14.9	9*
1945	47*	834	17.7	9
Total	488	7,991	16.4	100

* *Outstanding Performance.*

Earl (Curly) Lambeau

One chilly autumn morning in 1919, twenty-year-old Curly Lambeau entered the office of his employer, Frank Peck, owner of the Indian Packing Company in Green Bay.

"Yes, what is it, Curly?" asked the packing company executive.

"Mr. Peck," Curly began, "I've been talking to some of the other fellows and we think we could get together a football team. It would be great for Green Bay and the company. Will you back us up?"

Peck realized that his young shipping clerk was serious. It didn't take him long to reach a decision.

"O.K., Curly," he said, "we'll support you up to $500."

For young Curly Lambeau, who adored football with an almost consuming passion, this marked the beginning of his dazzling career. As a player and as a coach, Lambeau's stay in Green Bay spanned 31 years. His record included six National League titles, seven divisional championships and one first-place tie. In total, his Packer teams won 236 games, lost 111, and tied 23 in NFL competition.

Lambeau did even more. It was he, more than any other individual, who "put Green Bay on the map." "What he did for Green Bay borders on the miraculous," said Tony Canadeo, the "Gray Ghost of Gonzaga," a Packer player from 1941 to 1949. "He brought a small town into the big leagues."

Impatient and explosive—he was called the Bellicose Belgian by sportswriters—Lambeau's career was often marked by controversy. He left Green Bay early in 1950 following a dispute with the club's executive committee.

Curly was born in Green Bay on April 9, 1898, and was christened Earl Lambeau, but his dark, wavy hair won him his nickname. He attended East High which, for seven consecutive years, had been defeated by its traditional enemy, West High. Curly changed the pattern. In the 1916 game he put on a spectacular passing exhibition, and East rolled to an easy win.

In 1918 Curly enrolled at Notre Dame where Knute Rockne was the new head coach. Lambeau played both right halfback and fullback for the Irish and, although a freshman, was one of the squad's thirteen lettermen that year.

After the season Lambeau was bothered by a sore throat and returned home for a tonsillectomy. His recovery took six weeks and he was beginning to wonder if he should return to Notre Dame at all. It was then that Frank Peck offered him a position with the Indian Packing Company. The salary was to be $250 a month. "That was more money than I thought there was in the world," Lambeau once recalled. "So I stayed."

Once Curly had Peck's support for a football team, he began gathering players, a task in which he was greatly aided by George Calhoun, sports editor of the Green Bay *Press-Gazette*. The infant Packers were a powerhouse, and won ten straight games, turning back such rivals as Sheboygan, Racine, and Ishpeming, and athletic clubs representing Milwaukee and Chicago. They failed to win the Wisconsin state championship because of a 6–0 loss to the Beloit Fairies in the final game of the season. Lambeau crossed the Beloit goal twice, but each time a penalty nullified the play.

Each member of the Packer squad played practically the entire sixty minutes. "We did carry a few substitutes," Lambeau pointed out, "just in case somebody got killed or something." There was no fence around Hagemeister Brewery Field where the Packers played their home games, so the club couldn't charge admissions. It became the duty of the substitutes to pass the hat —an upturned helmet, actually—among the spectators who ringed the playing area. The money was banked and at the end of the season, after deducting expenses, the players divided the take. Each man got $16.75.

The next year, 1920, the Packers were again an artistic success, scoring 227 points to their opponents' 24, but the financial picture was a dismal one. Lambeau was able to land a new angel in the person of John Clair of the Acme Packing Company. On August 27, 1921, the Acme Company was granted a franchise in the American Professional Football Association. After the season, tragedy struck. Joe Carr, the new league president, revoked the franchise, charging that the new team had been using ineligible players.

Lambeau, though discouraged, was determined to see the Packers back in the league for the 1922 season. He had the $50 for the franchise, but no way to finance his trip to Cleveland for the league meeting in June.

Don Murphy, a friend of Curly's, came to the rescue. Murphy was the owner of a new Marmon automobile, and although he had high regard for the car, he had higher regard for the Packers. He sold the Marmon to pay Curly's expenses. Curly got the franchise, and Murphy got what he wanted—a chance to appear in the Packers' lineup. Murphy's career was exceptionally brief. He went into retirement after the opening game kickoff and one play.

The city of Green Bay loyally supported the Packers, but the club was dogged by bad fortune. Bad weather was a particular headache. For a game with the Columbus Panhandles, Lambeau and his associates had the foresight to take out a rain insurance policy. It rained on the day of the game, but missed the requirements of the policy by one one-hundredths of an inch.

Later in the season the Packers faced the Duluth Eskimos. It poured again. Lambeau considered calling it quits. The club owed $1,600 in back pay to the players, and the frightful weather meant that few customers would turn out. Lambeau was about to cancel the game, but Andy Turnbull, publisher of the *Press-Gazette,* convinced him to play the game in spite of the downpour. It cost the club $2,200, but in later years Lambeau said the game was a turning point. He admitted that if the game had been canceled, the Packers probably would have folded.

Later in the week, publisher Turnbull called a meeting of civic leaders to discuss the team. They arranged a loan of $2,500 to erase the Packers' most pressing debts. In 1923 the Green Bay Football Corporation was founded, with Turnbull as its president. Stock was sold at $5 a share, with each purchaser receiving a box seat for the season. There was $5,000 in the Packers' treasury when the 1923 season opened, making Green Bay one of the league's strongest clubs from a financial standpoint.

The men who worked most diligently to save the Packers were known as the Hungry Five. Besides Lambeau and Turnbull, they included Dr. W. W. Kelly, Gerry Clifford and Lee Joannes.

Most professional teams of the day featured a running attack, but the Packers were an exception. Lambeau preferred the passing game. "Why beat your brains out running against a pro line?" he declared. "It's easier to throw the ball and save your players. It's better business to pass the ball. It's better show business, too." Lambeau, as the Packers' quarterback, once threw 45 passes in one game, a startling statistic for the era.

In spite of their flashy attack, the Packers did not attain on-the-field success quickly. The club finished second in the twelve-team National League in 1927, their best performance up to that time.

After the 1928 season, in which the Packers slipped to third place in the standings, Lambeau brought in three players from other NFL teams who were to power Green Bay to the top. The three were Johnny Blood, a swift and elusive runner, and the premier pass catcher of the day; Cal Hubbard, a giant tackle, but quick and agile; and Mike Michalske, a fast, aggressive guard.

A crowd of 5,000, the largest opening day attendance in Green Bay history, watched Blood and Lindberg score touchdowns to sink Portsmouth, 14–0, to open the 1929 season. Actually, it was the beginning of an era. The Packers went undefeated that year, rolling to twelve victories and a tie. It marked the first time that any team had gone unbeaten since Canton turned the trick in 1923. In 1930 it was more of the same for Green Bay. Their winning streak reached twenty-two consecutive games before the club was stopped by Ernie Nevers and the Chicago Cardinals. But the Packers won the title in 1930, and again in 1931, to achieve three consecutive league championships, something no other team had done before, and something no team was able to do again until Green Bay teams of 1965 to 1967 duplicated the feat.

Lambeau had a sharp eye for talent and was always his own best scout. Each year after the football season it was his custom to make a trek to the Pacific Coast in quest of prospective Packers. In 1932, Lambeau signed a relatively "unknown" named Clarke Hinkle after watching him perform in the East-West Shrine game in San Francisco. Hinkle possessed a gifted toe that enabled him to lead the league in place-kicks twice, but his skill as a fleet halfback won him even greater renown. Hinkle led the league in scoring in 1938.

Lambeau's greatest find in the Golden West was a glue-fingered, snake-hipped young man named Don Hutson. He starred for Alabama in the 1934 Rose Bowl game. Hutson held down right end for Green Bay and developed into one of pro football's all-time greats. Hinkle and Hutson, and a strong-armed passer named Arnie Herber, fired the Packers during the late 1930's. In 1936, 1938 and 1939, Green Bay captured the Western Division title, and in 1936 and 1939 were NFL champions also.

The Packers were severely hurt when the All America Conference began operation in 1946. Green Bay could not afford to enter the wild bidding for draft choices, and the players they chose in the college draft were invariably signed by teams in the rival league. Inevitably, the club's on-the-field performance began to suffer. In 1948 Green Bay finished next to last in the Western Division, and in 1949 tumbled into the cellar.

Friction developed between Lambeau and the Packers' executive committee. The feud was fully covered in the press, and Green Bay was split into pro-Lambeau and anti-Lambeau camps. In February 1950, Curly resigned.

Lambeau coached the Chicago Cardinals in 1950 and 1951, and then moved on to the Washington Redskins until 1954, his last year as a coach. Lambeau died in 1965.

After he left Green Bay, Lambeau never experienced great success. In Chicago and Washington his teams lost many more games than they won. Arthur Daley, sports columnist for the New York *Times*, explained it best. "He left his heart in Green Bay," Daley wrote, "and the adjustment apparently never could be made."

Tim Mara

The National Football League was in its infancy and its future was bleak when, in August 1925, league president Joe Carr went to New York seeking a franchise holder for a team in that city.

Carr met with Billy Gibson, a local fight manager, who had previously, but unsuccessfully, invested in the pro game. Carr hoped that Gibson might be willing to risk his capital again. It must be said that Carr did not have much to sell. The NFL, then beginning its fifth year of operation, was a struggling and loosely organized eighteen-team league, with most of its franchises clustered in the Midwest states. Cities, to use the term loosely, like Duluth, Minnesota, Hammond, Indiana, and Kenosha, Wisconsin, were among those represented. Scheduling was haphazard; players came and went. People with good money to invest did not think of putting it into pro football.

Gibson was about to turn thumbs down on Carr's proposition when in walked Tim Mara, a bookmaker, and a very successful one. Gibson and Mara were old friends. "Here's something you might be interested in," Gibson said. Then he asked Carr to outline his proposal for Mara's benefit.

"I don't want to sound visionary," Carr began, "but the day is coming when professional football is going to be as important as big league baseball. But our league has to establish itself in New York. Without a franchise here we're never going to be big-time."

"What does it cost?" Mara asked.

"We want $2,500," Carr said.

Mara sat down and wrote out a check. "A New York franchise to operate anything ought to be worth $2,500," he said.

Although Mara had never seen a football game, and probably didn't know a tailback from a runback, in the years that followed he built the New York Giants into one of the most powerful, popular, and lucrative franchises in the National Football League. Carr got what he was looking for, and much, much more.

Mara was financially well established when he purchased the New York franchise, but his success had not come without a struggle. He was born on New York's lower East Side in 1887. As a thirteen-year-old, to help support himself and his widowed mother, he peddled newspapers after school and worked as an usher in a theater. He quit school because, in his words, "It got to be too much for a thirteen-year-old."

Many of young Timothy's newspaper customers were bookmakers, and he noticed that they were men who "had the best and worried the least." He began working as a runner, that is, collecting wagers from losing bettors (at a commission of 5 percent), and delivering payoffs to winners (for tips).

By the time Timothy was eighteen, he was covering small bets himself. Affable, with a wide smile, and a man of unquestioned integrity, Mara soon boasted a long list of clients. In 1921 he moved operations to the racetrack. He would sit on a high stool and his customers would throng around him. He held a slate that announced the betting odds in his left hand, and collected money with his right. As bets were made, the odds fluctuated. Mara, like other bookmakers of the time, could compute the changes in his head with all the speed and much the accuracy of modern pari-mutuel machines.

Being a financial wizard served Mara in good stead in his early years as the Giants' owner. But the job demanded many other attributes. Tenacity was one of them. A thick bankroll was another. There were many dark days.

Mara named Billy Gibson as president of the club, and Dr. Harry March, a Canton, Ohio, pro football promoter, as secretary. Since the club contracted to play its home games at the Polo Grounds, sharing the park with the baseball Giants, Mara decided to name his club the Giants, too.

Dr. March, an M.D. who preferred pro football to patients, hired Bob Folwell, a former coach at the U. S. Naval Academy, as Giant coach, and proceeded to sign some notable All Americans. They included Joseph Alexander from Syracuse, who became a standout lineman, tackle Century Milstead of Vanderbilt, and halfback Hinkey Haines from Penn State. But such names failed to enthrall New Yorkers. Mara, to whip up interest in the home opener at the Polo Grounds, advertised in local daily newspapers and hired a phalanx of publicity men, who were instructed to give out five thousand free tickets every week. Mara's young sons, John and Wellington, gave passes out to school friends. An estimated 25,000 fans showed up to watch the team in its debut. The Frankford Yellowjackets (who later became the Philadelphia Eagles) were the Giants' opponents. While the turnout was respectable, the gross was not. Less than half the spectators had paid their way in.

As the season progressed, attendance fell lower and lower. For a game against the Columbus Tigers, not many more than a thousand people—paid—were in the stands. Mara estimated his losses to be $45,000, an amount that put a severe strain on his bankroll. At this point Mara would have undoubtedly sold the team but, as he was to say in later years, "Where could I find anyone crazy enough to buy it?"

Mara had an inspiration. He felt that Red Grange, the spectacular college hero at Illinois, might be his salvation. He secretly went to Chicago hoping to sign the redhead. But he was too late. George Halas, owner of the Chicago Bears, had gotten to Grange first. The trip was not a total loss, however. Mara was able to make arrangements for a game at the Polo Grounds between the Giants and the Bears, featuring their new star. The remaining dates on the New York schedule were juggled a bit, and the game with Chicago was set for December 6, 1925, a Sunday.

The day dawned bright and unseasonably warm. Two hours before the kickoff, special police had to be called out to handle the great mob that had descended upon the Polo Grounds. By one o'clock an estimated 70,000 fans had packed their way into the stands. Grange carried the ball eleven times, gaining modest yardage, intercepted a pass, and scored one touchdown, as the Bears won, 19–7. But the big story was in the gate receipts, a record $143,000. Mara's losses were wiped out and he could even show a profit for the season.

Grange, the savior of the Giant franchise in 1925, almost destroyed it the next year. He and his manager, the canny C. C. Pyle, were unable to come to terms with George Halas on a new contract. They then demanded an NFL franchise to operate in New York. Though some of the owners were ready to give in to Pyle, Mara would not hear of it. "You're not going to muscle in here," Mara told him. "I'll fight you every inch of the way."

Fight they did. Pyle started a competing league, calling it the American Professional Football League, and took the New York franchise for himself and Grange. Hostilities lasted one season. Mara lost $60,000, but it cost Grange and Pyle almost twice that amount as their league failed dismally.

Time did nothing at all to diminish Mara's competitive zeal. In 1945, Dan Topping asked the National League to allow him to move his Brooklyn franchise to the Bronx and Yankee Stadium, in which he owned an interest. Mara turned him down. Topping reacted by deserting the NFL for the All America Conference. The AAC further imperiled Mara by putting a team in Brooklyn. All of this led to a fierce battle of checkbooks. Attendance fell to an average of 25,000 at Giant games, and at the same time the club's payroll for playing talent jumped from an estimated $100,000 in 1944 to almost three times that amount in 1947. Mara, at the risk of his own purse, fought to the bitter end—and won. The peace conference was held in 1949. The Giants were battered but recovered quickly, thanks to the reparations Mara demanded and got in the form of prize players from the New York-Brooklyn AAC interests.

It's significant that when the American Football League sought to set up shop in New York in 1959 with a team called the Titans, the Giants were so solidly entrenched that football fans scarcely noticed they were in town. Attendance was so poor that the club landed in bankruptcy court in three years. The Giants, meanwhile, were playing to sellout throngs each week. It was clear: New York was Mara country—exclusively!

Mara often quipped that he founded the Giants "on brute strength and ignorance," the brute strength being that of players, the ignorance his own. However, Mara was a keen-minded football man, although he did not concern himself with the game's technical subtleties. He hired Steve Owen, the Giants' coach for almost two decades, because he respected Owen's ability to handle men, not for his knowledge of football as a craft.

The Mara-Owen partnership was an eminently successful one, and won these championships:

1933—Eastern Division
1934—Eastern Division, NFL
1935—Eastern Division
1938—Eastern Division, NFL
1939—Eastern Division
1940—Eastern Division
1944—Eastern Division
1946—Eastern Division

In 1936, Mara installed his young son, Wellington, as secretary, and the older son, John, a lawyer, as president. Through the years the two took an ever-increasing role in the management of the club, and by 1953 they had assumed full control. When Tim Mara died in 1959, another Timothy, Jack's son, became the club treasurer. Jack Mara died in June 1965, and Wellington became the Giant's president the following August.

Thus, at a time when franchises, no matter the sport, are held by investment syndicates and even public ownership, the Giants are an extreme rarity—a family enterprise. That's the way old Tim Mara wanted it; that's what he fought for. And that's the way it is almost certain to remain.

George Marshall

Any attempt to explain pro football's high-flying popularity must include these reasons: the tenacity of the sport's pioneers, the men who would not let their dream fail; Red Grange's nationwide exhibition tour in 1925–26; the judicious use of television; and one more, the splitting of the National League into two divisions in 1933, with the winners of each playing for the pro football championship.

The man responsible for this last move was a Washington laundry tycoon named George Preston Marshall. To Marshall the word "mangle" had nothing to do with what happened on the gridiron; it was a machine for pressing sheets. Despite his early lack of experience, Marshall ranks as one of the most foresighted men in professional football. The innovations he championed brought benefits to everyone—club owners, players and fans.

Marshall was first, last and always a showman. After getting his schooling at Friends Select School in Washington and later at Randolph Macon, he became an extra in a stock company and also managed theaters in Washington and Baltimore. Then came a two-year hitch in the Army, during which time his father died. After his discharge George returned to Washington to support his widowed mother and assumed management of a small laundry the family owned.

It was now that Marshall's promotional genius came into full flower. When he sold the business in 1945, he had fifty-seven branches and his success had won him the title of the "Luxurious Laundryman." He dressed his employees in handsome blue-and-gold uniforms, and his delivery trucks and the laundry storefronts bore the same colors. "Long Live Linen" was the company's slogan; once Marshall took a full-page advertisement in a daily newspaper and the only message it contained was a line of type at the very bottom. It read: THIS SPACE WAS CLEANED BY THE PALACE LAUNDRY AND DRY CLEANING COMPANY.

In 1926, to further promote his wet-wash business, Marshall organized a basketball team, calling it the Palace Big Five, and entered the club in an early professional basketball league. Pro football was just a step away. The boss of the basketball league was Joe Carr, who also happened to be the president of the National Football League. The Chicago franchise was operated by one George Halas, who also was majordomo of the Bears.

In 1932, Carr and Halas convinced Marshall and three others to put up $7,500 each and get into pro football. Boston was to be the scene of operations, and Marshall was to be the boss. The team was named the Braves because they were to play their home games at Braves Field. One of Marshall's first acts was to hire Lud Wray as coach.

Boston took to the Braves about as kindly as they did to the British some years before. Those few fans who did turn out rattled around Braves Field like peas in a wash boiler. The club lost $46,000 in its first year of operation. His partners fled, leaving Marshall to stem the tide of red ink.

Marshall decided that a wholesale reorganization was in order. He renamed the team the Redskins. He switched to Fenway Park for the team's home games, and then he changed coaches—in typical Marshall fashion.

One day late in the season, Marshall suggested that Wray send in a certain play. A scowl came to Wray's face. "If you want to run the club," he fumed, "I'll go sit in the stands."

"Go ahead," Marshall told him. Wray did, the act leading to his early retirement.

To replace Wray, Marshall chose Lone Star Dietz who, despite his Indian heritage, could never get the Redskins on the warpath. In his two years with the club they won eleven and lost eleven.

Pro football of the early and mid-1930's was a loosely organized business. Each team made up its own schedule. Championships weren't won on the playing field; they were awarded. Marshall's forceful eloquence changed all this. He pleaded for a standardized schedule, with each team playing the same number of games each season. He also proposed that the league be split in two divisions—an Eastern and a Western division—with the winners of each meeting at the end of the season in a playoff for the world's title. Thanks to the support of George Halas, and Marshall's own irrepressibility, the changes were adopted.

Marshall also prodded the pros into livening up the game. He urged that passing be permitted from anywhere behind the line of scrimmage, instead of from five yards back; that the ball be spotted in 15 yards from a sideline; that the goalposts be returned from the end zone to the goal line. Pro football became a wide-open game as a result of these changes and fan interest skyrocketed.

Marshall pointed out that these rule changes had previously been advocated by college coaches, Pop Warner and Dick Hanley in particular. "I only pushed them through," he said.

While Marshall was a glorious success in the NFL meeting rooms, back in Boston it was an altogether different story. Boston fans continued to cold-shoulder the team. The crowning blow came in 1936.

Ray Flaherty had taken over as coach, built an explosive team, and steered it to the Eastern Division championship. Still Bostonians took little notice, newspaper editors included. A crucial late-season game with the Bears failed to earn a single line in the Boston newspapers.

Marshall was enraged. He decided to yank the team out of Boston and put it into Washington. There was still the matter of the league championship to be settled and, since Marshall would not play it in Boston, the game was assigned to neutral territory, the Polo Grounds in New York. There the contest drew a respectable turnout of 29,545, but the Redskins were overcome by Green Bay, 21–7.

Although Marshall was born in Grafton, West Virginia (in 1896), he had been brought up in Washington, and so returning to the capital was the same as coming home. He gave free rein to his promotional talents. "Football," Marshall once said, "is a game of pageantry. It derives as a spectacle from the gladiator shows of the Romans in the pages of history. It is strictly amphitheater. Its great success is due to the color surrounding it. It needs music and bands. Football without a band is like a musical without an orchestra."

The Redskins' marching band that Marshall instituted was worth the price of admission. It featured 110 members, all spirited volunteers, decked out in $25,000 worth of Indian costumes including headdress. "Hail to the Redskins," a stirring march which had been coauthored by Marshall's wife, was the team's official song. Besides the band, half-time entertainment at a Redskins' game might feature elephants, bears, trained seals, stars of the legitimate theater, a ballet troupe or, around Christmastime, Santa Claus.

The band was very close to Marshall's heart. In 1960 a fierce and unexpected blizzard struck Washington a few hours before the Redskins' game with the Giants. Marshall began a frantic effort to get equipment to clear off the field before game time.

Two hours before the kickoff the field was still blanketed with two feet of snow. A worried Jack Mara, president of the Giants, was looking dejectedly at the field when Marshall appeared, his face aglow.

"They're coming. They'll be here in plenty of time," he exclaimed.

"The snowplows?" Mara asked.

"No," said Marshall, his brow furrowing at his guest's lack of understanding, "the overshoes for the band."

When it came to attracting customers to Griffith Stadium, the half-time extravaganzas were only mildly successful. What really made the Redskins thrive and prosper was a slim young Texan with a shotgun arm named Sammy Baugh. In less than a season, Baugh became as well known in the capital as the Washington Monument and much more popular.

Baugh brought the Redskins home first in the Eastern Division in his rookie year of 1937. In the NFL championship game, he threw three second-half touchdown passes, as the Redskins whipped the Bears, 28–21. The club came close to a championship in 1939, but the following year they were on top again and were to meet the Bears once more for the NFL crown.

During the regular season, Chicago and Washington had played at Griffith Stadium and the Redskins had won, 7–3. The Bears, however, felt poor officiating had cost them a last-ditch touchdown. The game was argued in the press for days.

Marshall, whom no one ever accused of reticence, called the Bears "crybabies," "quitters," and "front-runners." In the weeks before the game, George Halas reminded his team of Marshall's comments. When the Bears took the field on the day of the play-off, Sid Luckman, the Chicago quarterback, observed, "There was a feeling of tension in the air, as though something tremendous was going to happen." Something did. The Bears won, 73–0. The game has become the classic example of a rout.

When the gun sounded to end the carnage, a press-box observer commented, "That's George Marshall shooting himself."

During World War II, professional football rosters were hard hit by the draft, and customers were hard to come by. Cleveland closed up shop. Pittsburgh and Brooklyn were on the brink. But Marshall left no doubts as to where he stood. "The Redskins won't fold," he declared. "If we throw in the towel, we're going to destroy everything we've worked to build in the last twenty years. Coming back after the war would be like warming up an old soufflé." The league stayed in business.

After the war, the Redskins fell on dismal days. There were many reasons. The All America Conference, which set up shop in 1946, was a principal headache. Marshall refused to be caught up in the bidding for players which became pandemic, and lost veteran players and draft choices to the insurgents. In 1949, when peace came, Washington was settled in last place in the Eastern Division.

The 1950's brought no resurgence. Coaches came and went with startling frequency. In one ten-year period, Marshall went through seven of them.

The team was also hurt by Marshall's refusal to hire Negro players. He denied that he was prejudiced, but it was 1962 before the Redskin roster ceased to be lily-white. That year Marshall made a trade which brought the Redskins Bobby Mitchell, a halfback who was converted to a flanker with excellent results. Mitchell's dazzling play was one reason the Redskins vacated the nether regions of the Eastern Conference.

Marshall was stricken with an organic brain disease in his later years, and was not able to maintain active control of the club. He was named president emeritus of the Redskins. Edward Bennett Williams became president.

In 1967 a marble likeness of Marshall was dedicated at Washington's magnificent new District of Columbia Stadium. But it was scarcely needed. The stadium itself, whose financing and construction were due largely to Marshall's efforts, stood as a monument to him.And sellout crowds and robust financial statements are part of the Marshall legacy, too, because the meaningful changes he championed in the 1930's helped lift the pro game to its present lofty status as much as television, Red Grange, or anything else.

Johnny "Blood" McNally

In the Hall of Fame in Canton his name is entered as "John Victor McNally" but in his playing days for the Green Bay Packers, and an assortment of less notable teams, he was called Johnny Blood. A halfback, Blood was fast and supremely confident. His slashing runs and extraordinary pass-catching ability helped Green Bay capture four world championships, the last coming in 1936. When John F. Kennedy met Blood during the Wisconsin primary campaign in 1960, he echoed the sentiment of many by saying, "Your name was a household word in our home."

Blood had another name. Otto Kuechle, sports editor of the Milwaukee *Journal,* dubbed him the Vagabond Halfback, a title that befits a man who had wandered all over the world. Blood had been an Air Force sergeant and cryptographer in China, and once was held prisoner in a Havana jail (for only one night). At one time or another, he served as a bartender, a hotel desk clerk, a laborer on a WPA project, a seaman and a newspaper stereotyper—the list is endless. Today he operates a thriving employment agency. Somehow he managed to crowd in twenty-two years playing professional football, fifteen of them in the NFL.

McNally adopted the name Johnny Blood in 1924. He and a friend, Ralph Hanson, had heard that a Minneapolis professional football team, called the East 26th Street Liberties, was looking for players. They decided to try out, but since they had a year of college eligibility left, they would have to use assumed names if they wanted to preserve their amateur standing. On the way to the ball park, they passed a theater. The marquee proclaimed: RUDOLPH VALENTINO IN "BLOOD AND SAND."

"That's it," Johnny cried, pointing excitedly. "You be Sand. I'll be Blood." Johnny Blood it thus became.

Blood made the team and helped the Liberties win the city championship. The next year he moved on to a pro club in Ironwood, Michigan, and from there to Milwaukee, then a member of the National Football League. Next he jumped to the Duluth Eskimos and then to the Pottsville Maroons. In 1928 his itinerant performing ended when he signed with the Green Bay Packers. He remained with the Green Bay team for nine years.

In negotiating his first contract with Curly Lambeau, the Packers' head man, Blood asked for $100 a game. Lambeau countered with an offer of $110 a game, provided Blood would agree to a clause in his contract that forbade him from drinking after the Tuesday of each week on which a game was scheduled. Blood was opposed to this but he had a compromise. He would accept $100 if allowed to drink through Wednesday. Lambeau agreed.

Tackle Cal Hubbard, a teammate of Blood's, once picked his all-time pro team. He selected Blood as a twelfth player, a clutch hitter, so to speak. Indeed, in pressure situations Blood had few equals. In a critical game against the New York Giants in 1929, Blood pounced on a fumble in the early stages of the game, and shortly afterward the Packers scored. Later he took a pass from Red Dunn and broke loose for a touchdown, the play covering 55 yards. The Packers won, 20–6, and clinched the first of three consecutive world championships.

Blood was slightly more than 6 feet tall and weighed 200 pounds. He could leap like a high jumper for passes and he was one of the fastest men of his era. When the great Don Hutson joined Green Bay in 1935, Blood was thirty-two years old and had lost some of the incredible speed of his heyday, yet Hutson was only a step or two faster than Blood over a sprint distance. Blood also played a fierce game on defense. "If we couldn't stay in there the full sixty minutes," he once said, "we felt we didn't measure up."

Jimmy Taylor, a Packer fullback of the 1960's, once observed that Blood's great skill was in improvising, in creating plays to fit the situation. As a result the opposition seldom knew what to expect. Once the Packers were battling the Providence Steamrollers in a close game. It was Green Bay's ball on their own

15-yard line. Blood called the signals. He was supposed to fake to the fullback and hand off to the halfback, or do the opposite, that is, fake to the halfback and hand off to the fullback. He did neither. He faked to both, kept the ball, and scored.

Poor Curly Lambeau found Blood as elusive off the field as he was on. Missed curfews and broken training rules were the norm. On one occasion the Packers departed from Green Bay for an important game with the Bears. Lambeau searched the train but could not find Blood anywhere. Shortly after leaving Green Bay, the train stopped abruptly. The Packer players threw open the windows and peered out into the darkness. It was Johnny Blood. He had parked his automobile on the railroad tracks to stop the train. The car was pushed from the rails and Blood, laughing merrily, clambered aboard to join his team-mates.

Blood needed a steady influx of cash to finance his life as a gay bon vivant, and borrowing was a common necessity. One time he approached Lambeau and asked for a salary advance. Lambeau turned him down. He told Blood not to bother him any more about it, that he was retiring to his eighth-floor room for the night, and taking the telephone off the hook. Blood was determined to make one more pitch. He took an elevator to the eighth floor, and climbed out onto a ledge leading to Lambeau's room. He worked his way along the narrow shelf until he came to Lambeau's half-opened window. He thrust it open and leaped in. Lambeau, jolted awake by Blood's thudding body, let out a startled scream. He reached for his trousers, grabbed a wad of bills from the pocket, and thrust it into Blood's hand. "Go! Go!" he shrieked. "Go anywhere you want, Johnny Blood."

Once Blood borrowed so much money from so many players that when it came to paying them back he hardly knew where to start. Before a game he put all his cash into a helmet and went from player to player asking each to dip in and take whatever amount he was owed.

Johnny was born in New Richmond, Wisconsin, in 1903. His homestead is still the house where he was born. A precocious youngster, he graduated from high school at the age of fourteen. He was too small to participate in sports until he entered St. John's College near Collegeville, Minnesota. He stayed at St.

John's for three years, winning letters in football, baseball, track and basketball, and then transferred to Notre Dame where he planned to get his degree. In the spring of 1924 he received a sixty-day suspension from Notre Dame for absenting himself from campus. He decided to make it permanent, and soon afterward he was playing for the East 26th Street Liberties, the start of his pro career.

In his years with Green Bay, Blood scored 37 touchdowns and 224 points. He scored 13 touchdowns in 1931, a season record at the time. He also held several league pass-catching records but these were eclipsed by Don Hutson. Blood liked Green Bay and the celebrating that went with winning. He once characterized Green Bay as the "greatest town in the world—the home of the perpetual fatted calf."

In 1937 Blood became head coach for Art Rooney at Pittsburgh. He was not a model coach. Training camp became a laugh; discipline was nonexistent. Road trips were joyous excursions. One piece of strategy that Blood employed was the slogan. When practice began each day, Blood would give the players a motto to be repeated over and over. One was "Packers easy to defeat." "Steelers can't be beat" and "Bear meat is good to eat" were others. Blood packed up his slogans and left the Steeler organization in the midst of the 1939 season.

The 1938 club was Blood's best. After five games the team had a 2-3 record; even so, Blood felt that they could be contenders. Then one afternoon he learned from a sportswriter that Rooney had sold the Steelers' Frankie Filchock to the Redskins. Filchock was indispensable to the Pittsburgh offense. Without him even slogans could not help.

Blood drifted to Kenosha and played there in the 1941 season. A sojourn in the Air Force, which took him to the China-India-Burma theater of operations, came next. In an exhibition game at Pittsburgh in 1945, Blood ran back a punt for Green Bay. He was forty-two then, and two behemoths flattened him before he had run very far. As he was pulling himself to his feet, his body aching in a hundred places, he suddenly realized that pro football was a younger man's game.

He returned to St. John's College in 1948 and accrued enough credits to get his degree. He remained at St. John's as an instructor and coached several sports.

In 1958 Blood was a candidate for sheriff in St. Croix County, Wisconsin. The principal plank in his platform was honest wrestling. Blood lost.

In 1963, when he was notified that he had been picked for the Hall of Fame, Blood remarked that his flamboyant reputation probably influenced the sportswriters and broadcasters in voting him in as a charter member. That is a safe statement.

Bronko Nagurski

Power, sheer power, was Bronko Nagurski's chief weapon. When he joined the Chicago Bears in 1930, he stood 6 feet 2 and weighed 230; he had a barrel chest and tree-trunk legs, and when he took the ball and poured into the line, he was as close to being unstoppable as any player before or since.

There was little subtlety to it. No dodging, no spinning. Just power. James T. Gallagher, a Chicago sportswriter, saw Nagurski play one day and summed up his performance in these words: "Those who were unlucky got in his way. Those who were lucky got out of it. The only thing that could stop him was a brick wall."

Tackling Nagurski in the conventional way, by ramming a shoulder into his legs and then wrapping one's arms about his knees, was done only by the foolhardy. It was sure to earn a jab from his powerful arm or, worse, a shoulder, which he would crash into the tackler's head or neck. Any normal tackle was not likely to cause him to slow down or even swerve. "Tacklers to Nagurski," Giant coach Steve Owen once said, "are like flies on the flank of a horse—a nuisance but not serious."

Red Grange, a teammate of Nagurski's, played against the Big Fellow in pre-season practice sessions. Said Grange, "When you hit Nagurski, it was almost like getting an electric shock. If you hit him above the ankles, you were likely to get yourself killed." In time, tacklers learned the best way to stop Nagurski, once he had gotten out into the open, was to hurl themselves horizontally at Bronko's legs.

Johnny Dell Isola, a center for the New York Giants, has never forgotten the first time he played against Nagurski. Dell

Isola was backing up the middle of the line for New York. It was first down and ten for the Bears. They handed Nagurski the ball and he charged into a hole opened for him in the center of the line. Dell Isola lunged forward to plug the gap.

"It was the hardest tackle I ever made," Dell Isola recalled. "I remember saying to myself, 'I guess that will show you, Nagurski.' But as they were unpiling us, I heard the referee turn to the Bears and say, 'Second down and two.' "

Bronko Nagurski was born on November 3, 1908, on the Canadian side of Rainy Lake, a body of water that spans the U. S.-Canadian border near International Falls, Minnesota. He attended schools in International Falls and in Bemidji, also in Minnesota, about one hundred miles to the south. Bronko played high school football, mostly fullback, but also tackle or any position where he was needed.

Despite Nagurski's presence in the lineup, his high school team had a dismal record, and in 1926 when he enrolled at the University of Minnesota, he was almost completely unheralded. But his skills did not go unnoticed for long. After Nagurski's freshman year, Doc Spears, the Minnesota coach, could tell the press, "I've got a tough kid who could pretty nearly be an All American wherever I use him. His name is Nagurski. He comes from International Falls, where it's so cold the mercury drops out of the bottom of the thermometer. But this kid is so tough that he doesn't even wear an overcoat." This was a day before college granted athletic scholarships, but Spears got Bronko a job firing the furnace in an office building. It paid him $50 a month.

Since the Gophers had All American Herb Joesting at fullback the Bronk was moved to tackle. He eventually played end, guard and fullback, too. In 1929 he was named to virtually every All American team, as a tackle on some, as a fullback on others. One newspaper solved the problem by naming a nine-member team plus Bronko—at both the tackle and fullback positions. Frank Menke, the noted sports authority of the day, declared, "Nagurski has solved the problem of what to do with the extra man when you are picking an All America. You can put him anywhere."

After Nagurski had achieved stardom at Minnesota, Coach

Spears was often asked how he had happened to find the Bronk. "I was driving past a farm," Doc would say, "when I noticed this big, strong farm boy plowing a field. I stopped to ask directions. The boy pointed—with his plow. That's how I found Bronko."

This is one of the many legends told about Nagurski. After he had joined the pros, the stories proliferated. One tall tale had it that the Big Fellow fell out of bounds one day and toppled a policeman's horse. According to another amazing story, Bronk once missed a wild tackle and sheared the fender off a Model-T Ford that was parked near the sidelines. Paul Bunyan had nothing on Bronko.

Nagurski graduated from Minnesota in an era before the football draft. Consequently he was available to every team. George Halas won him for the Bears. He contacted Nagurski through mutual friends, and then got Bronko to visit him in Chicago. Nagurski agreed to a two-year contract at $5,000 a season. When Bronko returned home, he was chagrined to find awaiting him an offer from the Giants of $7,500 for one year's play.

Bronko's debut as a Bear came in a game against the Green Bay Packers. Whenever Chicago went into punt formation, Nagurski and Red Grange were posted on the right side to protect the kicker. Grange was up close and Nagurski deep, close to the man doing the punting. Cal Hubbard, the mammoth tackle for the Packers, kept charging in on punts but he never got to Nagurski. Grange kept blocking him out.

Late in the game, Hubbard said to Grange, "Next time you kick, let me in. I guarantee you I won't block the kick. I just want to get a shot at Nagurski. I've been hearing how hard he is. I want to test him."

Grange agreed. The next time the Bears kicked, Grange let Hubbard through, then turned to watch. Hubbard charged toward Bronko like an express train, hit him, and bounced off as if he had run into the side of a building. Though dazed, Hubbard turned and ran downfield under the punt. When he caught up to Grange, he said, "Thanks, Red, but please don't do me any more favors."

In 1933, the Bears and the Portsmouth Spartans engaged in a season-long struggle for the Western Division lead. The two teams met in a critical game. Late in the final quarter, the Bears held a 10–7 edge. Portsmouth had to punt on fourth down, and when the Bears returned the ball to midfield, it appeared that the game was safely in hand. But the referee detected Nagurski holding, and the penalty gave the Spartans a first down. On the next play, Glen Presnell passed to Ernie Caddel for a touchdown, the play covering 65 yards. Portsmouth then converted to take the lead, 14–10. There was less than two minutes to play.

The Spartans' kickoff went to Nagurski and he returned it to the Bears' 45-yard line. In the huddle, his voice charged with emotion, Bronko said, "This is my fault, Brummy; give me the ball."

Quarterback Carl Brumbaugh complied. On the first play from scrimmage he pitched out to the Bronk who headed over left end, then arrow-straight downfield. His head down, his knees pounding almost as high as his chest, Nagurski sprinted for the Spartans' goal, providing his own blocking as he went. He was moving like a guided missile when he crossed into the end zone. His momentum was so great that he was unable to stop, and he barged into the brick wall of the dugout used by the Chicago Cubs. Observers swear that he chipped off a few bricks. "That last guy hit me awfully hard," Nagurski is supposed to have said.

After the 1933 season Nagurski took up professional wrestling, and somehow managed to combine his two careers successfully. It took a bit of doing, however, because the two seasons paralleled each other. In one three-week period in 1937, Nagurski appeared in the Bears' lineup for five games, and made eight mat appearances in such widely separated cities as Portland, Oregon, Vancouver, British Columbia, Seattle, Phoenix, Los Angeles, Oakland, Salt Lake City, and Philadelphia.

Nagurski developed a favorite method of flattening ring foes. He would grab the upper rope with one hand, then spring forward like an arrow from a bow, hurling his body to strike athwart his opponent's midsection. But even if he failed in this, he would still inflict serious damage. He would hit his man with an arm, a leg, his hip or a shoulder. Something. There could be no escape.

In the latter stages of his career, Nagurski was beset with arthritis and assorted aches and pains, the consequence of more jolts and collisions than anyone's flesh should ever be heir to. By 1935 he was no longer able to play a full sixty minutes of every game. An operation to remove a bone spur from his hip sidelined him for part of the season.

In 1937 rumors began to circulate that Nagurski was all through. The story was repeated to Steve Owen. "Nagurski's through?" Owen declared, "He's slowed down? I'll tell you how much he's slowed down. Now he only gains an average of six yards a try."

Nagurski did retire after the 1937 season. A big factor was that wrestling had become more profitable for him than football. He continued wrestling for four more years.

In 1943, with playing rosters decimated by the wartime draft, the Bears sent out an emergency call for Nagurski. Now thirty-five, he appeared as trim and powerful as the day he left the team six years before. Instead of playing fullback, however, he limited himself to playing guard.

In the final game of the season the Bears faced their crosstown rivals, the Cardinals. They had to win in order to clinch the Western Division championship. But the Cards were being stubborn. In the fourth period they held a 24–14 edge.

Nagurski paced nervously in front of the Bears' bench. Suddenly he clamped on his helmet, walked up to Bear coach Hunk Anderson, and announced, "I guess it's time for the Bronk to get to work." He ran out onto the field to take his old place at fullback.

It was the Bears' ball on the Cardinals' 38-yard line. The Bronk carried. Three plays later the ball was on the eleven. Four more plays and the ball was in the end zone.

Later in the game the Bears called on Bronko again when they couldn't move the ball. With fourth down and four to go, quarterback Sid Luckman handed off to the Big Fellow, and he rammed into the line for a first down. Luckman passed for the winning touchdown.

In the championship game against the Redskins that year, Nagurski's three-yard plunge into the line cracked a tie and put Chicago into the lead at half time. But in the second half Sammy Baugh's passes sent the Bears down to defeat.

Nagurski played a total of nine years with Chicago, and won All NFL honors six times. It's not known precisely how many yards he gained during his career since nobody kept accurate records in his early days with the Bears. Those statistics that are available credit him with 4,301 yards in 872 attempts, an average of 4.6 yards per carry. He scored 242 points. The fact is often overlooked, but Nagurski was a clever passer, too. He threw 80 passes and completed 38 of them.

What the statistics don't reveal, of course, is that Bronko was undoubtedly the strongest player of his era, perhaps of all time.

Steve Owen of the Giants had the only sound defense against the Bronk. "The thing to do," said Stout Steve, "is shoot him before he leaves the dressing room."

Ernie Nevers

Ernie Nevers, who has been called "America's all-time one-man team," would doubtless have become a member of the Hall of Fame anyway, but he guaranteed himself such status one cold and dreary Thanksgiving Day morning in 1929 when he led his team, the Chicago Cardinals, in a rout of the Chicago Bears. The score was 40–6. What is remarkable about the game is that Nevers, with six touchdowns and four conversions, scored every point. It's a record that still stands; indeed, very seldom has it ever been threatened.

Ernie Nevers was born in Willow Grove, Minnesota, on June 11, 1903. When he was a youngster, his parents moved to Superior, Wisconsin. At Superior Central High, Ernie's athletic skills first began to attract attention. He was a tailback on the football team, a feared hitter in baseball, and one of the very first practitioners of basketball's hook shot.

His folks moved to Santa Rosa, California, when Ernie was still in high school. After graduation he went to Stanford. "I would have enrolled at Wisconsin," Ernie says, "but nobody there offered me a job." The oversight must be ranked as grievous.

Ernie was an 11-letter man at Stanford, and as the fullback in the double wing installed by Pop Warner, an awesome triple threat. Not long before the end of his senior year season, Ernie injured one ankle and broke the other. Stanford had been selected to play in the Rose Bowl against Notre Dame and the vaunted Four Horsemen—Elmer Layden, Jim Crowley, Harry Stuhldreher and Don Miller. Though his ankle still wasn't sound, Nevers convinced Warner that he should play. With a pair of shears and a hammer, Warner fashioned an artificial ankle joint out of sheet aluminum and rubber inner tubing, then taped it to Nevers' lower leg.

Ernie played the entire sixty minutes and put on one of the greatest individual performances that the Rose Bowl game has ever known. His bullet passes were deadly accurate and his assaults into the line accounted for more yardage than the entire Notre Dame team was able to accrue. One account of the game credited Ernie with more than one-half of the Stanford team's tackles. Nevers alone was not quite enough, however, and Notre Dame won the game, 27–10.

After college Ernie became a professional—in three sports. He played a few basketball games for a Chicago team in a league that was a forerunner of the National Basketball Association. He signed with the St. Louis Browns in the American League as a pitcher, receiving a bonus of $10,000 and a salary of $7,000 for the season. He pitched three seasons of big league baseball before a back injury ended his career. Baseball's record book has given Nevers lasting fame, but he probably wishes that his name wasn't there. It is set down that Ernie twice served home run pitches to Babe Ruth the year that the Babe hit his classic sixty.

Ernie played only exhibition games during 1926, his first year in professional football. The money was good—$20,000 for the season. Only Red Grange, often Nevers' opponent on the gridiron, had ever received more.

The next year Ernie signed to play with the Duluth Eskimos in the National Football League. He received $25,000. "But I made one mistake," Ernie recalls. "I forgot to ask how long the season was going to be."

Renamed the Ernie Nevers Eskimos, the team played all but one of its games on the road, and just about every place in the East and Midwest where there was an open field. The squad left Duluth early in September and returned late in January, after having traveled 17,000 miles, playing 29 games, 19 in league competition and 10 exhibitions. During one stretch, they played 5 games in eight days—in St. Louis on Saturday, Detroit on

Sunday, New York on Thursday, Philadelphia on Saturday, and Pottsville on Sunday. Little wonder that they were often referred to as the Iron Men of the North. Of the 29 games they played, they won 19, lost 7, and tied 3.

Nevers was indestructible during the grueling campaign. He missed only 27 minutes of play. But it was no cinch. When the season started he weighed 210; at the finish he weighed 185.

In a game against Milwaukee, the doctor told Nevers not to play, that the pains he was suffering signaled an appendicitis attack. Through the first quarter and most of the second, Ernie remained on the sidelines, writhing in frustration as he watched the Milwaukee team build a slim lead. "What else could I do?" Nevers recalls. "I had to put myself in." He promptly threw a 62-yard touchdown pass to end Joe Rooney, the longest pass on record at the time. Then he booted the extra point. The Eskimos won, 7–6.

The Eskimo squad numbered only thirteen players, a fact that was often the source of chagrin to Dewey Scanlon, the coach, and Ole Haugsrud, the owner. Both used to don uniforms before each game and warm up with the regulars, so that the crowd wouldn't realize that the club was so pathetically undermanned.

On the Eskimos' first visit to New York to play the Giants, New York owner Tim Mara rented a sight-seeing bus to show the visitors the town. The bus pulled up in front of their hotel, and the Eskimos, all thirteen of them, climbed aboard. Mara greeted each man. After they were seated, he turned to Haugsrud and said, "C'mon, Ole; get the rest of your guys out here. I'm paying for this bus."

Ole was unwilling to admit that this was his entire squad. "I guess," he lied, "they're still asleep in their rooms. Let's go without them."

In the game later that week, Ernie intercepted a pass on the Eskimo 45-yard line. Then he carried the ball nine straight times to score his team's first touchdown.

He was injured in the fourth period and forced to the sidelines. A regulation in effect at the time prevented a player from reentering the game, but because the Eskimos were so shorthanded, the Giants agreed to relax the rule. Besides, most of the spectators had paid to see Nevers. Once back in the game,

Ernie carried the ball on every play and scored a second time. But he missed the extra point. The Giants won, 14–13.

"I was wondering where Nevers was hurt," said Giant coach Steve Owen after the game. "It could only have been his big toe."

Sometimes called the Blond Bull, Nevers stood 6 feet and weighed 210, not big for a running back by today's standards. But he was indomitable. It was always his aim to go *through* the line, never around it. He would try over and over again. Some observers believe that if he had been a more devious runner he would have had much greater success as a professional.

Ernie not only handled the Eskimos' ball-carrying and place-kicking, but he did the passing and punting, and he returned punts and kickoffs. He also called the signals and served as captain, and, in time, became player-coach.

Ernie had many remarkable days for the Eskimos. He once kicked a punt 80 yards against Green Bay that went out of bounds on the Packers' one-yard line. One day at Pottsville he threw seventeen consecutive completions and scored 27 points. And in a game at Hartford, Connecticut, Ernie booted five field goals at distances of 21, 25, 26, 28 and 42 yards.

The Duluth club was sold in 1929, and Nevers' contract went to the Chicago Cardinals for the 1929 season. He served as player-coach. He was twenty-six at the time.

It was during his premier year with the Cardinals that he went on the scoring orgy against the Bears. Ernie's performance that day is responsible for this entry in the NFL Record Manual: "Most Points, Game—40, Ernie Nevers, Chicago Cardinals vs. Chicago Bears, November 28, 1929 (6 touchdowns, 4 points-after-touchdown)."

The feat is all the more amazing when one realizes that typical scores of the day were 6–0 or 3–0. The emphasis was on the running game, with plunges into the line and occasional sweeps the accepted methods of attack, and to have a team—much less one player—score 40 points was unheard of.

The game was played on the Cards' home grounds, Comiskey Park, before 8,000 fans who cheered wildly for Ernie throughout the day. Both teams were far down in the league standings, but the game had importance because it was to decide the city championship, a title the Cardinals had never won.

It was bitter cold and the field was frozen. Because the footing was so poor, the Cardinals, who operated out of a double wing, were unable to use their tricky spinners and reverses. "All we could do," says Nevers, "was shoot our power between tackles."

Nevers' first touchdown came in the first six minutes of play. After an exchange of downs, Nevers and Mickey McDonald, a halfback, worked the ball deep into Bear territory. Nevers then splintered the line for a 20-yard touchdown run, his longest of the day. His place-kick attempt went wide.

Minutes later Ernie scored again, this time on a five-yard plunge. His point-after attempt was good; the Cards led, 13–0.

Nevers scored his third touchdown in the second quarter on a six-yard run, and again he added the extra point. This made the score 20–0, Cards.

The Bears went to the air when the third quarter began, because of their lack of success on the ground. Walt Holmer connected on a short pass to Garland Grange, Red Grange's brother, who outraced the Cardinal defenders to the end zone. That made the score 20–6. This feat encouraged the Bears and minutes later they had possession of the ball on the Cardinals' 30-yard line, but there their attack bogged down and they never threatened again.

But it was a different story with Nevers. He scored his fourth touchdown late in the third quarter in a one-yard plunge; his kick was good. The Cardinals now had a 27–6 lead.

Ernie's fifth and sixth touchdowns came in the final period on a one-yard buck and a 10-yard gallop. A poor pass from center prevented his try for the extra point after the fifth touchdown, but the other attempt was good.

With about five minutes remaining in the game, Ernie signaled the bench for a substitute. When he trotted from the field, the 8,000 frenzied fans sounded like 80,000.

Knute Rockne, the famed Notre Dame coach, was in the stands that day, surrounded by the Notre Dame team. They had come to Chicago from South Bend especially for the game. Rockne seldom smiled, but when Nevers scored his sixth touchdown, Rockne beamed. "That, gentlemen," he said, "is how to play football."

Often overlooked in the accounts of the game is the fact that Ernie had scored all 19 of the Cardinals' points in a game against Dayton the previous Sunday. Added to his 40 points against the Bears, this gave him a total of 59 consecutive points. Many records that Nevers set have been surmounted, but this one seems "unbreakable."

Only twice in recent years have players come close to netting 40 points in a game. In 1951, Dub Jones of the Cleveland Browns scored six touchdowns against the Chicago Bears to give him 36 points for the day. And in 1965, Gale Sayers did the same against the San Francisco 49ers. Nevers watched Sayers on television. Afterward, he said, "I felt that the Bears should have kept the boy in—to let him try to break that forty-point record with another touchdown."

The year 1931 was Ernie's last as a professional player. His body had become so battered by this time he almost had to tape himself together to play. Sometimes he had to resort to black electrician's tape because the Cardinal management complained that he was spending too much money. Yet his spirit never dimmed, and he played nineteen games that year, and a full sixty minutes in each.

One game that year documents his pride and pluck. The Cardinals were playing Brooklyn. Nevers carried the ball for a short gain. Right after the whistle blew, a Brooklyn player, unable to stop himself, crashed down upon Ernie and his knees dug into the middle of Nevers' back. Nevers was knocked unconscious. The referee allowed the Cardinals two minutes to carry him from the field.

Phil Handler, the Cardinals' player-coach, and a trainer had gotten Nevers almost to the sidelines when his eyes opened and he looked about dazedly. "Where are we?" he asked. "What's going on?" Handler explained.

Ernie became enraged. He pulled free of Handler's hold. "You're not taking *me* out," he roared, and he raced back out onto the field.

To underscore his well-being, he called his number until he had scored a touchdown. It took sixteen consecutive plays.

Ernie returned to the Cardinals in 1939 as a coach. But the team had a cheerless season, winning only one game. He was fired at the end of the season. In 1946 he coached the ill-starred Chicago Rockets in the All America Conference.

Nevers now makes his home in California. He feels that today's players are every bit the equal of those in his day. "The ball is smaller and the equipment is better," he says. "But the players are just as tough. A team still has to block and tackle to be good. And the backs still have to cross the goal line to score." He is a director of the California Clippers, the Oakland soccer team. But though he is a soccer enthusiast, most of the interviews that he grants concern his football exploits with the Eskimos and Cardinals.

Pop Warner, who coached both Nevers and the fabled Jim Thorpe, was once asked who was the better player of the two. "Nevers," Warner answered without a moment's hesitation. "He could do everything Thorpe could do and he tried harder. No man ever gave more of himself than Ernie Nevers."

Jim Thorpe

Anyone who ever saw him play agrees: Jim Thorpe was the best, the absolute best ever to pull on a pair of cleated shoes.

Like all great players of his time, Thorpe was a triple-threat man; he could pass, run or kick, but he could do each of these as no human before or since. He could score by drop-kicking from the 50-yard line. Once, in a game against Lafayette, his shortest punt was 70 yards.

He ran with an effortless spring in his stride, but he had the power of a Sherman tank. He eluded tacklers by "showing them a leg and then taking it away," but often it pleased him to hurtle into a foe, smashing him to the ground as he rolled on his way.

Tackling was his special pleasure. To be hit by Thorpe was similar to being wiped out by a telephone pole. When he struck a man he invariably cudgeled him with one of his mighty shoulders. If the victim remained conscious, he was likely to hear Thorpe bend low and say, "A fellow can get hurt playing this game. If he don't take care."

Thorpe starred in every sport he ever participated in, but football was his favorite. Body contact—to carry the ball into the line, to nail a runner—that was the ticket.

Pro football was born in Latrobe, Pennsylvania, in 1895 but grew to manhood in the steel and coal towns of northeastern

Ohio during the early years of the next century. Massillon organized a pro team in 1903, and Akron, Youngstown, Canton and Shelby soon after. In time Massillon and Canton became the acknowledged powerhouses and bitter archrivals. In 1906 Massillon beat Canton, 12–6. After the game the Canton coach was accused of bribing one of his own players to throw the game. This incident soured local residents on the pro game and the sport dropped out of sight.

In 1915 Canton decided to resume operation and in an effort to rekindle interest in the club, the Bulldogs hired Thorpe as a player-coach. Jim quit his job as an assistant coach at Indiana University to go with the team.

Thorpe was no wide-eyed, rawboned youngster. He was twenty-seven, and he had already conquered several worlds. His gridiron exploits with the Carlisle Indians had won him every collegiate honor there was to win; indeed, he had become a living legend at the school. He had startled the world with his stunning performance at the Olympic Games in Stockholm in 1912. And he had two boisterous seasons in professional baseball with the New York Giants under his belt.

He was still a supple giant of a man, with thick arms, a massive chest, broad shoulders, and a great shock of black hair. But crinkles were beginning to etch his face, and he was fleshier now than in the good days under Pop Warner at Carlisle.

Canton paid Thorpe $250 a game, a princely sum. The going rate for a player in those days was $75 to $100 a game.

Relatively little is known of this early phase of Thorpe's pro career. There was no league, no organization. Nobody kept records. It is known, however, that Canton had other fine players besides Thorpe. There was Greasy Neale, who once scored six touchdowns in one game; Indian Joe Guyon, a fast and durable halfback, who had been a teammate of Thorpe's at Carlisle; and Howard "Cub" Buck of Wisconsin, a lineman who went on to fame at Green Bay.

Canton and Massillon renewed their rivalry for the mythical "championship." Before each meeting the two clubs would load their rosters with talent gleaned from other pro teams, and people would pour in from miles around to watch the savage battles.

One year Massillon had a fellow named Knute Rockne holding down left end. On the first play from scrimmage, Rockne hurtled through Canton's defenses to nail Thorpe for a loss. Then he did it a second time.

Thorpe showed anger. "You shouldn't do that to Jim," he told Rockne firmly. "All these people came out to see Jim run."

"Well go ahead and run—if you can," came Rockne's flip answer.

On the next play Thorpe swung wide and Rockne knifed through to meet him. He missed the tackle but he caught Thorpe's knees, a shoulder and bludgeoning stiff-arm. Undeterred by the encounter, Thorpe galloped 60 yards for a touchdown. As he trotted to the Canton bench, he noticed the battered, bloody Rockne being helped from the field. Thorpe went over to him. "Nice going, Rock," he said. "You sure let old Jim run."

Gus Dorais, a passing sensation at Notre Dame, and Fritz Pollard, a fast, elusive scatback from UCLA, also played with the Massillon Tigers. Pollard was known as the Shadow because he was so difficult to put down. When Thorpe encountered Pollard, he made no effort to tackle him the first time he carried the ball. He merely studied Pollard's style.

Then Pollard streaked for the sideline on an end sweep. Thorpe went after him. As Pollard neared the sideline, Thorpe shouted, "Out! Out! Get out!" Pollard's answer was an extra burst of speed. Thorpe leaped and locked one arm around Pollard's neck, crashed him to the ground and landed on top of him.

Thorpe got up but Pollard was out cold. Then his eyes opened and he looked up to see Thorpe standing over him. "Mr. Thorpe," Pollard said, "you are a mean man."

In the fall of 1920, representatives of the most powerful teams of the day met in the showroom of Ralph Hays' automobile agency in Canton and organized the American Professional Football Association. (It was renamed the National Football League two years later.) They elected Thorpe their president and Stan Cofall, a Massillon man, as vice-president.

Professional football of the day being what it was, the league paid Thorpe no salary. He quit as president in 1921 to devote his full energies to playing and coaching. That year he left Canton to organize the Cleveland Indians but in 1922 he returned to the Bulldogs.

The following year Thorpe started up the Oorang Indians,

named for a dog kennel in La Rue, Ohio, that specialized in Airedales. The Oorang team was largely Indian in makeup—Lone Wolf, Wrinkle Meat, Gray Horse, and Eagle Feather were some of the players, and often they would play wearing Indian buckskins over their football pads. One year they represented Marion, Ohio, in the NFL and finished near the bottom in the league standings.

After two years with the Oorang club, Thorpe moved on to the Toledo Maroons, and then to the Rock Island Independents. He didn't play every game, but when he did play his team usually won.

People everywhere went to see him and he earned good money, as much as $15,000 a year. But it went fast. Personal tragedy haunted him. A cherished son died. There were broken marriages. He drank too much. At forty, Thorpe was still playing football, still trying for the smashing tackle, still hurling himself into the line.

James Francis Thorpe was born in 1888 (some sources say 1886) in a tiny farmhouse near the Oklahoma settlement of Prague. He was a twin. The other child, a boy named Charles, died at eight.

Thorpe's ancestry was Sac and Fox, the names of two Indian tribes. In later years he joked about his heritage: "My father, Hiram Thorpe, was half Sac-Fox and half Irish. My mother was three-fourths Sac-Fox and one-fourth French. That makes me five-eighths Indian, one-fourth Irish, and one-eighth French. I guess you'd call me an American Airedale."

The Thorpe family lived on a 160-acre ranch-farm. As a youngster Jim and his two brothers tracked game, hunted deer and fished in the nearby North Canadian River. Jim was sent to the Sac-Fox reservation school, and later he attended the Haskell Institute in Lawrence, Kansas.

At this stage Thorpe's life took a significant turn. The traveling superintendent of the Carlisle (Pennsylvania) Institute (officially known as the United States Indian Industrial School) selected Jim from a group of candidates. The reason Thorpe was chosen has been lost to history, but his enrollment there served as the launching pad for all that was to come.

Jim was fifteen when he arrived at Carlisle and, in his own

words, "just a skinny little jigger." He stood only 4 feet 10 and weighed about 115. But he was growing fast. A tailor apprentice, he played guard on the tailor's football team in the school's shop league. The tailors captured the school championship and seven members of the team, Jim included, were elevated to varsity status.

Enter Pop Warner.

Glenn Scobie Warner, who was to become one of college football's most famed coaches, was coach at Cornell University in 1898 when the Big Red journeyed to Pennsylvania to play Carlisle. They won, 23–6, but Warner came away with a deep-seated admiration for the scrappy Indian squad. The next year Warner was casting about for a better job and an offer came in from Carlisle. Warner grabbed it. The two—Warner and Thorpe— were to rocket to fame together.

At first Warner paid no attention to Thorpe. There was no reason to. Carlisle had a splendid team, and Thorpe, who had been converted from a guard to a halfback, was not adjusting smoothly to his new position.

One afternoon during a tackling drill Thorpe made his first impression and it was a lasting one. He was sent downfield to catch punts and return them, without blockers, against first-string defensive tacklers. He gathered in a punt near the goal line, tucked it to his side, and stormed toward the other end of the field with his characteristic bounding, hip-swinging style. Some tacklers hit him and bounced off. Others dove and missed. And Thorpe romped into the end zone.

Warner fumed. "Who do you think you are?" he roared. "This is tackling practice, understand?"

Thorpe looked at him grimly. "Nobody tackles Jim," he said.

"Let's run the drill again," Warner ordered. "This time really hit. Bang him so hard he won't get up."

Again Thorpe caught the ball. He was hit harder this time, but it didn't change the outcome. Once more he made the end zone.

This performance didn't win Thorpe a starting position right away. But a few weeks later Carlisle faced Pennsylvania in a rugged game at Franklin Field. Carlisle's halfback, Albert Payne, was injured and Warner sent Thorpe in.

Thorpe didn't know the signals; he didn't know how to use

his interference. It didn't matter. He took the pass from center, blasted his way through the line of scrimmage, then thundered 65 yards for a touchdown.

"That's fun," Thorpe said in the huddle. "Let me do it again." Late in the game, they did. Thorpe swept 85 yards through the hapless Penn team for another score.

So began Thorpe's gridiron career. In 1908 Walter Camp listed Thorpe on his All America third team, an unprecedented honor for little Carlisle. Thorpe was also making headlines in other sports—in baseball, as a hard-hitting first baseman, in track and field, as an unbeaten hurdler, in basketball, wrestling and lacrosse.

When school let out in the spring of 1909, Thorpe didn't feel like returning home to work on the farm. Two of his Carlisle teammates, Joe Libbey and Jesse Young Deer, were going to North Carolina to play baseball and they asked Thorpe to go along.

The three caught on with Rocky Mount, Thorpe as a third baseman at a salary of $15 a week, and his two friends as outfielders. Later Thorpe became a pitcher and in typical Thorpe fashion won 23 out of 25 games.

Thorpe did not return to Carlisle that fall or the next year either. Instead he spent most of the time playing baseball. From Rocky Mount he moved to Fayetteville, Arkansas, and played until the league folded because of lack of attendance. This interlude in Thorpe's career had little bearing on his development as an athlete. It is important because, in later years, his playing baseball at Rocky Mount was to be cited as a violation of the amateur code. To Thorpe it was merely innocent fun; he did it openly. Yet he was to be thrust into deep disgrace because of it.

Thorpe went on the warpath when he returned to Carlisle in 1911, and he personally manhandled every opponent on the Indians' schedule. In seven of nine games that season, he broke loose for touchdown runs of 70 yards or more. In 1912, it was more of the same. He scored 25 touchdowns and 198 points, a record which is untouched to this day.

In the Olympic Games of that year, Thorpe's performance was just as outstanding. No event in Olympic competition is more grueling, requires more in the way of strength, skill and stamina, than the decathlon. Thorpe won the decathlon with ease, and set a new record doing it. He was first in the shot put, the high hurdles, the high jump and 1,500 meters, and no worse than fourth in any of the other six events. For good measure, he also won the pentathlon.

At the conclusion of the games, Thorpe ascended the victory podium and King Gustav of Sweden presented him with a huge jeweled trophy, shaped like a Viking ship, and said to him, "You, sir, are the greatest athlete in the world."

A tumultuous welcome greeted Thorpe on his return to the United States. There was a ticker tape parade up Broadway, banquets in his honor, and President Taft called him "the highest type of citizen."

After the football season of 1912, the story broke. Thorpe, it was said, was no amateur when he won his Olympic titles. He had played professional baseball. Jim didn't deny it. He was stripped of his titles and had to send back the trophies and the medals. The furor bewildered him, but later it was to cause him deep sadness.

Thorpe signed with baseball's New York Giants after he left Carlisle. In all, he spent seven years in the major leagues, but it was largely a dismal experience. He feuded with Giant manager John McGraw, not a good man to feud with, and spent many an afternoon on the bench as a result. He was traded to Cincinnati and later Boston and in neither city did he manage to impress anyone. "No one ever bothered to teach Thorpe any of baseball's fundamentals," says one of his teammates. "They just wanted him for his name."

In 1920 the Boston Braves sent Thorpe to Akron. It was all downhill after that. Toledo, Portland, Oregon, Hartford, Worcester, Massachusetts—the towns kept getting smaller and the spectators fewer.

In pro football, it was the same. The New York Giants hired Thorpe in 1925. He was so rusty and out of shape that they paid him a salary of $200 for a half game, and would not allow him to play a full game until he got himself in playing trim.

Thorpe's last appearance in a pro football game came on November 30, 1929, when he played briefly for the Chicago Cardinals in their annual Thanksgiving Day game against the Bears.

According to the Associated Press, he was "muscle-bound . . . a mere shadow of his former self."

Thorpe died in 1953. In his last years, when his once proud and powerful body had been sapped of its fire and strength, football provided him with warm memories. "That was the best time of my life," he said in recalling his days with the Canton Bulldogs. "I'll never forget it."

In his prime, Thorpe could do anything on the football field as well as any specialist. He could run with the elusiveness of Red Grange, hit the line with Nagurski's power, and pass with Sammy Baugh's finesse. Time eroded his skills. But he was—simply—the best, and that is the way to remember him.

1964

Jimmy Conzelman

"Give us a story on Jimmy Conzelman," the editor of *Sport* magazine wired its Chicago correspondent. "Very well," the answer came back, "but which Conzelman, the coach of the Chicago Cardinals, the professional baseball player and executive, the newspaper publisher, songwriter or orator?"

James Gleason Conzelman has been all of these—and more, much more.

Conzelman's most glittering achievements in professional football came during three seasons late in the 1940's when he coached the Cardinals, then based in Chicago, to two division titles and a world championship.

Conzelman returned to the Cards in 1946 and quickly welded them into a team to be feared. They had the kind of a backfield that most coaches only dream about. It included halfback "Mad Marshall" Goldberg, a dangerous runner and an exceptional defensive player; quarterback Paul Christman, a good short passer and a great long passer; and, beginning in 1947, a young halfback named Charley Trippi.

A friend had written to Conzelman describing Trippi's skills while the young man was still at the University of Georgia. Jimmy passed the report along to Charles Bidwill, owner of the Chicago team, and the Cards went after him, just managing to snatch Charley from the grasp of the New York Yankees of the All America Conference.

Jimmy had a keen eye for talent. He drafted Elmer Angsman of Notre Dame, and in his rookie year Angsman supplanted

Goldberg as a Cardinal halfback. "I drafted Elmer third," Jimmy recalls, "and I had a good reason. He'd had eight teeth knocked out in Notre Dame's game against Navy on Saturday and the following Monday he reported for practice. A guy that tough I wanted."

The Cards finished with a 6-5 record in 1946, but the next year, Trippi's rookie season, they were ready to make their move. The division race came down to the final day of the season, a game against the Chicago Bears, with the two teams deadlocked for first place. It was a bruising battle, but the Cardinals won, 30–21. The outcome, however, was decided on the very first play from scrimmage.

Conzelman's scouts had reported that Mike Holovak, the Bears' defensive halfback, invariably picked up the first eligible receiver to come his way. So the Cards decided to send two men into Holovak's territory on the first play of the game. The first man, end Mal Kutner, was to be merely a decoy, while the second, Boris Dimancheff, was to get a Christmas pass.

Dimancheff was not let in on the strategy until the day before the game. He had become a father during the week and had missed the team's practice sessions. Even after he had been told, Conzelman refused to let him practice the play because he was afraid a spy from the Bear camp might be around.

"The first thing we had to do on the day of the game was win the toss," Conzelman remembers. "Luckily we did."

The kickoff soared over the Cards' goal line. With first down and ten on their own 20-yard line, the Cards put the plan into action. To further bewilder the Bears, Conzelman had Dimancheff, who in all previous games that season had lined up at left half, now line up at right half. Christman took the hand-off from center, and Kutner and Dimancheff sprinted downfield. It worked to perfection. Holovak came over to defend against Kutner. Dimancheff grabbed Christman's pass at midfield and galloped into the end zone. It was a stunning blow and the Bears were unable to recover.

The championship game was played in Comiskey Park and the Philadelphia Eagles were the opposition. The Cards' "dream backfield" was never better. Twice Elmer Angsman went 70 yards to score. Charlie Trippi returned a punt 75 yards for a touchdown and streaked 44 yards for another. It was all too much for the Eagles. They fell, 28–21. It was the first title win for the Cardinals since 1925.

The next season the Cardinals won eleven and lost one to take the Western Division crown again, but in the championship game the Eagles got revenge by winning, 7–0.

Throughout their two winning seasons the Cardinals had been struck by one tragedy after another. Owner Charles Bidwill died in April, 1947. During the 1947 season halfback Jeff Burkett was killed in an airplane crash. And following the opening game of the 1948 season, tackle Stan Mauldin collapsed and died in the Cardinal dressing room. Conzelman, heartbroken over the chain of ill fortune, retired after the season.

The Chicago Cardinals of 1946–1948 were not the first pro team Jimmy Conzelman ever coached, not by any means. They were merely the most successful. Conzelman's involvement with the pro game goes back to the lean and hungry days before the founding of the National Football League.

Jimmy Conzelman (christened James Ryan Dunn) was born in St. Louis on March 6, 1898. He starred in basketball, baseball and football at McKinley High, and set a prep school record by scoring 26 touchdowns in one season, nine of them in one game.

He attended Washington University in St. Louis and later was a member of the Navy's splendid Great Lakes team, one of the finest football squads ever to represent a branch of the service. They defeated the Mare Island Marines in the Rose Bowl on January 1, 1919. One of his teammates was George Halas. When Halas organized the Staleys of Decatur, Illinois, in 1920, the team that was to become the Chicago Bears, he signed up Conzelman.

The next season Conzelman joined the Rock Island (Illinois) Independents. This was 1921, the year that the NFL was founded. "Pro football players of that period were looked upon as toughs and bruisers, men who couldn't get a job anyplace else," Conzelman remembers. "I was almost ashamed to go home to St. Louis after the season. People forgot that most of us had gone to college."

Early in his first season with the Independents, the team faced the Staleys. Conzelman scored a touchdown and kicked a field goal to give Rock Island a 10–0 lead at halftime. But the Staleys rolled for two touchdowns in the second half to win, 14–10. The game launched a long and spirited rivalry between Halas and Conzelman.

The first of many distinctions that were to befall Conzelman took place during his first year at Rock Island. He was named coach of the team, and it happened while a game was in progress. The opposition was running play after play through right tackle, a position that happened to be manned by the coach. During the second half a substitute came in from the bench to tell Conzelman, "The owner says you're the new coach; so get busy." Conzelman did. The Independents won.

Conzelman spent two seasons with Rock Island and became so idolized by the fans that he was offered a job managing the town's baseball team in the Missouri Valley League. Besides managing, he filled in as a catcher, third baseman and outfielder.

After Rock Island, Conzelman was player-coach of the Milwaukee Badgers, another NFL team of the day. He had been with Milwaukee for two years when one day he received a telephone call from Joe Carr, the NFL commissioner.

"Come down to Columbus [Ohio] and see me," Carr said. "I want you to put a pro team in Detroit. The franchise fee is $1,000, but I'll let you have it for $100." Conzelman quickly agreed to the offer.

Jimmy took in Henry Horner, a future governor of Illinois, as a partner, but one of the Rockefellers would have been a better choice. The Panthers, as he christened the club, were powerful and talented, and achieved a fine 8-2-2 record during 1925, but Detroit hardly noticed their existence. The citizens of Detroit were football fans all right, but they supported the University of Michigan. Besides, Conzelman's home dates were invariably struck by rain. At the end of the season, as Conzelman puts it, "We were hurtin' in the ready-cash department."

Jimmy felt that he could hold back the great red wave that was threatening to engulf him by booking Red Grange and the Chicago Bears for an exhibition game. Grange, the fabled Galloping Ghost, had joined the Chicago club after a sensational career at the University of Illinois and was attracting big crowds everywhere. Detroiters remembered him for the four touchdowns he had scored against Michigan in the space of eleven minutes.

"Tickets started selling like mad," Conzelman recalls. "I could see that we were going to take in about $20,000. It meant we'd get off the hook, wipe out our debts and see daylight for the first time."

A few days before the game, George Halas called and told Jimmy that Grange had been hurt and might not be able to play. "I thought the fair thing to do was to tell the newspapers; so I did," Conzelman says.

On the day of the game, Conzelman looked out the window and saw a line a block long at the Panther box office. This is the greatest sports city in the world, he thought to himself. Grange is hurt, but they still want to see him.

What Jimmy didn't know at the time was that the fans weren't *buying* tickets; they were lined up for refunds. "We drew about 4,500 people," he says. "But it wasn't enough."

The 1926 version of the Panthers was less successful on the playing field and no better at the gate. "I couldn't afford to keep going," Conzelman says, "so I handed the franchise back to the league." In 1951 the franchise sold for $250,000, and two years later for $6 million. Today its value is approximately twice that figure, and the money the management spends for cleats would probably have been enough to have kept Conzelman solvent.

After the demise of the Panthers, Jimmy moved on to the Providence Steamrollers as a player-coach and stayed four seasons. In 1928, he piloted the club to the NFL title. It was during his years with the Steamrollers that a knee injury ended Jimmy's career as a player.

At this point Conzelman took stock. He had spent almost a decade in professional football, and about all that he had to show for it was a bantam-sized bank account and a bad knee. He decided that it was about time to seek something more secure.

For a time he published a weekly newspaper, the Maplewood (Missouri) *Press* by name, and he saw duty as a reporter, editor and business manager. The journalistic skills he acquired attracted considerable attention in 1946 when articles he wrote appeared in a number of national magazines. One, entitled "I'd Rather Coach the Pros," which he sold to the *Saturday Evening Post,* was judged to be one of the finest sports features of the year.

In his spare time, Jimmy was an actor on the St. Louis stage, an avocation that fitted well with another of his talents, songwriting. Jimmy had nine songs published, including one entitled "What a Baby," which enjoyed mild popularity in the mid-1920's. He was never a threat to Irving Berlin, however.

By 1932 Jimmy was back on the football scene, returning to Washington University, his alma mater, as head coach. He held the post for eight seasons and won the Missouri Valley Conference three times.

As a college coach, and a successful one, Conzelman was in great demand on the chicken-and-green-peas circuit. The only trouble was that he was no speaker. Whenever he mounted the rostrum, his knees quivered and the words would only trickle out. To overcome this deficiency, Jimmy began accepting every speaking engagement he could get, sometimes as many as four or five a day. His determination paid off. A commencement day address he delivered at the University of Dayton in 1942, entitled "The Young Man's Mental and Physical Approach to War," was twice read into the *Congressional Record* and became required reading at West Point. Today Conzelman is widely recognized as a brilliant orator, and he has been the principal guest speaker at virtually every important football function.

In 1940, when Cardinal owner Charles Bidwill was looking for a coach, George Halas, a close friend of Bidwill's, suggested Conzelman. Twice before Jimmy had rejected offers to coach the Cards but this time he relented. If Conzelman was grateful to Halas, he didn't show it on the football field. The first time that the Cards met the Bears they beat them soundly.

But this game was but a candle in the darkness. In general, these were woeful days for the Cards. They lost many more games than they won, and Jimmy was never able to get them higher than fourth place in the division standings. What made the situation even worse was the brilliance of the Bears, the Cards' crosstown rivals. Halas' club completely dominated the league during this period, and the Cards lost seven straight to them before achieving a rare victory in 1945.

Jimmy resigned as the Cardinals' coach in 1942 to become assistant to Don Barnes, president of the St. Louis Browns baseball team. Four years later, when Jimmy returned to the Cards, it was all very different. He quickly nailed down the club's second NFL title.

A football coach, both pro and college, a baseball executive, an actor, a writer, a raconteur—Jimmy Conzelman has won great renown for his amazing versatility. But Marshall Goldberg, after a testimonial dinner to Conzelman some years ago, described him best. "He is," said Goldberg, "one of the sweetest guys you'd ever want to meet."

Ed Healey

In 1921, not long after the Bears had set up shop in Chicago, the team played host to the Rock Island Independents. George Halas, the Bears' boss and, at the time, their right end, played across the line from big and rugged Ed Healey.

Early in the game Halas decided to try a new block, one that involved a bit of holding. The ball was snapped. Halas held Healey. And Dutch Sternaman gained seven yards.

Healey boiled with rage. "Holding!" he roared. "You were holding me! Do that again and I'll knock your block off!"

The same play was called. Again Halas held Healey. Again Sternaman gained.

"I was on my hands and knees when some sixth sense told me to duck," Halas recalled. "I pulled back, and just in time to see Healey's big fist whistle past my nose. It was traveling so fast it buried itself up to the wrist into the ground."

It was at that moment that Halas decided he wanted Healey playing on his side, not against him. On November 27, 1922, he purchased Healey's contract from Rock Island for $100. It was, incidentally, the first player sale in the history of professional football, according to Howard Roberts, the Bears' historian.

Healey was happy to join the Bears. The clubhouse at Rock Island had no shower facilities and no trainer. The Bears had both.

Healey played his college football at Dartmouth where he won three letters in the sport under coaches Frank (the Iron Major) Cavenaugh and Dr. Clarence W. Spears. He played two years with Rock Island before Halas grabbed him.

Healey's most memorable game in professional football came in early 1926 when the Bears were in Los Angeles to play the Tigers, one of their opponents on the Bears' fabled Red Grange tour of 1925–1926. Some 60,000 fans turned out, anxious to see Grange match talents with one George Wilson, a halfback for the Tigers, whose speed and elusiveness were regarded the equal of Grange's by West Coast fans. Early in the game the Tigers had the ball deep in their own territory. The ball was snapped to Wilson who knifed his way through the right side of the Bear line and broke into the open. Healey, hurtling fallen Bears, went after him. He chased the fleet Tiger almost the full length of the field and at the last possible moment launched a flying leap. Wilson went flat. The crowd's groan could be heard all the way to Long Beach.

"That was my greatest moment in football," Healey says. "I lost a tooth on the play when Wilson's heel hit me in the mouth —but it was worth it."

Healey was a lineman through and through. He enjoyed the violence of the game. Tackling, any bodily contact for that matter, was high pleasure. Healey played the game with such distinction that he won All Pro honors five times during his eight-year career.

Healey was one of the few Bears that Halas permitted to hold a regular job during the football season. The truth was that Healey played the game more for the fun of it than the money. When the demands of his business career became too great, he quit the gridiron, though reluctantly. Now in retirement, Healey lives as a gentleman farmer in Niles, Michigan.

Clarke Hinkle

The history of the National Football League is replete with the exploits of battering-ram fullbacks. In days gone by there were Ernie Nevers and Bronko Nagurski, and more recently, Cleveland's Jimmy Brown and Green Bay's Jim Taylor. But to the late Curly Lambeau, who saw them all in his thirty-year career as player and coach of the Packers, the "greatest all-around fullback ever to play in the National Football League was Clarke Hinkle."

"Hinkle runs the middle, runs wide, and blocks and tackles viciously," Lambeau said. "He punts and place-kicks with the best. He can do a good job as a pass receiver. And in defense against aerial attack, Hinkle has no superior in professional football."

Lambeau, it must be said, had a deep-seated personal interest in Hinkle. He scouted the young Bucknell star in 1932 at the annual East-West Shrine game for crippled children, and signed him for Green Bay right afterward. Hinkle stood 6 feet, and weighed 200 pounds—not big, but he had tremendous acceleration and power.

How much power? Power enough to win butting contests with Bronko Nagurski more than once.

In a game at Chicago it was the Packers' ball at midfield. Hinkle carried off tackle and Nagurski came up to meet him head on at the line of scrimmage. Instead of tackling a runner, it was Nagurski's style to flatten him with an explosive block, often causing a fumble. When Nagurski struck, Hinkle was hurled back several yards but he didn't go down. He landed on his feet and, churning his legs, instantly stormed right through the same hole for a touchdown.

Another memorable Nagurski-Hinkle meeting took place at Green Bay. The Packers had the ball on their own 20-yard line, with third down and fourteen to go. Hinkle dropped back to punt. (Teams often punted on third down in long yardage situations in those days.)

Hinkle took the pass from center, but instead of kicking he raced to his right. As he neared the sideline, Nagurski closed in, ready to unleash a bone-jarring block. But Hinkle was ready. He lowered his shoulder and smashed it into Nagurski's face. He stayed in bounds and managed to reach midfield before a tackler brought him down from behind. This was a day before face guards and Nagurski incurred considerable damage. His nose was broken, and he suffered bruised ribs and a fractured hip. He was kept on the sidelines through most of the rest of the season.

"I learned a lot from watching Nagurski play," Hinkle once said. "He taught me how to use my shoulders. He never played dirty, but if you had to play against Nagurski you had to use the same tactics he did."

Few players of the day pursued the game with Hinkle's dedication. He was a cinch for Lambeau to sign. "He could have had me for nothing," Hinkle once said. "I just wanted to play."

Cecil Isbell, the Packers' incomparable passer, once observed that Hinkle "didn't know how to lose." Said Isbell, "He'd get so fired up before a game he'd be glassy-eyed. If we lost, he wept."

Hinkle was named to the All League team four times: in 1936, 1937, 1938 and 1941. He led the league in scoring in 1938, and led it in field goals in 1940 and 1941. His 1,171 ball-carrying attempts on which he averaged 3.2 yards were both Green Bay records until eclipsed by Jim Taylor in the 1960's.

Three years after Hinkle joined the Packers, a young man named Don Hutson became a member of the team. Hutson rewrote the record book grabbing passes from Arnie Herber and later Cecil Isbell. Hinkle played an important but often unsung role while Hutson worked his magic. He frequently hit the line without the ball to decoy the defense, giving Herber or Isbell time to fade back and toss to Hutson.

During Hinkle's tenure with the club, the Packers were seldom out of contention. They won the Western Division crown in 1936, 1938 and 1939. The 1936 and 1939 teams went on to win NFL titles.

Oliver E. Kuechle, sports editor of the Milwaukee *Journal*, who saw Hinkle play in almost all of his games, best summed up his career: "They don't ever come any better than the "Hink!"

Clarke Hinkle Career Rushing Record

Year	Carries	Yards Gained	Average Gain	Touchdowns
1932	95	331	3.4	2
1933	139	413	2.9	4
1934	144	359	2.4	–
1935	77	273	3.5	2
1936	100	476	4.7	4
1937	129	552	4.2	5
1938	114	299	2.6	3
1939	135	381	2.7	5
1940	109	383	3.5	2
1941	129	393	3.0	5
Total	1,171	3,860	3.2	32

Roy (Link) Lyman

In 1925, after the Bears had returned to Chicago following their grueling tour of Eastern and Midwestern cities to display Red Grange, Halas' troops were in woeful shape. Every man on the squad was a casualty. Even Grange himself was in agony with an injured arm. But Halas and C. C. Pyle, Grange's manager, were determined to press on, and they arranged additional games for the club in Florida and on the Pacific Coast. Fresh talent had to be hired. One of the new recruits was an experienced 246-pound tackle named Roy (Link) Lyman. He was a wise choice. Halas held on to him until the day Link retired.

When Lyman joined the pros in 1922, each lineman had a fixed area of responsibility. The better linemen shifted with the play, of course, but they did not have much freedom to move. Lyman was one of the first to change this. He was tremendously agile and shifted much more than anyone else. Often he changed position just as the ball was snapped. Nobody did that in those days. Steve Owen, coach of the New York Giants, declared that Lyman's ability to diagnose a play and switch accordingly was a major factor in the development of the sophisticated defensive patterns introduced in the 1950's.

Lyman was born in Table Rock, Pawnee County, Nebraska, in 1898. He did not play football at McDonald Rural Federated High because only seven boys attended the school. Basketball was the only sport played.

Lyman's lack of experience in football was no great drawback when he entered the University of Nebraska. He quickly learned the game as a freshman. In 1918, as a sophomore, he started every game for the varsity. He played in 1919, then dropped out of school for a year, but in 1921 he returned to become a vital cog in what is considered one of the most powerful Nebraska teams ever assembled. They scored 283 points to a mere 17 for the opposition, roaring to seven victories and losing only to Notre Dame. Pop Warner's mighty Pittsburgh team was one of their victims. The Cornhusker line that year was rated as one of the strongest ever in the Midwest. Walter Camp singled out three players for special praise—Clarence Swanson at end, John Pucelik at guard, and Lyman.

After graduation Lyman signed with the Canton Bulldogs, who were coached by a fellow Nebraskan, Guy Chamberlin. The Bulldogs won the NFL title in 1922, Lyman's rookie year, and again the next year. Both seasons they were undefeated. Lyman moved on to Cleveland in 1924 and that team promptly won the league championship. Lyman won All Pro honors each of these years.

Link returned to Canton as a part owner in 1925. The following year his career with the Bears began.

He was a bulwark in the Bear line from 1926 through 1934, helping the Chicago team to win the NFL title in 1933 and a division crown in 1934. In 1929 he took a leave from the Bears to play semipro football in San Antonio, Texas, and during the 1932 season business conditions compelled him to remain on his ranch.

Lyman surely had a winning way. In his sixteen seasons of football, college, semipro and pro, he played on only one losing team. When Lyman retired in 1934, Bear owner Halas said that Link was tougher and stronger than when he had first joined the club.

After leaving the Bears, Link returned to the University of Nebraska as a line coach. He now resides in San Marino, California, near Los Angeles, where he owns an insurance agency.

In days gone by it was said of tackles that they were merely fullbacks with their brains knocked out. But no one ever made that pronouncement about Link Lyman.

August (Mike) Michalske

Playing guard in the rough and rugged pro football days of the 1930's was perhaps the toughest assignment of all. A guard in those days had to be able to block, head on, the biggest of opposing linemen, and had to be able to pull from the line and lead interference for the ballcarrier.

This was only 50 percent of his job. When the other team had the ball, the guard was the key man in stopping the enemy running attack. Last, he had to be capable of storming into the backfield to thwart a pass.

No guard in pro football history was more adept at carrying out these manifold duties than Iron Mike Michalske, whose most glittering days came in the nine years he spent in the green and gold uniform of the Green Bay Packers. Though not a big man—he seldom scaled more than 210—Michalske had the speed, agility and intelligence to win All League honors six times. It is also significant that he is one of the few linemen of his time and the only guard to have won Hall of Fame status.

Michalske broke into pro football during one of its early wars. After graduation from Penn State, where he was a Walter Camp All American in 1925, his senior year, he joined the New York Yankees, a team created by promoter C. C. Pyle. The team played in the American Football League, another Pyle creation. The Yankees featured Red Grange, and one season they played thirty-six games in an effort to display Grange's talents to the greatest number of people possible. "We played every other day for ten days during one period," Michalske recalls. "And we had only fifteen men—seven backs, seven linemen, and our coach, Ralph Scott, who played whenever he had to."

The American Football League, in spite of Red Grange's presence, was a financial failure and broke up. Pyle's Yankees were taken into the National Football League. There, with the Giants as their competition, they fared no better, and in 1929 they threw in the towel for good.

Pyle owed Michalske $400 when the Yankees flopped. In lieu of payment, he made Mike a free agent. Michalske promptly sold his services to the Packers. "I didn't want to stay in New York," he recalls. "There were too many bright lights there and I couldn't save any money."

Michalske quickly won a starting assignment at Green Bay. Two other players who were to become all-time greats for the Packers joined the club that year—swift and elusive Johnny (Blood) McNally, and 255-pound tackle Cal Hubbard. These two, along with Michalske, provided the driving force as Lambeau's charges stormed to three consecutive league championships, a feat that went unequaled until the Packer teams of 1965–1967 turned the trick.

Michalske was christened August when born in Cleveland, and was nicknamed Mike. But because of his indestructibility he came to be known as Iron Mike. Like all players of the day, Mike played both ways—offense and defense, almost sixty minutes of every game. "I just didn't get hurt," he recalls, "not until my last season of pro ball when I injured my back. The players used to kid me. They used to say I must have been getting paid by the minute."

Michalske is noted for more than just fortitude, however. He had played fullback in high school and he sold Lambeau on the idea of using former fullbacks at the guard position because they were fast and explosive. Russ Letlow and Pete Tinsley, notable Packer guards of the late 1930's and early 1940's, were cast in this mold.

Michalske is also rated as one of pro football's first red-doggers. "It was referred to as 'blitzing' in those days, too," he says. "But it was legal then to rough the passer, even after he had gotten rid of the ball. Sometimes we worked him over pretty good."

Michalske and Hubbard, before the ball was snapped, used to switch positions or move in or out of the line to confuse the offense. Today this is called "stunting." "We always figured," Michalske says, "the best time to stop them was before they got started."

Packer coach Curly Lambeau placed a high value on Michalske's services. How great a value is apparent from this incident. When Arnie Herber broke in as the Packers' quarterback in 1930, he was paid $75 a game. Once he got Michalske's paycheck by mistake. He stole a look at it. It read $175.

Michalske's last season with the Packers was 1937, but he had launched a career as a coach even before then. In 1936 he worked with Ernie Nevers at Lafayette, where he coached basketball. After his departure from the Packers, Michalske coached at St. Norbert College in West De Pere, Wisconsin, and was head coach at Iowa State from 1942 to 1947. He was later line coach at Baylor, Texas A. and M., and the University of Texas. In the pro ranks, he was an assistant coach with the Baltimore Colts for two seasons.

Michalske gave up coaching in 1957 because, as he put it, "I was always finding myself out of a job. I got tired of getting fired, so I quit." He now lives in De Pere, Wisconsin.

If Michalske played football today, he'd be a linebacker. He had the mobility this position demands plus the capacity to hit hard. There's no doubt about it—he'd be a great one.

Art Rooney

Art Rooney acquired the Pittsburgh Steeler franchise in the National Football League because of his warm friendship with Joe Carr, then president of the league, and, equally important, because he had the $2,500 purchase price. That was in 1933. Since then Rooney has become a millionaire, but thanks to his racing interests, not professional football. The Steelers are notable for their lack of success, financial and otherwise. They have never won an NFL championship. "That's right," says Rooney wistfully, "I've yet to break my maiden."

His years of gloom with the Steelers have scarcely bruised Rooney's good nature, however. A grin still comes easily to his map-of-Ireland face. It must be said that in pro football circles most of the people with Rooney's style and charm have gone the way of the dropkick.

The Steelers' continued failure on the field has become a football legend. One day in 1941 Rooney visited the team's training camp in Hershey, Pennsylvania, to see how things were progressing. He sat in the stands and watched a lackluster intrasquad game. The players happened to be wearing brand-new uniforms.

After the game a sportswriter asked Rooney what he thought of the team. Art's remark was to live until this day. "It's the same old team," he said. "The only thing different is the uniforms."

For years afterward, newspaper accounts of the Steeler performances often bore the headline: SAME OLD STEELERS. It used to bother Rooney; it still does, but not as much. He has turned the operation of the Steelers over to his son Dan, and although the club remains one of his principal interests, he has others, particularly a harness racing track near Philadelphia in which he is a major stockholder, his own stable of forty running horses, and Shamrock, a 400-acre Thoroughbred breeding farm in Sykesville, Maryland.

Art Rooney was born in 1900 in Coulterville, a small mining town near Pittsburgh, the oldest in a family of six boys and two girls. Almost all of his relatives worked in the coal mines or steel mills except his father, who, as Coulterville's only innkeeper, operated the Rooney Saloon, famed for its nickel beers and the fact that it barred its doors to women.

Art and his brother Dan were fascinated by sports and developed into first-rate athletes. Art was such a fine football player that Knute Rockne tried to persuade him to attend Notre Dame, and two major baseball teams, the Chicago Cubs and Boston Red Sox, sought his services. Dan, who also seemed headed for a career as a major-leaguer, chose the priesthood instead, entering a Franciscan seminary. Later he became a missionary in China. Art's decision was to stick to sports, but to organize and coach, not play.

His first club was a semipro venture called the J. P. Rooneys, named for another brother, Jim, who had been a star kicker at the University of Pittsburgh. Art went on to operate the Hope Harveys and the Majestic Radios. The last named later became the North Side Majestics and won the West Penn semipro championship in 1932. "We had some great teams in those days," Art once recalled. "They may have been called semipros but there were some teams comparable to teams in the National League when it was first formed."

When Rooney took over the Steeler franchise in 1933, he endowed the club with a strong local flavor. Coaches and players were recruited from Pitt, Washington and Jefferson (in Washington, Pennsylvania), Duquesne (in Pittsburgh), and Carnegie Tech (also in Pittsburgh). To Rooney, football first of all had to be fun. Winning was important, but secondary. Thus practice sessions were languorous, and strategy meetings were often excuses for story swapping and more serious forms of conviviality. The team was popular—once 25,000 customers turned out to watch the Steelers play the New York Giants—despite the fact it seldom won. The Steelers finished dead last in the Eastern Division during their first two seasons in the National League.

Although the Steelers have established a tradition of nonwinning for themselves, the club has experienced some moments of splendor. In Rooney's cluttered office in Pittsburgh, three pictures of players hang on the wall—photographs of Johnny Blood, Byron (Whizzer) White, and Bill Dudley. Each one in his way represents a period of Steeler grandeur, however brief.

The amiable Johnny Blood took over as the Steelers' coach in 1937, late in his career. On the first play of his first game as the team's field general, he took the kickoff at the goal line and sprinted 100 yards for a touchdown. "Follow the example of your boss, boys," he chortled afterward. Unfortunately, there was no one who could.

Blood was thoroughly footloose, and if he found something to capture his interest he was likely to go AWOL. "On every team," Rooney once said, "it's usual for the coach to worry about the players. But when Blood was around the players had to worry about the coach, whether he was going to show up."

One of the Blood-coached Pittsburgh teams actually beat the Chicago Bears. It happened in an exhibition game in 1939. Pittsburgh won, 10–9. No Steeler team had ever beaten the Bears before.

But Blood received a major assist from Danny Rooney, Art's seven-year-old son. The Bears and Steelers were quartered in the same hotel. A few hours before the game Rooney happened to be walking through the hotel corridor with young Dan, when he heard the voice of George Halas giving the Bears a pre-game lecture. He whispered to his son and sent him to the doorway. While Danny knocked, his father got out of sight.

"Who's there?" Halas asked, then added: "What do you want?"

"My name," came the little voice, "is Danny Rooney, and my old man sent me here to tell you to take it easy on his team tonight."

The Bear players roared. Even Halas had to laugh. He realized any further serious talk about the game would be futile, and dismissed his players. In later years Halas declared, "Rooney's kid was the main offense the Steelers showed that night."

Whizzer White signed with the Steelers in 1939, fresh from an All America career at the University of Colorado. Rooney paid White, the nation's top collegiate scorer, $15,000, the first five-figure salary ever given out in the NFL. He repaid Rooney's generosity by leading the NFL in ground gaining and scoring 24 points for a run-of-the-mill Steeler team. "I have seen many players with greater ability than White's," Rooney once said, "but no player ever put out as much effort. He gave 100 percent." White stayed with the Steelers only one season, then used the $15,000 to pay his way through law school. He went on to an outstanding law career, climaxed by his appointment to the U. S. Supreme Court in 1962.

The most notable player in Steeler history was Bill Dudley. Rooney has called him his "all-time favorite." Dudley, an All American from the University of Virginia, joined the Steelers in 1942. Though small in stature, he became the team's best runner, best punter and leading defensive player. He kicked off and booted field goals and points after touchdown. Rooney paid him the supreme compliment; he named a horse after him.

Rooney also named a horse after Johnny Blood. The steed finished far out of the money in his first four races. "I'd sell him, but my trainer told me not to," Rooney said. "I'm attached to the names, not the horses."

Money never meant a great deal to Rooney. He often looked upon it as something to be given away. Once the Steelers won a game in a torrential rainstorm with more people on the playing field than in the stands.

"A financial disaster," said Bert Bell, Rooney's partner at the time.

"So what?" said Art. "We won, didn't we?"

Rooney once made a fantastic killing at the racetrack. Some say it served as his stake for the founding of his football and racing enterprises. According to the legend, Rooney ran $300 into $21,000 one Saturday at the old Empire City racetrack in New York. The following Monday he went to Saratoga and bet heavily. One wager was for $10,000, and the horse won 8–1. It was that kind of a day. Rooney left the famous spa with $256,000 and his own personal Pinkerton. Later he gave $50,000 of his winnings to his missionary brother in China.

In 1946 Rooney hired Jock Sutherland of the University of Pittsburgh to coach the Steelers. Sutherland had formed the Pitt Panthers into one of the most formidable college teams of the day, and he came close to achieving preeminence for the Steelers. The team attained an 8-4 record in 1947 and ended the season in a tie with the Philadelphia Eagles for the division championship. The Eagles won the playoff game. That is the closest Pittsburgh ever came to winning a title.

Sutherland, who died suddenly in the spring of 1948, also brought box-office success to the Steelers. His popularity was such that sellout followed sellout. One year Rooney sold 23,000 season tickets, almost capacity. Rooney says that if it had not been for Sutherland he would not own the Steelers today. "He came along at the right time," Rooney once said. "He gave the fans the kind of teams they had been looking for, and he came at a time when the All America Conference had begun its costly war. I wouldn't have been able to continue in pro football if it wasn't for Doc Sutherland."

After Sutherland's death the Steelers resumed their losing ways. In 1957 coach Buddy Parker brought his favorite quarterback, Bobby Layne, to the Steelers. "I had heard about Rooney all my life and what a great guy he was," Layne recalled once. "Well, everything I heard was true. When I went into his office to sign my contract, I figured there might be some trouble. 'Are you satisfied with what you're getting in Detroit?' he asked me. I told him I was. 'Then it's O.K. with me, too,' he said. It was the easiest contract I ever negotiated."

Layne got the Steelers as high as third place in the standings in 1957 and 1958, but could do no better. He retired after the 1962 season.

During the 1960's the Steelers lost many more games than they won. Empty seats were no rarity, and many of the fans who did attend came to boo. Once a reporter asked Rooney if the booing bothered him. "Not at all," Rooney said. "Tell all the booers to come out and watch the Steelers. I'd like to see 40,000 booers at each of our home games."

George Trafton

"Trafton was the only guy I ever met who claimed he was the world's greatest at his position," says onetime Cardinal coach Jimmy Conzelman. "Of course, he actually was."

Trafton's position was center. A handsome, happy-go-lucky

giant, he was not only good, he was good and tough. Extreme violence often characterized professional football in Trafton's day, and Trafton was one of the most violent players of all. Red Grange, Trafton's teammate on the Chicago Bears, once said that Big George was "the toughest, meanest, most ornery critter alive."

Trafton was the original Bears' center, joining the team in 1920 when it was based in Decatur, Illinois, and known as the Staleys. For years he ranked as *the* center in professional football, winning All League honors eight times in the thirteen seasons that he played.

Trafton's football skills first attracted attention when he played for Oak Park High School in Chicago. He enlisted in the Army in 1918, and was captain of the Camp Grant team. Scores of colleges wanted Big George. He chose Notre Dame. His career there was an especially abbreviated one. Knute Rockne caught him playing semipro football on a Sunday and personally had him expelled.

As center for the Staleys, Trafton's roughhouse tactics caused him to be disliked in every city of the league except Green Bay and Rock Island. In these two he was hated.

One bright fall afternoon at Rock Island in 1920 the game was more sanguinary than usual. Every play ended in a ferocious pileup, with Trafton always in the center. Four Rock Island players were knocked cold in the space of twelve plays, and the blame for this was directed at Trafton. He could hear the snarling threats of the Rock Island fans who were aching to tear him limb from limb.

Big George had figured in advance the kind of day that it was going to be. He had learned that Rock Island had hired a player and assigned him to remove Trafton from the game by any means he felt necessary. But Trafton disposed of the hatchet man early in the game. When they led him from the field, the imprint of cleats could be discerned from his forehead to his chin.

"Rock Island had a halfback named Chicken," Trafton recalls, "and I tackled him on the right side. There was a fence close to the field and after I hit him, he spun up against the fence and broke a leg. After that, the fans really got on me."

When the final gun sounded, Trafton made a jackrabbit sprint for the nearest exit. As he passed the Bears' bench, trainer Andy Lotshaw tossed him a sweat shirt. "Quick, put it on!" he shouted. "Cover up your uniform number." A rock whistled by Trafton's head and he armed himself with a couple of empty milk bottles from the water bucket.

A teammate had a cab waiting. George leaped in. Rocks came crashing through the windows. George leaped out and bolted down the highway, a pack of angry rock-throwing Rock Islanders after him. He had not gone far when a shiny blue Mercer pulled up alongside.

"Where are you going, kid?" the driver asked.

"Out of town," Trafton shouted between puffs, "and in a helluva hurry."

"Hop in," the man said, and he whisked Big George to safety.

Bear owner George Halas took note of all this. A year later when the Bears played in Rock Island again, the club's share of the gate receipts amounted to about $7,000. Halas handed the money to Trafton.

"I knew," Halas explained, "that if trouble came, Trafton would be running for his life. I'd only be running for the $7,000."

Another afternoon at Rock Island, Trafton hooked up in a rowdy feud with Lou Kolls, center for the Independents, a man whose size and temperament were similar to Trafton's. Throughout the afternoon they fiercely punished one another. The officials ignored their sundry infractions. Afterward, referee Bobie Cahn explained, "If we tried to discipline them, we'd be calling penalties all day long. We figured we might as well let them kill each other."

Trafton, however, did not just roughneck his way to eminence. He was a skilled defensive player, and he had the moves and reactions of a halfback to go with his size and strength. He was also very slick.

One day against the Packers, Vern Lewellen, Green Bay's splendid punter, dropped back to kick from his own goal line. Trafton ripped through the Packer defenses to block the kick for a Bear touchdown.

"Who blocked that?" a disgusted Lewellen asked after the play.

"Hewitt did," Trafton replied, and he pointed to the Bears' rookie end.

Later in the game the same situation developed again. This time, however, the Packers overshifted to stop the innocent Hewitt.

The ball was snapped and Trafton roared through. Again he blocked the kick; again he scored. The final read: Bears 14, Green Bay 10.

Trafton, like all players of the time, played a full sixty minutes of every game. "We had only fifteen players on the squad," he recalls. "Halas used to come into the dressing room between halves and shout out, 'Now, boys, this half Trafton will replace Trafton; Hunk Anderson will take over for Hunk Anderson, and Healy, you'll relieve Healy.' "

Although Trafton was a demon on defense, he was not quite such a stalwart when the Bears had the ball. In his early days with the team, he had a habit of standing around with his hands on his hips after he had snapped the ball back. Herb Stein, Trafton's opposite number with the Pottsville Maroons, cured Big George of this habit.

He spotted the unwary Trafton while a play was in progress, got a running start, and butted Big George squarely in the belly with his head. The blow jolted Trafton backward about five yards and knocked him cold. After that, Trafton got so he would flop down on his belly once he had passed the ball back.

While he was with the Bears, Trafton also pursued a career as a prizefighter. It was both brief and undistinguished. In his first bout Big George was matched against Arthur "the Great" Shires, a first baseman with the Chicago White Sox who had a reputation as a brawler. Incredibly, 5,000 people paid $18,000 to see the fray. Chicago's old White City Stadium was the scene.

Trafton floored Shires in the first round, and staggered him in the second. But after that, both men stopped fighting and concentrated on staying alive. Trafton apologized to his teammates. "I couldn't knock him out," he said. "My arms each felt like they weighed a hundred pounds."

Big George got the decision, however, and his ring career was off and winging.

After he had had a few bouts, someone talked Trafton into fighting Primo Carnera, who was then being groomed for a heavyweight title match. It took Carnera only 54 seconds to convince Big George that he was never going to be a Jack Dempsey.

Trafton had more success as a manager of boxers. When his pro football days were over, he launched a prosperous career handling fighters.

In 1930, Trafton was not offered a contract by Halas. Undismayed, Big George simply reported to the Bears' new coach, Ralph Jones. Jones told him to be in uniform at 9 o'clock the next morning. Trafton, never noted for his punctuality, showed up at 9:30. Jones ordered him off the field. But the next day Trafton was back at 8:45. Promptness became one of his hallmarks, and when the season opened, Trafton was back in his familiar spot in the middle of the line. He stayed on with the Bears through the 1932 season, helping the club to win the league championship that year.

One day in 1944, Trafton met Curly Lambeau, coach of the Packers. "What's wrong with your club?" Trafton asked. "They don't scrap back like the old Green Bay teams. Why I could chase half those mugs right out of the park."

Lambeau smiled. "O.K.," he said. "You're hired. Report to Green Bay on August 20."

As an assistant to Lambeau, Trafton helped steer the Packers to a world championship that year. The next season he went to Cleveland as an assistant coach and the Rams promptly won the title.

Although a splendid coach, it is for his playing skills that Trafton will be remembered. Mel Hein of the Giants, Bulldog Turner of the Bears, and Trafton—these three are invariably cited as pro football's greatest centers. And many experts name Trafton the best of the trio.

1965

Guy Chamberlin

One word best describes the rather brief but brilliant playing and coaching career of Guy Chamberlin. "He was," said Steve Owen, coach of the New York Giants, "the 'winningest.' "

Chamberlin, appropriately nicknamed "the Champ," never played on a losing team in his two years of varsity football at the University of Nebraska. And five of the six years he was active in NFL ball, his club won the league championship.

Chamberlin was born in 1894 on a Gage County, Nebraska, farm, and attended high school in Blue Springs. The school wasn't large enough to support a football team. Guy gained his first experience in the sport by joining a group of boys from Blue Springs and Wymore who traveled to Beatrice to scrimmage against the powerful high school team there. For two years, playing without a coach, this group of youngsters acted as practice opposition—"cannon fodder," one observer called them—for the skilled and experienced Beatrice crew.

Chamberlin attended Nebraska Wesleyan University after graduating from high school. He chose a relatively small college because he felt he would have a better chance of making the football team. In 1912, his freshman year, he won All State honors and came to the attention of Jumbo Steihm, head coach of the University of Nebraska, who convinced Guy to transfer to the state university campus. At Nebraska, Guy starred as both a defensive end and an offensive halfback, scoring nine touchdowns in 1914, and fifteen in 1915, to lead the Cornhuskers to two undefeated seasons. Chamberlin won All America honors both years and a niche in the college football Hall of Fame.

In his book *Spotlighting the Husker Greats,* Walt Dobbins described Chamberlin in these terms: "Hula-hipping his way through opposing lines, slashing around the ends—knees high and possessing a potent left arm, Chamberlin was the most feared, the most talked about runner in the Midlands."

Guy served in the Army in World War I, and was discharged in 1919. That year Jim Thorpe asked Chamberlin to join his Canton Bulldogs. Thorpe, who won enduring fame with the Carlisle Indians beginning in 1908, had been an idol of Chamberlin's, and he was quick to accept the big Indian's offer. The Bulldogs went undefeated during Chamberlin's rookie season and were rated the No. 1 pro team in the country. This was a year before the founding of the National League.

George Halas is said to have "discovered" Chamberlin on a scouting trip through the Midwest in 1920. "He was a tall boy and very fast," Halas once recalled. "There was no bidding for his services, however. No one had any money to give away in those days."

Chamberlin played two seasons for Halas' Decatur Staleys, the team that was later to become the Chicago Bears. Like most of the other players, Chamberlin worked part-time in the Staley starch factory. During the two years that Guy was with the Staleys, they completely dominated pro football, attaining a 21-2-2 record.

One of the losses came on a fluke. The Staleys were playing the Chicago Cardinals at the old Cubs Park in Chicago. During the game the wooden bleachers on one side of the field collapsed and the spectators moved down to the sidelines. Late in the game the Cardinals completed a screen pass. The receiver was about to be tackled when he ducked behind a cluster of fans who had spilled out onto the playing field. He kept behind the protecting screen of spectators all the way down the sideline for the winning touchdown.

The only game that Halas' team lost in 1921 was to the Buffalo All Stars. In a rematch later in the season the Staleys won, 10–7, and thereby claimed the league championship. Chamberlin's heroics were vital to the Staleys' victory. He intercepted a Buffalo pass early in the game and scampered 70 yards for his team's only touchdown.

The next year Chamberlin returned to Canton, this time as a player-coach. The Bulldogs did not lose a single game in his two-year tenure although they tied two in 1922, one in 1923. Naturally, they were league champions both years.

In 1924 the Canton team was moved almost *en masse* to Cleveland. There Chamberlin promptly produced another title winner. It was a habit by now.

"Before Guy came to Cleveland, we just met on Sunday afternoons, ate lunch and then played the game," one of his players now recalls. "But he made us work; he had us start practicing every day."

Chamberlin's Cleveland team did lose a game—but only one.

Chamberlin was disappointed by the failure of Cleveland fans to support his club, and he transferred the franchise to Frankford, a Philadelphia suburb, and rechristened the team the Yellowjackets. In 1925 the Yellowjackets finished sixth in a twenty-team league, the first time a Chamberlin-coached team had ever failed to win the NFL title. The next year, however, Chamberlin returned to form. The Yellowjackets finished with a 14-1-1 record and a clear claim to the NFL crown.

The championship that year was decided late in the season when the Yellowjackets met the Chicago Bears, who were riding a ten-game winning streak. According to Howard Roberts, the Bears' historian, the Chicago team might have won if Guy had been content merely to coach. But he played end and his brilliance spearheaded the Yellowjackets' win. He broke through to block Paddy Driscoll's try for an extra point following a Chicago touchdown, and late in the game he blocked Driscoll's attempt at a field goal. Frankford scored in the dying minutes of the contest, then added the extra point, to eke out a 7–6 win.

Chamberlin retired after the 1926 season. No one has ever matched his gaudy record. In five years of coaching, he produced four league titles. In his three years as a player (two of them before the NFL was established), his teams never failed to win the national championship. During the Hall of Fame ceremonies honoring Chamberlin, Earl (Red) Blaik, Army's famed coach, remarked that "Chamberlin never learned how to lose."

Guy died at his home in Lincoln, Nebraska, in 1967. After

his death, the state of Nebraska established the Guy Chamberlin Athletic Scholarship, awarded each year to the outstanding high school football player in the state. Nebraska will not soon forget Guy Chamberlin. Neither will pro football.

John (Paddy) Driscoll

In the 1920's, field goals and extra points were scored chiefly by means of the dropkick, a fairly simple maneuver but one that required split-second timing. The kicker would drop the ball on its nose in front of him, and boot it just as it rebounded from the ground. Charley Brickley, Frank Nesser, Jim Thorpe and Paddy Driscoll were artists when it came to drop-kicking, but Driscoll is rated by many as the greatest of them all. His skilled right foot rendered him the greatest name in Chicago football until a fellow named Red Grange exploded upon the scene in 1925.

Driscoll also was uncannily accurate as a punter. The most famous story concerning him has to do with this particular skill. In 1925 George Halas, owner of the Chicago Bears, plucked Red Grange from the campus of the University of Illinois, and set his debut as a professional for Thanksgiving Day that year with Driscoll's team, the Chicago Cards, as opponents. A capacity crowd of 36,000 jammed Wrigley Field anticipating that Grange would run wild. But the redhead never shook loose once. The reason was Driscoll. He punted the ball twenty-three times, but always sought to angle the kick away from Grange. Red got to run back only three punts all day.

The contest ended in a scoreless tie. As the teams were leaving the field, several thousand fans booed lustily. Paddy stopped for a moment to speak to his wife.

"It's a shame to hear the fans boo Grange," he said. "It wasn't his fault."

"Don't feel sorry for him," she said. "They're booing *you!*"

The next year Grange again figured prominently in Driscoll's career. Red and his manager, C. C. Pyle, started a league of their own, the American League, and they put a team in Chicago called the Bulls. The new club immediately tried to lure Driscoll away from the Cardinals. Chris O'Brien, the Cards' owner, knew he could not match the Bulls' salary offer because of the limited size of the Cardinals' home grounds. George Halas had no wish to see the Bulls land Driscoll either, so he went to O'Brien and offered him $3,500 in cash for Paddy. O'Brien took it.

Driscoll was an immediate hit with the Bears. In his first game he booted a field goal and threw a touchdown pass as Chicago tripped the Detroit Panthers, 10–7. In the next game he scored all the points in the Bears' 7–0 win over the Giants. And in his debut against his old teammates, Paddy kicked three field goals and an extra point in the Bears' 16–0 victory.

Driscoll's reputation began building during his high school days in Evanston, Illinois. In 1914 he entered Northwestern and was named captain of the team in 1916. He scored nine of Northwestern's ten points in the team's conquest of the University of Chicago, the Purples' first win over Chicago in fifteen years. The field goal he booted traveled 43 yards. Northwestern lost only one game that year. Paddy was a top-notch baseball player, too, and had a brief stay with the Chicago Cubs.

During World War I, Paddy was stationed at the Great Lakes Naval Station and was a standout on their fabled football team. He paced the Bluejackets in their win over the Mare Island Marines in the 1919 Rose Bowl game, booting a 30-yard field goal and passing to George Halas for a touchdown. The final score was 17–9.

After he was discharged from the service, Paddy returned to Northwestern as an assistant coach. While he was there a Hammond, Indiana, sports promoter approached Leo Fischer, a sportswriter for the Chicago *American,* and asked him if he thought Driscoll would be interested in playing baseball for Hammond.

"Baseball, hell!" Fischer said. "Get him to play football." The promoter went to Driscoll and offered him $50 a game.

Driscoll demanded $75 but the owner refused to go that high. "It's $50 or nothing," he said. Driscoll reluctantly agreed.

In his debut with Hammond, Driscoll ran 63 yards for a touchdown and kicked a field goal. "Before I took my shower I demanded $75 for my next game," Driscoll recalls. "And I got it!"

In 1920, when Chris O'Brien entered his Chicago Cardinals in the newly founded National Football League, he hired Driscoll as the club's gate attraction, and he paid Paddy a fancy fee— $300 a game.

The Cards were in direct competition with the Chicago Tigers (named after their striped jerseys). O'Brien and the Tiger owner, agreeing that their box-office rivalry was suicidal, arranged a game in which each owner staked his team. The loser would fold. One touchdown was scored that day and Driscoll was the man who scored it. The Cards won, 6–3, and the Tigers were never heard from again.

The Cardinals' mascot in those days was a small and lively pig. He was kept on a leash near the Cards' bench and was paraded up and down the sidelines whenever the team scored, much to the delight of the fans, who referred to the porker as "Paddy's pig."

After George Halas switched his franchise from Decatur, Illinois, to Chicago in 1921, a spirited rivalry sprang up between the Bears and the Cardinals. Driscoll also seemed to be at his best when facing Halas' team, surely a factor in the Bears' bid for Driscoll after the 1925 season. Paddy flattened the Bears single-handedly in 1922. He drop-kicked two field goals in the first meeting of the two teams that year, and three more in their second contest. The Cards won by scores of 6–0 and 9–0.

One of Driscoll's most celebrated days in pro football was October 11, 1925. He kicked four field goals as the Cards buried the Columbus Tigers. His kicks traveled 23, 18, 50 and 35 yards. What was perhaps Driscoll's longest recorded field goal kick came when he was a member of the Hammond team. He booted the ball 55 yards. Legend has it that he was "out on his feet" at the time he kicked as a result of a pileup on the previous play.

Driscoll's stay with the Bears was to prove one of the most enduring in professional football. He retired as a player after the 1929 season, but continued to serve the club as an assistant coach. In 1956 and 1957 he was the Bears' head coach, and he steered the team to the Western Conference championship in 1956. Later he was director of research and planning for the Bear organization.

Danny Fortmann

Linemen are often the forgotten men of pro football, but Danny Fortmann, a guard with the Chicago Bears during their days of glory in the 1930's and 1940's, is a notable exception.

Fortmann became a Bear almost by chance. In February 1936, the National Football League adopted the draft, the system whereby pro teams select college players from a pool, with the team that finishes last in the team standings choosing first; next to last, second, etc. Scouting systems of the day were not nearly as efficient or thorough as they are today, and as a result teams came to the draft meeting prepared to pick only a few players. In the final round, when it came to George Halas' turn to select, he stood and stared blankly at the huge blackboard. Not a name on it was known to him.

Suddenly he flashed an impish smile. "Daniel Fortmann," he declared, "of Colgate. Fortmann. I like that name. I'll take him."

When Halas got around to investigating Fortmann's background, he had cause to regret his inspiration. Reports were that Danny was too young and too small for pro football. But despite these seeming shortcomings, young Fortmann fought his way into the Chicago starting lineup.

Though he weighed scarcely 200 pounds, Fortmann held his own in the company of such rugged giants as Joe Stydahar, Lee Artoe, George Musso and Clyde "Bulldog" Turner. For six consecutive seasons, Fortmann was an All League selection, and anytime George Halas picked an all-time all-professional team Fortmann's name was on it.

On offense, Fortmann called signals for the linemen and was a battering-ram blocker. On defense, he was a genius at diagnosing enemy plays and a deadly tackler.

Only nineteen when he reported, Fortmann was the youngest man on the Bears' roster; indeed, the youngest starting player in the league. The same draft that brought in Fortmann also landed Joe Stydahar, the Bears' mighty right tackle for many years. Fortmann and Stydahar played cleat to cleat in the East-West game in San Francisco on New Years' Day in 1936, in the

All Star game in Chicago that fall, and through better than half-a-dozen pro seasons. "It helped me tremendously to play next to the same player for so many years," Fortmann once said. "A partnership built up. We got to know exactly what to expect from one another."

Fortmann is high in his praise of George Halas, and calls him firm but fair, tough-minded, and a master of psychology. He says that Halas reached his peak as a psychologist in preparing the Bears for the 1940 championship game, the one in which they beat the Redskins, 73–0.

"For three weeks he kept reminding us that the Redskins had beaten us earlier in the year. We had lost, 7–3," Fortmann recalls. "When the Bears took the field for the playoff game, they were keyed the highest emotionally I ever saw them." The half-time score was 28–0, and although Halas used every player on the bench, the Bears kept scoring touchdowns.

One of Fortmann's prized mementos is the silver dollar used in the coin-flipping ceremony that preceded the game. The Bears won the toss and elected to receive. Then the lightning struck—eleven touchdowns and seven points after conversions.

The Monsters of the Midway, as the Halas-coached team was called, did not rely on brute force exclusively. They had the slick ball handling of Sid Luckman. They were also very tricky, and mastered the method of stretching out playing time. The rules of the day permitted an injured player to be taken from the game with no time-out being charged. Chicago made the most of this. During the 1938 season, the Bears stretched the final two minutes of three games—a total of six minutes of playing time—into almost a full hour. A total of 27 Bear "injuries" were recorded in that period.

Once Fortmann was the unfortunate victim of this practice. Halas spotted both Danny and tackle Del Bjork lying prone after a play. He rushed in a substitute for Bjork, who was feigning injury. But Fortmann, who was actually hurt, had to stay in the game. Not long after, Halas proposed a rule change that served to outlaw clock-beating.

Fortmann was a brilliant student at Colgate with ambitions to become a doctor. After graduation, he applied to the University of Chicago Medical School. The way Fortmann tells it, there was one remaining vacancy on the freshman class and fifty applications. Dean B. C. H. Harvey eliminated all the applicants but two, Fortmann and one other. Then he asked his secretary, "Which one should I select? Both are Phi Beta Kappas. One is a football player, the other is a violin player." The secretary happened to be a football fan.

Fortmann used pro football to pay for his medical education. After being drafted by the Bears, Fortmann sat down with Halas and Dean Harvey and they worked out a schedule that enabled him to play football and continue his studies. The success of the plan is apparent. Today Danny is known as Dr. Daniel J. Fortmann, and he is Chief of Staff at St. Joseph's Hospital in Burbank, California.

Dr. Fortmann is a dedicated fan of pro football. Once he was asked to name the biggest changes he has seen in the game since his retirement as an active player. He named several—more passing, more sophisticated offense, and more money for the players. As a rookie, young Danny Fortmann earned $1,700 for the year. His last season with Chicago he reached his zenith—$6,000.

Otto Graham

"The test of a quarterback is where his team finishes. So Otto, by that standard, was the best of them all." This tribute to Otto Graham was delivered by his coach, Paul Brown.

Indeed, by this yardstick, Otto was the greatest—by far. He played ten seasons as a pro, four in the All America Conference, and six in the National Football League. Each of the ten years his team participated in the title game; seven times they won the league championship.

Paul Brown's esteem for Otto Graham predated Otto's career as a pro quarterback. In 1944, when Brown began putting together the Cleveland team, Graham was the first player he signed. Otto was in the service at the time, and his football talents were being utilized by North Carolina Pre-Flight. He had played as a tailback, although he had been an outstanding passer. Brown wasn't worried because Graham had almost no T experience. Later he said, "He had the basic requirements of a T quarterback—poise, slick ball handling and, above that, distinct qualities of leadership. We were never afraid that he wouldn't be able to adapt himself to the T."

Brown's confidence was well placed. In his first season with the Browns, Otto completed 95 out of 174 passes, 17 of them for touchdowns. Only five of his tosses were intercepted. The Browns won 13 of 15 games, including the championship. But statistics don't tell the story. Otto was the heart of the Cleveland football machine. "He's the kind of guy you want to do your best for," said Mike Scarry, the Browns' center. "We don't always give him all the protection he needs but he never complains. He'll get us in the huddle and say, 'I could use a little more time back here, fellas. They're making me rush the passes.' That's all. No griping. How could you help liking a guy like that?"

As a member of the All America Conference, Cleveland was seldom less than awesome. Over the four years that the league operated, the Browns won 52 games, lost four and tied two. They won the league championship every year. Otto earned a helmetful of records. He gained the most yards passing in one season—2,785 in 1949. He had the fewest passes intercepted in one season—five in 1946. He had the best completion percentage in one season—a gaudy .606 in 1947. Graham and the Browns were good all right, too good. People stopped coming to see them play. Why bother? The outcome was known in advance.

In 1949, the AAC came to the end of the road and the Browns were taken into the NFL. ("We simply absorbed the National League," is the way that Otto once put it.) Supporters of the older league had long held that the AAC was of strictly minor status, and the Browns would be lucky to win a single game in NFL competition.

The Browns' first game saw them matched against the fearsome Philadelphia Eagles, the league champions in 1949. The game was played on a warm Saturday night in September in Philadelphia's Municipal Stadium before 71,000 fans. It is doubtful if any one of them was prepared for what happened.

The Eagles jumped off to a 3–0 lead. Then the Browns took over the ball. On the first down, Graham called a short pass, a hook to left end Mac Speedie. As Graham darted back into the protective pocket and got set to throw, he spotted Dante Lavelli speeding downfield. He had gotten behind the Eagle safetyman. Otto fired; he was right on target. Lavelli raced into the end zone.

The long bombs were bad enough, but what really unhinged the Eagles were the short passes. Speedie and Lavelli would race downfield angling toward the sideline. Otto would hit them just before they went out of bounds. These patterns were almost unstoppable. The final score saw the Browns on top, 35–10. Graham completed 21 of 38 passes for 346 yards and three touchdowns.

Cleveland went on to win the championship of the American Conference of the NFL, although it required beating the New York Giants in a playoff game. Then the Browns met the Los Angeles Rams, winners of the National Conference, and turned them back, 30–28, thus adding the National League title to their string of All America championships. There could not be the slightest doubt about it now; they belonged!

Otto Everett Graham, Jr., was born December 6, 1921, at Waukegan, Illinois, the son of a music instructor at Waukegan High School. Otto's father had been a semipro baseball pitcher and he encouraged his son's athletic pursuits. Otto's mother taught music in a rural school district, played the organ at church, and gave piano lessons. Naturally, all the Graham boys— there were four of them—were taught to play at least one instrument. Eugene's specialties were the oboe and English horn. Victor played the oboe; Richard the French horn. Otto learned to play the cornet and violin, but he was most accomplished on the French horn. He majored in music at college despite his involvement with athletics, and he managed to squeeze in a year with the French horn in the Northwestern orchestra.

Sportswriters often attributed Otto's great sense of timing to his musical background. Otto did nothing to discourage this. "Music means rhythm," he once said, "and rhythm means timing. I always know when my left foot is supposed to follow my right. Music has taught me everything."

Otto won letters in track, basketball and football in high school, but football was secondary in importance. Waukegan, like many cities in the Midwest, went wild over basketball each winter. Members of the high school basketball team were authentic local heroes, while football players received little more than amiable respect. And Graham was an outstanding basketball player. Schoolboy sports expert Pat Harmon, then writing for the Champaign *News Gazette,* called Otto "the greatest high school player since Lou Boudreau roamed the hardwood for Thornton Township." Lightning-fast and a deadly shooter, Graham led the Waukegan team to a regional championship in the state tournament in his junior year. When scholarship offers began to come Graham's way, they were for basketball, not football.

Later, Cleveland end Dante Lavelli observed that Otto's varied sports career gave him a distinctive quality that made him a great quarterback. "Otto has amazing coordination between hand and eye," Lavelli said. "It's the kind of coordination that comes from competing in many sports. I think it comes especially from basketball. Otto could react in a split second when he saw his receiver head for an open spot, and at the same moment he was anticipating not only the receiver, but what the defensive man would do."

A number of colleges wanted Otto. "Just plain tuition scholarships," he recalls. "No Cadillacs." He chose Northwestern on the advice of Ade Schumacher, a close friend. Otto, judged to be a basketball specialist, wasn't even invited to try out for football in his freshman year. He played intramural football, however, and that is how he caught the eye of the coaching staff. Unfortunately, his career was sidetracked by a knee injury. He tore a cartilage, and head coach Pappy Waldorf recommended that he take a year's hiatus to have an operation. By withdrawing from school for a year, he would be able to preserve a year of football eligibility. Otto followed the coach's advice.

Otto's football career was launched in the fall of 1941. He understudied Bill De Correvont and alternated with him at halfback. He showed brief glimpses of the daring and imagination that were to characterize his play in later years. In the 1941 game at Minnesota, which the Wildcats lost, 8–7, Northwestern had possession deep in Minnesota territory. The Gophers were looking for an off-tackle power play, a Northwestern favorite. Otto noticed that a Minnesota defensive halfback had moved in very close. He told end Bob Motl to fake a block, and then whip around the halfback. Otto, who played left halfback, took the ball from center and started straight toward the off-tackle slot. Then he suddenly straightened up and rifled a pass to Motl, who grabbed it and stepped into the end zone. Otto's future role as a master strategist was signaled that day.

In three seasons at Northwestern, Otto completed 157 passes in 321 attempts for 2,162 yards, a Western Conference record. In 1943, his senior year, Otto was awarded the Chicago *Tribune* Trophy as the most valuable player in the conference. He graduated the following February and became a Naval Aviation Cadet. Eventually he was sent to Chapel Hill, North Carolina. There he played fullback and later quarterback on the powerful team of Pre-Flighters that upset mighty Navy in 1944. After Chapel Hill, Graham was assigned to Glenview, Illinois, Naval Air Station. It was while at Glenview that Paul Brown visited him and signed him. Otto's final tour of duty was at Pensacola Naval Station. He was there when the war ended.

One of Otto's trademarks as a professional was the long pass. He threw it with uncanny accuracy. It arched high and settled softly in the hands of his receivers. He could achieve incredible distance with it, putting the ball out where either his own men could run under it or defenders couldn't. His career record shows an extremely low percentage of interceptions. Of course, he could also throw the bullet. Graham and Mac Speedie made the quick sideline pass a glorious art.

One aspect of Graham's career is the subject of controversy—play calling. Paul Brown often called plays for the team. Coaches at various vantage points connected by phone to the bench, and players coming out of the game, constantly fed information to Brown. He would digest their thinking and send in a play. He developed a messenger service to do this, with two players alternating in carrying his directives to the team.

Otto once told Al Silverman of *Sport* magazine that when Cleveland was in the All America Conference, Brown didn't call more than six or seven plays a game. Once the team entered National League competition, the coach increased the number of calls. In Otto's final years with the team, Brown was making as many as 95 percent of the calls.

Otto didn't think kindly of this strategy, believing that the quarterback could run the team with better results than the coach on the sidelines. But never once did Otto question

Brown's right to run the team in the manner he thought best. "He's the coach; he's the boss," said Otto philosophically.

There were occasions, however, when Otto would override the coach's strategy. In a close game against the Eagles, the Browns were in desperate need of a touchdown. Cleveland had the ball on the Philadelphia three-yard line. The team huddled, and in came the messenger with instructions from Brown calling for a "dive" play. Otto was to hand off to the left halfback who was to blast his way over left tackle. But the whole Eagle team converged on him and he barely made the line of scrimmage. Otto noticed that if he had kept the ball he could have waltzed around the right side into the end zone.

The team went into the huddle, and the second messenger left the bench. But Otto waved him back. He called the play that had just been stopped, but this time he faked to the half-back. There was another pileup, but Otto scampered around right end untouched.

"You'd better be right when you overrule your own boss," Otto said afterward. "If you're wrong too often, you could be out on the street looking for a job."

Graham, though seemingly relaxed and carefree most of the time, retired at the end of the 1954 season because the pressure of the pro sport was becoming more than he wanted to bear. Pre-game tension weighed heavily upon him. When the 1955 pre-season schedule got under way, Otto was in the insurance business in Cleveland. The team looked horrible without him, and Brown sent an SOS to Graham, asking him to put aside his retirement plans. Graham obliged. He rejoined the team the week of the final pre-season game.

Graham was rusty, and the team sputtered at the start. Then one win began to follow another. After a loss in the season's opener, the Browns ran up a streak of six straight victories before dropping a decision to the Eagles. They did not lose again, however, rolling to their sixth straight Eastern Conference title. In the 1955 NFL championship game, Graham threw a pair of touchdown passes and scored two touchdowns himself to lead the Browns to a victory over the Los Angeles Rams, 38–14, and their second straight pro title.

Again Graham announced his retirement. A reporter asked

Brown if he would try to get Otto to reconsider. "No," said the coach. "I imposed upon him once; that's enough."

Graham's greatness is not based so much on his individual attainments. After all, he played only six seasons in the NFL. Sammy Baugh's record figures were accumulated over sixteen seasons. Bobby Layne was a fifteen-year man; Norm Van Brocklin played twelve. One of Graham's outstanding achievements is his percentage of completions, a stunning 55.7, less than a percentage point behind Sammy Baugh, the all-time leader in that category.

Graham's name is preeminent in the individual records for NFL championship play. He completed the most passes (86), for the most yards (1,161), and for the most touchdowns (10). In the Cleveland-Los Angeles championship game of 1950, Graham completed 22 of 32 passes, for a startling 68.8 percentage. No one in any championship game has ever come close to that. Otto also holds an array of other title game records including the most touchdowns scored in one game (3) and total number of touchdowns (5).

But Graham's most convincing claim for football immortality lies in the record of the teams he quarterbacked. No team has ever approached the ten-year reign of the Cleveland Browns. The chances are good that no team ever will.

Otto Graham Career Passing Record

ALL AMERICA CONFERENCE						
Year	Attempts	Completions	Pct.	Yards	Touchdowns	Interceptions
1946	174	95	54.6	1,834	17	5
1947	269	163	60.6	2,753	25	11
1948	333	173	52.0	2,713	25	15
1949	285	161	56.5	2,785	19	10
Total	1,061	592	55.2	10,085	86	41

NATIONAL FOOTBALL LEAGUE						
Year	Attempts	Completions	Pct.	Yards	Touchdowns	Interceptions
1950	253	137	54.2	1,943	14	20
1951	265	147	55.5	2,205	17	16
1952	364	181	49.7	2,816	20	24
1953	258	167	64.7	2,722	11	9
1954	240	142	59.2	2,092	11	17
1955	185	98	52.9	1,721	15	8
Total	1,565	872	55.7	13,499	88	94

Sid Luckman

In any discussion of the greatest quarterbacks of all time, three names come to the fore immediately. One is Sammy Baugh of the Redskins, the second is Otto Graham of the Browns, and the third is Sid Luckman.

Luckman, who played with the Bears in their most glittering days of the late 1930's and 1940's, and is now a Chicago coach, was the first, and many say the most brilliant, of the T-formation quarterbacks. Sportswriters of the day referred to him as "Mr. Quarterback," and George Halas, the Bears' owner-coach, once stated that Luckman never called a wrong play in his twelve-year career.

Luckman's name will be forever linked with what has been rated as the most perfect game of football ever played by one team, the Chicago Bears' performance in their fabled 73–0 win over the Redskins in the NFL championship game of 1940. Luckman quarterbacked the Bears that day, and although he only played the first half, it was he who steered the Bear machine and set it upon its devastating course.

On the first play from scrimmage, Luckman called a feeler play to test the Redskin defenses. As the Bears broke from the huddle, Ken Kavanaugh spread out 15 yards from his left-end position. Washington's right halfback followed him. Ray Nolting, the left halfback, went in motion to the right, Washington's linebacker trailing. Luckman had found out what he needed to know, that the Redskins had not changed their defenses from what they had been earlier in the season. On the play, Sid handed to George McAfee who got eight yards off right tackle.

On the next play, Chicago lightning struck. McAfee, the right halfback, went in motion to his left, and Luckman, making a reverse pivot, handed off to Bill Osmanski on a run to the spread side. McAfee was supposed to take out the Redskins' right end but he missed his block. No matter. Osmanski altered his course and swept wide past the outstretched arms of the enemy and streaked into the clear. At the Redskin 35-yard line a pair of defenders closed in, but George Wilson, racing from the other side of the field, barreled into them both, and Osmanski romped into the end zone.

After the kickoff, the Redskins got within striking distance of the Bears' goal, but a dropped pass and a missed field goal attempt short-circuited their scoring threat.

Now Luckman took over again. He brought the Bears to within a football of the Washington goal line in seventeen plays, and then sneaked over for the touchdown. The next time the Bears got the ball, Luckman called almost the identical play that had sprung loose Osmanski, but this time Joe Maniaci did the running, and instead of getting a hand-off he took a shovel pass. But the results were the same—a touchdown.

Luckman passed to Ken Kavanaugh for another score before the end of the half to make it 28–0. The die was cast. Arthur Daley, who covered the game for the New York *Times,* said of Luckman, "No field general ever called plays more artistically or engineered a touchdown parade in more letter-perfect fashion."

The Bears' exercise in perfection had great significance. True, it won them the NFL title, but more important, it triggered a stampede to T-formation football. The single wing, the double wing, and all their variations soon went the way of the cloche helmet.

It's ironic that Sid Luckman, the man who played such a decisive role in this football revolution, never saw the T in college; never, in fact, until two weeks before he came under Halas' wing.

Sid Luckman was born in the crowded Williamsburg section of Brooklyn on November 21, 1916. As a youngster he played touch football on the street in front of his house. "I was the big man on the block," he once said. "I owned the football."

Sid played his scholastic football at Erasmus Hall High School in Brooklyn. Dave Eisenberg, a sportswriter who covered many of Luckman's high school games, remembers him as a sensational runner and a deadly safety on defense, and called him the "greatest player ever in Brooklyn scholastic history."

Young Luckman was inundated with offers from colleges, but one college that *didn't* enter the bidding was Columbia, and that's where Sid wanted to go. He received no scholarship, only the promise that the university would try to help him work his way through. He washed dishes, ran messages and served as a baby-sitter—at 50 cents and hour—to support himself.

Under Coach Lou Little, Luckman developed into an outstanding triple-threat tailback. Running was his strong suit, but he was a fine passer and a better-than-average punter and placekicker.

George Halas followed Luckman's college career closely. At the football draft in December 1938, Pittsburgh had first choice, and named Luckman. But under the terms of an agreement that had been worked out in advance, the Steelers handed over the handsome dark-haired Brooklynite to the Bears in exchange for another player. Such folderol is not permitted today, but in 1938 it was accepted practice.

In August 1939, two weeks before he became a Bear officially, Luckman was in Chicago for the College All Star game. Luke Johnsos, an assistant to Halas, visited Sid in his hotel room and brought him one of the Bears' thick playbooks. This was Luckman's introduction to the T formation, and the originality of the system astonished and alarmed him. His fears were confirmed the first time he tried the T. He fumbled in his attempts to hand off or feint, and he fell over his feet when trying to pivot. In general, he more or less resembled a Vassar undergraduate.

Luckman looked so inept that Halas temporarily junked the idea of making him a quarterback and tried him at half. But late in the 1939 season, he resumed Luckman's tutoring and started him at quarterback against the Packers. Luckman was slick, a magician; and he led the Bears to a 30–27 victory, tossing the game-winning touchdown in the process.

But Luckman knew it would take years to become proficient as a T quarterback using the Bears' system. It contained 400 plays, approximately 60 of which were used in each game. Luckman had to learn the assignment of every man on every play. He made it a practice to report to training camp a month ahead of the rest of the squad to sit with Halas and Johnsos studying movies of past games. He practiced pivots, feints and hand-offs constantly, even in his hotel room on road trips.

In 1941, the Bears turned back the Packers in a Western Division playoff. They did it with relative ease, 33–14. "I was just getting the idea of the T then," Luckman told Howard Roberts, who chronicled the history of the Bears.

The 1941 Bear team is often cited as one of the most powerful of all time. Besides Luckman, McAfee, Nolting, and Osmanski, it featured ends George Wilson and Hampton Poole; and Norm Standlee, Hugh Gallarneau and the hard-driving Gary Famiglietti in the backfield. They ran roughshod over almost every team in the league, trouncing their city rivals, the Cardinals, 53–7, and the Detroit Lions, 49–0. They lost just once, to Green Bay, 16–14. In the championship playoff they found the Giants to be child's play. The final score was 37–9.

Luckman's career is riddled with days of glory, but many feel his most brilliant performance came in November 1943 at the Polo Grounds. Sid's fans in New York honored him with a "day," and his mother was in the stands to watch him play for only the third time in her life. After the gifts had been presented and the speeches recited, Sid put on a fantastic display. Seven times that afternoon he hit his receivers with touchdown passes to set a league record. (The record has since been tied twice.) The Bears waltzed to a 56–7 victory. It was Sid Luckman Day, all right—in spades!

"It was strictly luck," Sid said afterward. "All I could think of when the seventh touchdown pass went in was the day I saw Lou Gehrig hit four home runs in Yankee Stadium."

The NFL championship game that year between the Bears and the Redskins was billed as a decisive duel between Luckman and Sammy Baugh. Both stars were at their peak, or close to it. Sportswriters predicted the sky would be darkened by flying footballs when the two incomparable passers met.

But the match was terribly one-sided. Chicago won, 41–21, with Luckman tossing five touchdown passes. It was a bad day for Baugh. Early in the game Luckman gathered in one of Sammy's punts and streaked for the Redskins' goal at full speed, his thigh-heavy legs pumping high and hard. Baugh dove at him, head on, and Luckman's right knee struck Sam in the forehead. Baugh spent most of the rest of the afternoon on the bench.

Luckman enlisted in the U. S. Merchant Marine in 1944, and saw tanker duty in the North Atlantic. He was discharged the next year. He was a bit below par in 1945, but the next season he was razor-sharp again, and he led the Bears to another division title.

One of Luckman's last great days on the gridiron came in the championship playoff that year. The Bears faced the Giants at the Polo Grounds. The first Chicago touchdown came on a Luckman pass to Ken Kavanaugh, a play that covered 21 yards. Deep in the fourth quarter, the score was tied, 14–14, and Chicago had the ball on the Giants' 19-yard line.

Halas seldom allowed Luckman to run the ball for fear of injury, but this looked like an appropriate time. Sid called a time-out and walked to the sideline.

"Now?" he asked Halas. Papa Bear nodded.

Luckman faked a hand-off, hid the ball behind his right hip, and strolled to the goal line behind some splendid downfield blocking which cleaned out the New York secondary. The play gave the Bears a 21–14 win and another league title.

Luckman became one of Chicago's all-time sports favorites. His conduct off the field was just as exemplary as it was on. Modesty and good manners were two of his virtues. In 1960 he was elected to college football's Hall of Fame with eight others, one of them his college coach, Lou Little.

When it was time to pay tribute to Little, Luckman stepped to the microphone and began, "Lou . . ." And then stopped in embarrassment.

"You know," he explained, "that's the first time I ever addressed him as Lou."

Loyalty was another quality Luckman had. When the Chicago Rockets of the All America Conference came into being in 1946, they sought to hire Sid. They offered him $25,000, a generous sum in those days, to serve as a player-coach. Sid rejected the offer without a second's hesitation.

"How could I possibly have taken it?" he asked. "How could I quit a club that's done so much for me?"

Luckman played seldom after the 1948 season. When he retired as a player in 1950, he could look back on a record of achievement few players have equaled. He was the quarterback on five Western Division championship teams, and four of these won the league title—in 1940, 1941, 1943 and 1946. He was the NFL's All League quarterback in 1941, 1942, 1943, 1944 and 1946, and the league's most valuable player in 1943.

In the twilight years of his playing career, Luckman worked diligently with talented Johnny Lujack of Notre Dame who was meant to succeed Sid. A serious shoulder injury put an end to Lujack's career, however.

After Luckman retired there was a ghastly gap in the Bears' backfield. Through the years the club struggled to fill it. Quarterbacks came and went but never one who was nearly the equal of "Mr. Quarterback" himself, Sid Luckman.

Sid Luckman Career Passing Record

Year	Attempts	Completions	Pct.	Yards	Touchdowns	Interceptions
1939	51	23	45.0	636	5	4
1940	105	48	45.7	941	6	9
1941	119	68	57.1	1,181	9	6
1942	105	57	54.2	1,023	10	13
1943	202	110	54.4	2,194*	28*	12
1944	143	71	49.6	1,018	11	11
1945	217	117	53.9	1,725*	14*	10
1946	229	110	48.0	1,826*	17	16
1947	323	176	54.4	2,712	24	31
1948	163	89	54.6	1,047	13	14
1949	50	22	44.0	200	0	1
1950	37	13	35.1	180	0	1
Total	1,744	904	51.8	14,683	139	128

* *Outstanding Performance.*

Steve Van Buren

During the late 1940's, professional football was dominated by the Philadelphia Eagles, who won three Eastern Division titles and the NFL championship twice. This preeminence was due largely to the efforts of a big, broad-shouldered halfback who loved to tuck his chin to his chest and blast his way over enemy tacklers. His name was Steve Van Buren.

There was little that was fancy about Van Buren. Most of his yardage was amassed through the line of scrimmage, with right tackle his favorite target. Once in the secondary, however, he was an immediate scoring threat, and he could twist and change direction in a way that made one think of Red Grange. At one time Van Buren held six different NFL records for rushing and scoring, and when the Philadelphia club observed its silver anniversary in 1957, Van Buren was honored as the Eagles' "greatest player." Nothing has happened since that would serve to change that designation.

One of Van Buren's greatest performances came in the NFL championship game in 1948. The Chicago Cardinals were the opposition, but an even greater foe was the weather. On the day of the game, Philadelphia was struck by one of the worst blizzards in the city's history, so fierce in intensity that NFL Commissioner Bert Bell left it up to the players to decide whether the game should be played or postponed. They voted to play, but before they could take the field they had to pitch in and help the ground crew remove the snow and peel away the tarpaulin from the frozen field.

For three quarters the teams played like snowmen. Neither could score. With less than a minute remaining in the third period, the Eagles got a break. Frank Kilroy recovered a Cardinal fumble on Chicago's 17-yard line. The Eagles ran one play before the end of the quarter, gaining six yards. Then the teams changed sides.

Falling snow had obliterated the yard markers at the new end of the field and the referees almost had to guess where to put the ball down. Joe Muha made three yards over center. Then Tommy Thompson ran a quarterback sneak, moving the ball to the Cardinals' five-yard line and gaining a first down. Now the near-frozen fans began to chant, "Steve! Steve! Give it to Steve." That's exactly what Thompson had in mind. He handed off to Van Buren who slid triumphantly into the end zone for the only score in a 7–0 game. It was the first championship ever for the Eagles. Steve's contribution that day was 98 yards rushing in 26 carries. The Cardinal *team* accounted for 96 yards.

Van Buren had another brilliant game in the championship playoff of 1949. This time the Los Angeles Rams were the Eagles' opponents. Again the weather was a major factor. This time it was rain, torrential rain that turned the field at Memorial Stadium into a sea of mud. But Van Buren was seemingly unbothered by the heavy going. He sloshed through the Rams' defenses for a spectacular 196 yards on 31 carries, and the Eagles won, 14–0. Both the yardage he accumulated and the number of carries he totaled that day set records for an NFL championship game, and the records still stand.

Van Buren's performance caused Greasy Neale, the Eagles' coach, to say, "Maybe Grange was better than Van Buren. Maybe Bronko Nagurski was. But I'll bet nobody ever ran better than Van Buren did in this mud."

Van Buren's background has a bit of the bizarre to it and it is surprising that he ever played football at all, and even more amazing that he became one of the game's standouts. He was born in 1921 in Tele, Honduras, where his father was a fruit inspector. Both his parents died when he was very young, and he was sent to New Orleans to live with his grandparents. He began to develop an interest in football as a sophomore at Warren Easten High School. He wanted to try out for the team, but the coach advised him not to since he weighed only 125 pounds.

Steve dropped out of school after his sophomore year and went to work in an iron foundry for two years. When he returned to Easten High, he was a muscular 155-pounder. Boxing had become his main interest. But he played football well enough to win a scholarship to Louisiana State University, and this persuaded him to forget the prize ring.

Van Buren toiled in relative obscurity as a blocking back during his freshman and sophomore years, but coach Bernie Moore converted him to a running back in his junior season and he began making headlines. He had a splendid senior year, accounting for a total of 832 yards rushing.

Coach Moore tipped off Greasy Neale as to Van Buren's value. He called the Philadelphia coach and reported, "This kid can make your team. Give him as much as you can." As a result Van Buren was the Eagles' No. 1 choice in the 1944 draft.

Philadelphia knew much more about him than he knew about Philadelphia. "We didn't pay too much attention to pro football in those days. The Bears and the Redskins were the only teams I knew about," Steve once revealed. "In fact, when the team sent me my railroad ticket to Philadelphia, I rode right past the North Philadelphia station and ended up in New York."

Van Buren was an impressive sight at the Eagles' training camp. He stood 6-1, and weighed slightly more than 200 pounds. But it was the way in which he was put together that cheered

Greasy Neale. He had wide, powerful shoulders, a tremendous chest, and his body tapered down to the slim legs of a track man. He could run 100 yards in 9.8 seconds. An eye ailment impaired Van Buren's vision on the right side, and caused him to be rejected by the armed services. But if the affliction ever had an adverse effect upon his football talents, no one ever discovered it.

When Philadelphia opened the season against the Boston Yanks, Van Buren was suffering from an influenza attack, but Neale started him. The first time Steve was handed the ball he turned right end and sprinted 47 yards for a touchdown. Neale, fearing his star might collapse, quickly yanked him from the game. Steve didn't return until late in the fourth quarter. In five frantic minutes, he carried the ball three times, for gains of 8, 10 and 20 yards, and then he caught a pass from Ray Zimmerman for a touchdown. As soon as the final gun sounded, he returned to his sickbed.

An appendectomy sidelined Van Buren for several games during his rookie season. Even so, he carried the ball 88 times for 444 yards, and averaged a very respectable 5.5 yards per carry.

In 1945, his sophomore year, Van Buren ran wild. He led the NFL in rushing with a total of 832 yards. The sixteen touchdowns he scored on runs stood as a record until the days of Cleveland's Jimmy Brown and Green Bay's Jim Taylor. Beginning in 1945, Van Buren's value was increased by the presence in the lineup of a dead-eye passer named Tommy Thompson. Despite the fact that Van Buren and Thompson gave the Eagles an almost unstoppable offense, they finished second that year. They were runners-up again in 1946, a year in which Steve was hampered by injuries.

The Flying Dutchman, as Steve came to be called, was a splendid blocker, a sure-handed receiver on short passes, and a better-than-average punter. "He could have been a better kicker," Greasy Neale once remarked, "but all he wanted to do was run. In practice, he'd only practice running."

Van Buren preferred not to dodge tacklers; he liked to run right over them. Like many ballcarriers who hew to this style, Van Buren ran with his head down. Once Neale attempted to correct this habit and sent Steve into a game with instructions to keep his head erect so he could see where he was going. Early in the game Steve came to the bench. His face was puffed up from the pummeling he had taken and one eye had been blackened.

"Now I know," he told Neale, pointing to the eye, "why I have been keeping my head down all these years."

Van Buren scored several touchdowns by catching passes, but he never tried, or even wanted to try, throwing the ball. In fact, he sometimes scorned the pass as an offensive weapon. Once he declared, "The fellow who threw the first pass must have been someone too tired to run with the ball."

In 1947 the Eagles ended the season in a tie with the Steelers for the Eastern Division title by beating Green Bay, 28–14, in their final game. Steve's performance was the feature of the day. He gained 96 yards rushing to break the NFL mark set by Beattie Feathers in 1934. (The record now belongs to Jimmy Brown.) He also stunned the Packers with a 101-yard kickoff return, but a clipping penalty nullified the feat.

The Eagles then beat the Steelers in the playoff, only to be turned back by the Chicago Cardinals in the championship game. The Cards managed to keep Van Buren in check.

The year 1949 saw Van Buren at his peak. His slashing rushes accounted for a record 1,146 yards, a mark that stood until 1958. In one game that season, against the Pittsburgh Steelers, he carried the ball 27 times and gained 205 yards. Few men in the history of the National League have gained more than 200 yards in a single game.

In 1950, Van Buren's career went into a decline and simultaneously the reign of the Eagles came to an end. Steve had a foot operation that failed to heal properly. No longer was he feared. The Eagles suffered a late-season collapse and managed to win only half their games. The next year, with Van Buren still in poor health, was even worse.

Steve's career came to an abrupt end early in the 1952 season. He said he was "feeling as good as he has ever felt in his life." During a practice session Steve carried the ball and was stopped by several tacklers but was held erect amidst them. Suddenly another tackler came crashing in from the side and crumbled Van Buren to the ground. His leg was severely twisted as he went down and he suffered a torn ligament in his left knee. The big halfback with the No. 15 on his green jersey did no more serious running after that.

Van Buren served as a scout for the Eagles after his playing days ended. For a time he was vice-president of the Newark Bears in one of football's minor leagues. Later he joined the Philadelphia Bulldogs as a backfield coach and assistant director of personnel.

It would have been interesting to see how Van Buren might have fared against today's defenses, which are aimed more to thwart passes than to halt rushes. "I'd love to have been able to run against those four-man lines," Steve once said. "If one man is blocked out you have space to run before the linebacker can move up to stop you. In my day it was tough just getting past the line.

"I never got to run such a thing as a draw play [where the quarterback fakes a pass and hands off to a charging back]. In my time it was mostly off tackle or around the end. And I played defense when the other team had the ball."

As it was, with the defenses always concentrating on him, Van Buren still managed to set a helmetful of records. Only in recent years, with teams playing an increased number of games, have Van Buren's marks begun to be challenged and toppled, and it is likely that some of them may never fall.

Steve Van Buren Career Rushing Record

Year	Carries	Yards	Average Gain	Touchdowns
1944	80	444	5.5	5
1945	143	832*	5.8	15*
1946	116	529	4.6	5
1947	217*	1,008*	4.6	13*
1948	201*	945*	4.7	10*
1949	263*	1,146*	4.4	11*
1950	188*	629	3.3	4
1951	112	327	2.9	6
Total	1,320	5,860	4.4	69

* *Outstanding Performance.*

Bob Waterfield

What kind of player was Bob Waterfield? Unbelievably versatile. The best. Consider this evidence:

On October 3, 1948, the Los Angeles Rams played host to the Philadelphia Eagles, a team destined to win the NFL championship that year. Four minutes of the third quarter remained, and Los Angeles trailed, 28–0. Fans in the Coliseum were leaving in disgust. Suddenly Waterfield, the Rams' quarterback, hit Jack Zilly in the end zone. Then Waterfield ran and passed his team 54 yards in nine plays for the second score, closing the drive with a touchdown pass to Bill Smyth. Waterfield converted a second time to make it 28–14.

Midway in the fourth period, Waterfield struck again, this thrust featured by a 40-yard pass to Tom Fears. Bob Hoffman bulled across. With less than two minutes left, Waterfield passed to Red Hickey for 20 yards, to Dante Magnani for 10 yards, to Fears again for 14 yards. Once more Waterfield peddled back, shook off one tackler, then another, and finally found his receiver—Zilly—and fired 24 yards for the score. He calmly booted the extra point, his fourth. Final score: 28–28.

"The Eagles will never be able to explain what happened when they get home," said a Philadelphia newspaperman. "Who will ever believe what Waterfield did to them?" Besides the twelve passes to six different receivers, good for 212 yards, Waterfield place-kicked without a miss, punted, intercepted a pass, recovered a fumble, and streaked for six yards on a crucial third-down play in the final quarter.

Indeed, Bob Waterfield could do it all. He was a brilliant field general, and a precision passer. He could boot gorgeous 70-yard punts. Three times he led the National League in field goals, and four times in point-after-touchdowns. As Jack Teele, the Rams' public relations director, once put it: "Waterfield was a specialist, but his specialty was everything."

During the years Waterfield served as quarterback, the Los Angeles Rams were the most feared offensive team in pro ball.

Four times the club won division championships during Waterfield's eight-year career, and twice they captured the NFL title.

Winning had become something of habit to Waterfield by the time he reached the pros. He was born in Elmira, New York, on July 26, 1920, and when he was a youngster his parents moved to Van Nuys, California. He played high school sports, but was not an outstanding athlete. "I loved playing," he once said, "but I was small during my high school days. I weighed less than 150 pounds."

After he graduated from high school, Bob took a job in an aircraft plant in Los Angeles and worked on the assembly line. He spent virtually all his spare time playing football, with long hours devoted to passing and kicking practice. His mother kept after him to get more education. He entered UCLA in 1940. The following year he won varsity status, and in 1942 really blossomed, leading the Bruins to the Pacific Coast Conference championship and to a win over Georgia in the Rose Bowl.

His private life was also marked by success, for in 1943 he married his high school "steady," Jane Russell, whose career in motion pictures later rivaled and, at times, even overshadowed her famous husband's. The same year Bob entered the Army and was sent to Officer Candidate School at Fort Benning, Georgia. (Jane went along.) He injured a knee and received a medical discharge in 1944. Returning to UCLA, he had another splendid year. He climaxed the season with an unforgettable performance in the East-West game. In leading his underdog West team to a 13–6 victory, he passed for one touchdown, scored the other himself, and averaged a stunning 59.4 yards punting.

A draft choice, Bob began dickering with the Rams, who were based in Cleveland at the time. The negotiations lasted months. "He's married to Jane Russell, the movie star," said Chile Walsh, the Rams' vice-president, "and that doesn't make it any easier to sign him." On June 15 Waterfield and the Rams came to an agreement. Bob was to receive an annual salary estimated to be $7,500. Even by the 1945 pro wage scale, the Rams had gotten a spectacular bargain.

Waterfield was an immediate sensation at the Rams' training camp. He tossed two touchdowns in his first pre-season game, and took over the starting quarterback assignment from veteran Albie Reisz.

Waterfield's rookie year can only be classed as sensational. He pitched for 1,192 yards and nine touchdowns, and led the league with a 6.3 yards per carry average, as the Rams, who had been no more than mediocre in 1944, roared to nine wins in ten games. Clinching the Western Division title hinged upon a late-season game against the Lions at Briggs Stadium. The day of the game Waterfield could hardly raise his throwing arm above his shoulder. In a game the week before against the Cardinals, he had taken a severe beating.

"It's torn rib muscles," said the trainer. "We can't use him today."

"The hell you can't," said Waterfield. "Tape me up and give me a shot."

With the aid of Novocain and a wide strip of tape around his body, Waterfield put on a spectacular exhibition. Despite freezing weather and a constant pummeling from the Lions, he completed ten passes to Jim Benton for 303 yards, a record at the time. The Rams won, 28–21. A Cleveland paper headlined: WATERFIELD BEST CLEVELAND PITCHER SINCE BOB FELLER.

In the championship playoff against the Redskins, Bob connected 14 times in 27 tries, and hit Benton and Jim Gilette for touchdowns. The Rams came out on top, 15–14. Amazingly, the young rookie had taken his team all the way. He was the top vote getter on every All Pro team, and voted the league's Most Valuable Player, the first time ever for a rookie. A fellow named Sammy Baugh finished runner-up. Rams' owner Dan Reeves signed him to a three-year contract at $20,000 a year, making him one of the highest-paid performers of the day. Said Reeves, "I wouldn't trade Bob for the Brooklyn Bridge, with any player you can name thrown in."

After the 1945 season, Reeves gained permission from the other NFL owners to move the Cleveland franchise to Los Angeles. There Waterfield and the Rams were to enjoy their most glorious days, winning the Western Conference crown three consecutive years—1949, 1950 and 1951.

In 1951 the Rams ended the long championship reign of the Cleveland Browns. The title game was played in the Coliseum before a record crowd of 59,475. After a scoreless first period,

Waterfield's passes brought the Rams to within a yard of the Browns' goal. Then Dick Hoerner bucked into the end zone. Late in the third quarter Waterfield contributed a field goal. A pass from Norm van Brocklin to Tom Fears provided the final score in Los Angeles' 24–17 victory.

Although Waterfield was a recognized demon as a punter, place-kicker and passer, his skill as a runner was often overlooked. But in executing "sneak runs" he had no equal. There were times his wizardry as a bootlegger even fooled the officials. Before one game the defensive coach of the Chicago Bears told Mac Berry, "If Waterfield bootlegs around you this afternoon, it'll cost you $25."

In the dressing room after the game, Berry lamented his lost money. "I hawk him all afternoon," he cried, "and the one time I'm not looking for it, he sneaks around me."

Despite his successes, Waterfield never received great adulation from the Los Angeles fans. His most magnificent deeds were usually rewarded by no more than polite applause. One reason may have had to do with his personality; he was notably reserved and taciturn. Later, when Bob took over as the Rams' field general, Jim Murray of the Los Angeles *Times* called him "the Great Stone Coach." Indeed, there was not a flamboyant bone in his body, and in Los Angeles flamboyance counts.

Bob could list modesty as one of his virtues. "What made you a great quarterback?" a reporter once asked him. "Benton, Fears and Hirsch didn't hurt me any," Waterfield replied.

Quarterbacks of today can thank Bob Waterfield for one of their most lethal weapons—the bomb, the long pass. Prior to Waterfield's day, coaches looked upon the bomb as no more than a desperate expedient. The quick kick was common on third down and long yardage situations, but Waterfield scorned such strategy. He preferred to rear back and throw a long arcing pass—sometimes it would travel half the length of the field—and he developed this skill to such a high degree of sophistication that the bomb became a part of the Rams' offensive plan. Today, of course, it is used by every team.

Bob's last year as a player was 1952. Late in the season the fans honored him with a "day," perhaps his return for a day he had given them earlier in the year. In a game played at Green Bay, the Rams trailed the Packers, 28–6, with only twelve minutes to play. Waterfield had often won games that were apparently lost, but this time the burden seemed much too great. Working methodically, he brought the Rams to the Packers' one-yard line, and then sent Dan Towler into the end zone. Now the Packers' lead was 15 points. A field goal and a touchdown that followed a recovered fumble cut Green Bay's edge to only five points and set the stage for Waterfield's last-ditch heroics.

The game was in its dying minutes when the Rams took over the ball on their own eight-yard line. Waterfield, as cool as a deep freeze, mixing his plays beautifully, marched the team relentlessly the full 92 yards. Dan Towler scored the winning touchdown. The game brought forth this comment from Vincent X. Flaherty of the Los Angeles *Examiner:* "Games such as the Rams and the Rifle (Waterfield) played on Sunday are the kind that set pro football apart, give it that extra touch of quality which makes it the finest game in the land."

The win enabled the Rams to tie the Detroit Lions for first place in the conference standings. But the Detroiters won the playoff game.

After his retirement as a player, Waterfield tried a movie career, but before long he was back with the Rams as an assistant coach. In 1960 he was named head coach. This was the beginning of a dark period for Los Angeles, however, with the club beset by frequent clashes among the owners. The Rams won only four games in 1960, the same number in 1961, and had a 1-7 record in 1962 when Waterfield announced his retirement. "He didn't resign," said Jim Murray, "he escaped." He continued to serve the Rams as a scout.

There may have been quarterbacks in the league who could pass with greater efficiency than Waterfield; there were men who could run faster and punters who could kick farther. But no one could do so many things as well as Bob Waterfield. It was this rare versatility that made him one of the game's immortals.

Bob Waterfield Career Passing Record

Year	Attempts	Completions	Pct.	Yards	Touchdowns	Interceptions
1945	172	89	51.7	1,653	55	16
1946	251	127	50.5	1,747	18*	17
1947	221	96	43.4	1,310	8	18
1948	180	87	48.3	1,354	14	18
1949	296	154	52.0	2,168*	17	24
1950	213	122	57.3*	1,540	11	13
1951	176	88	50.0	1,566	13	10
1952	109	51	47.7	655	3	11
Total	1,618	814	50.3	11,893	99	127

* *Outstanding Performance.*

Bob Waterfield Career Punting Record

Year	Number	Total Yards	Longest Punt	Average	Blocked
1945	39	1,588	68	40.70	1
1946	39	1,745	65	44.69*	0
1947	59	2,500	86	42.40	1
1948	43	1,843	88*	42.60	2
1949	49	2,177	61	44.40	0
1950	52	2,087	61	40.10	2
1951	4	166	52	41.50	0
1952	30	1,276	88*	42.60	0
Total	315	13,382	88	42.48	6

* *Outstanding Performance.*

1966

Bill Dudley

He didn't look like a football player. He was 5-9 and weighed 170. His hands were small and he passed with a herky-jerky side-arm motion that sent football purists home in disgust. They called him "the Bullet," but the name didn't fit. He had little speed afoot, and once in a sprint race before an All Star game he finished a plodding fifteenth among fifteen runners.

But Bill Dudley always seemed to find a way to beat you. Though he did lack speed, he was as elusive as a wisp of smoke and uncanny in his use of blockers. Twice—in 1942 and 1946—he led the National Football League in rushing yardage. His place-kicking style was all his own. He took no steps, merely swung his foot into the ball pendulum-style. But rarely did he miss a field goal or a place-kick. One of the last of pro football's sixty-min-utes-a-game performers, Dudley was a demon on defense with his fierce tackling and in 1946 he led the league in pass interceptions.

All his life Dudley was dismissed as being "too small" to play football. Yet his size, or lack of it, never seemed to hinder him. He was a star of his high school team, an All American at college, and the NFL's Most Valuable Player in 1946, a year in which he held down halfback spot for the Steelers. Often he is rated as the greatest player in the history of that club. Indeed, even today, Dudley's name is revered as much as U. S. Steel by Pittsburgh fans.

Dudley's interest in football started in his grade school days in Bluefield, Virginia. He read all there was to read about the sport and went to local games. Harry Newman, the 5-foot-8, 176-pound bullet-passing All American at Michigan, was his idol. When Dudley entered Graham High School, he tried out for the team but the coach turned him down. The school didn't have a uniform small enough to fit him.

As a high school junior he made the team but he never got to play in a game. Finally, as a senior, he blossomed. Kicking was his forte. He was the best punter on the team, and in all his high school career he never missed an extra-point attempt. The colleges he wanted to attend weren't interested in granting a football scholarship to a 5-foot-9, 152-pound halfback. However, Bill's coach managed to get him a partial scholarship—$500 a year—to the University of Virginia.

Despite his pint size, Bill was the team's star, their best runner, best punter and a stalwart on defense. In a game against North Carolina, he called the team's signals, did all the punting, booted extra points, ran back punts, and played a devastating game on defense. He passed for one touchdown, scored himself once on a three-yard plunge and a second time on a 60-yard run. For a third touchdown, he faked a punt, then wove his way 89 yards to pay dirt. It was one of the greatest individual performances ever seen on a college gridiron.

Bill was twenty in 1942, the year the Steelers made him their No. 1 draft choice. Easygoing Walt Kiesling was the Pittsburgh coach, and there was considerable speculation as to how the diminutive Dudley would fare among the monster pros.

When he reported to the Steelers' training camp, he had a bad ankle, but he played the first game of the season and in the opening seconds of play he ran 55 yards for a touchdown against the Philadelphia Eagles. As if to prove that this was no fluke, the very next week, against the Packers, he took the second-half kickoff and raced the length of the field for a score.

Dudley played with fiery determination and he expected every other player on the team to do the same. If a player appeared to be shirking his duty, Dudley would lecture him. For this he was sometimes accused of trying to coach, but, in general, the players accepted his leadership.

The Steelers, after getting off to a shaky start, rebounded to win seven of the last nine games on their schedule to finish second in the Eastern Division. This may seem like a modest achievement, but not to Steeler fans. It was the first winning season in the history of the team. Dudley, the darling of the fans, gained 696 yards rushing, tops in the league. He was named Rookie of the Year.

After his first year, Bill entered the Army Air Corps and served as a pilot. At Randolph Field and March Field, where he played football before being sent to the Pacific, he was an All Service halfback.

Once Dudley was on an Army team that faced a powerful Navy squad. Through the afternoon the teams battled to a scoreless tie. Then Dudley intercepted a pass and cut, dodged, and pivoted his way into the Navy end zone for the only touchdown of the day. Buster Ramsey, a sailor lineman who played civilian football with the Chicago Cardinals, pursued Dudley most of the way. In the end zone he said to him, "Dudley, you're the luckiest man who ever played pro football."

A couple of years later, when Dudley and Ramsey had returned to their respective clubs, the same thing happened again: the Steelers edged the Cards on a frantic run by Dudley. Again Buster was the man in pursuit.

"I still say it," Ramsey declared. "You're the luckiest man who ever played football."

Dudley smiled. "Want to know something?" he said. "I'm beginning to believe you."

Bill traded in his khakis for a Pittsburgh uniform late in 1945. The hapless Steelers had not won a game, but Dudley gave them a lift. In his first appearance in the lineup, he showed that he had lost none of his improvisational gusto when it came to running the ball. He scored two touchdowns and led the Steelers to an upset win over the Chicago Cardinals. The next morning a headline in a Pittsburgh paper read: THAT MAN IS BACK. Although he played in only four games, Bill still managed to outscore all the other Steeler backs that year.

The 1946 season was bizarre. It began when Jock Sutherland, the so-called "dour Scot," and a stern disciplinarian, took over as the Steelers' head coach. The personalities of Sutherland and Dudley clashed sharply, with the coach mistaking his star performer's "suggestions" as a usurpation of his authority. Often the coach reacted with sarcasm.

One day in a practice session Dudley was throwing passes. He missed three or four in a row.

Sutherland was standing at the sidelines and Dudley called out to him. "I think," he said, "that I'd do a lot better if you'd use different-colored jerseys so I could tell the receivers from the defenders."

Sutherland flared. "Are *you* coaching this team?" he said icily.

"No, sir, I'm not," was Bill's calm reply.

"Then you follow instructions like everyone else," Sutherland ordered.

Though Dudley was often disconsolate, it scarcely affected his play. Sutherland considered him as good on defense as offense, and used Bill for as much as 57 minutes in a game. He took many a physical beating as a result. Nevertheless, he led the league in interceptions with 10, and again he topped the league rushing yardage. But the feuding with Sutherland was more than he could stand. At season's end, his contract having expired, Dudley abruptly quit.

"I'm too small for the pro game," he announced. "I think it would be best for everyone if I played somewhere else. Under Jock I've had to play too much for my size."

Dudley planned to return to the University of Virginia and become a backfield coach, but this phase of his career never got off the launching pad. During the summer, the Detroit Lions gained permission to bid for Bullet Bill's services and dispatched an emissary to California (where Bill was honeymooning) to talk to him. They quickly came to terms. The contract Dudley signed called for a salary of $25,000, the highest amount paid any player since Red Grange's percentage deal with the Bears two decades before. The Lions had to give the Steelers two players and the draft rights to two others as well.

It must be said that the Detroit players were not enthused by the club's acquisition of Dudley. There were rumors he would try to run things. There was talk he would be only a part-time performer. But when Dudley showed up at the Lions' camp, he set to work like an eager rookie. He became "one of the boys" during an exhibition game in Battle Creek. Coach Gus Dorais told him he didn't have to play but Bill insisted on starting. It was a rough game and on one play Bill's lip was deeply gashed. He came to the sidelines, had the cut stitched, and then reentered the game. None of his teammates doubted his dedication after that.

Just before the season's opening game with the Steelers, the Detroit players held a meeting to elect a captain. Dudley got every vote but one—his own.

One other matter was resolved that day. As captain, Bill went to the center of the field before the game for the coin toss. At the conclusion of the ceremonies, Jock Sutherland walked out to where Bill was standing, extended his hand and said, "I wish you luck, Bill. Good luck—but not too much against us."

As a Lion, Bill picked right up where he had left off with the Steelers, and many an afternoon he delighted Detroit fans with his long runs. In 1947 he intercepted a pass and ran 41 yards for a touchdown, ran a kickoff back 78 yards for a score, and returned a punt 84 yards for still another touchdown. He established team records for the longest punt and longest field goal, and he continued his sparkling defensive play.

Bill's exploits, however, could not win many games. In 1946, the season before Dudley joined the Lions, the club had lost all but one contest. Winning football could not come to Detroit until there was a wholesale change.

After three years with the Lions, Bill was dealt to the Washington Redskins, another club that had fallen upon evil days. There Bill spent the final three seasons of his career. One day, when the Redskins were playing the Steelers, Bill made the record book on what many people believe was his greatest run.

It was part of Bill's playing philosophy that *every* punt should be caught and run back. Often he went to great extremes to achieve this. In the game in question, Joe Geri of the Steelers got off a tremendous punt. Following a diagonal course, the ball sailed downfield more than 60 yards, and appeared to be going over the goal line or, worse, out of bounds inside the Redskins' five-yard line. Dudley was at the right spot when the ball came down. To make the catch, he had to reach out of bounds, being careful his toes didn't touch the sidelines. His fingers plucked the ball from the air; then he clutched it to his chest. He faked out the first tackler who threatened to spill him, and then his blocking began to form. He clung to the sideline all the way and went 96 yards for a touchdown.

Dudley's stunning runback took place on December 3, 1950.

No one since has equaled the feat. (The longest punt return in NFL history is 98 yards, a record established in 1933 by Gil Le-Febvre.)

While Dudley is invariably remembered for his brilliant offensive skills, he also must be rated as one of the top defensive men of all time. Steve Owen, the Giants' coach, called him "the best defensive back in the league."

In 1950, professional football adopted the unlimited substitution rule. Every pro team then began to develop separate offensive and defensive squads. The day of the specialist had arrived. With this rule, the man who played both ways, the man who could run or pass, block or tackle, went into quick decline. Bullet Bill Dudley was one of the last of them—and one of the best.

Bill Dudley Career Rushing Record

Year	Carries	Yards Gained	Average Gain	Touchdowns
1942	162*	696*	4.3	
1945	57	204	3.5	3
1946	146*	604*	4.1	3
1947	80	302	3.8	2
1948	33	97	2.9	0
1949	125	402	3.2	4
1950	66	339	5.1	1
1951	91	398	4.4	2
1953	5	15	3.0	0
Total	765	3,057	4.0	15

* *Outstanding Performance.*

Joe Guyon

In pro football's grim infant days, player contracts were virtually unknown. A player might change teams from season to season, or even from game to game. He went to the highest bidder or wherever he had the impulse to play.

The career of Indian Joe Guyon, a brilliant runner and a devastating blocker, is a case in point. Guyon switched teams with the ease a player of today changes his shirt. Though his career was relatively short, Guyon played with seven different clubs.

Guyon started in pro football three years before the National Football League was founded. Jim Thorpe invited him to join the Canton Bulldogs in 1918. Guyon stayed with the Bulldogs for three years, his longest tenure anywhere, and in that period Canton didn't lose a single game. After Canton, Guyon played with the Buffalo Bisons, the Kansas City Cowboys, the Cleveland Indians, the Oorang Indians, and the Rock Island Independents.

He finished his career with New York in 1927, the year the Giants won their first championship. They boasted an 11-1-1 record that season, scoring 197 points and allowing only 20. A 179-pound halfback, Guyon contributed by running, passing, blocking, tackling and punting. "I did everything but sell programs," he recalls.

The most famous story about Guyon happened while he was with New York. The Giants met the Chicago Bears in a decisive game, and one that has become noted for its violence. In the third quarter, Guyon drifted back to pass. George Halas, playing right end for the Bears, gave chase, intent upon putting Guyon out of commission by any means, legal or otherwise. Guyon's back was to Halas when the Big Bear leaped to strike, but Guyon whirled around and swung a knee that caught Halas in the chest. Then he fell backward, screaming that Halas had clipped him.

His teammates carried Halas from the field with four broken ribs, and the referee penalized the Bears 15 yards for clipping. The penalty led to a Giant touchdown.

Guyon's teammate, Steve Owen, who later coached the Giants for many years, walked to the groaning Halas, peered down at him, and declared, "George, you should know better than to try to sneak up on an Indian."

Bone-crunching play was standard practice in Guyon's time. Once, when playing with the Kansas City Cowboys, he flattened the Giants' little Heinie Benkert with a vicious tackle, then did a high-stepping war dance around Benkert's inert form. New York swore revenge. A few minutes later, two Giants hit Guyon like a pair of arrows. Lynn Bomar got him high; Century Milstead got him low. Guyon did no more war dances that day.

Guyon, of the Chippewa tribe, was born O-Gee-Chidaha on the White Earth (Minnesota) Indian reservation in 1892. "The government only gave us a sixth-grade education," he remembers, "and as a result it was hard trying to make anything out of yourself. Sports were one of the few ways a youngster could pull himself up."

There were many fine Indian players in football's early days. Besides Guyon, there was Pete Calac, Woodchuck Welmus, Mount Pleasant, Red Fang, Little Twig and Big Twig. The last-named often wore Indian garb over his uniform when running plays for the Buffalo Bisons. Sometimes he'd even don it at nights and parade the streets of the town in which he was playing.

Of course, the most renowned Indian player of all was Jim Thorpe. He was a teammate of Guyon's at Carlisle, and they were close friends. Guyon believes that Thorpe was the greatest athlete of all time. After Thorpe's death, Guyon helped establish the Thorpe Memorial in Pennsylvania, near the Carlisle School.

Guyon succeeded Thorpe as an All American at Carlisle, and then transferred to Georgia Tech. There he was a member of the 1917 national championship team. To say that this team was a powerhouse is to be guilty of gross understatement. They went undefeated in nine games, and won by such scores as 83–0 over Vanderbilt, and 98–0 over Carlisle.

Despite the fact that professional football players were a great deal more truculent in Guyon's time than they are now, he believes that teams of the present day would be capable of murdering clubs like the Kansas City Cowboys and Canton Bulldogs. "There have been tremendous changes in equipment," he says, "and play today is much more deceptive and scientific."

Guyon was also a professional baseball player with the Louisville Colonels of the American Association.

After he retired, Guyon settled down in Louisville. He coached junior football in that city each fall. At age seventy-five, he played golf frequently and always carried his own clubs. He shot in the 90's. And he still looked capable of making a slashing tackle or turning an end.

Arnie Herber

Green Bay fans have become used to the fact that Packer teams are passing teams. Curly Lambeau, who founded the club, learned the air game under Knute Rockne at Notre Dame. Since Lambeau's time the Packers have always had young men who could throw the football—Red Dunn, Vern Lewellen, Cecil Isbell, Irv Comp and, in recent years, Bart Starr. But none of these did more to uphold the Packers' tradition for aerial finesse and marksmanship than a homegrown piece of talent by the name of Arnie Herber.

Herber joined the Packers in 1930 and quickly established himself as one of the first great passers of professional football. He was the NFL passing leader in 1932, 1934 and 1936. His career record gives him 481 completions for 8,033 yards. His best performance came in 1936—77 completions for 1,239 yards.

Herber was completely unheralded as a rookie. He had been born in Green Bay, grew up there, and attended Green Bay's West High where he had been a high-scoring guard in basketball, and a triple-threat back in football. He sold programs for the Packers so he could get into the games.

After high school, Arnie attended the University of Wisconsin as a freshman, then transferred to Regis in Denver to play football for coach Red Strader. Regis planned to build a football powerhouse, but the idea fizzled with the stock market crash and the depression that followed. Herber returned to Green Bay to become a handyman around the Packer clubhouse.

The players nicknamed Herber "Dummy," and Curly Lambeau, the Packer coach at the time, didn't like it. One day during a practice session he sent Herber into town on a fake errand. Then Lambeau called a meeting of the team and declared that anyone who used that nickname again would be hit with an automatic fine of $50. No one did.

For a time Arnie was known as "the Kid" or simply "Herber." But as he won respect with his firing arm, he came to be called "Flash." The dictionary says that "flash" means "to sparkle or gleam; to be brilliant." This definition, in Herber's case, is just about perfect.

Lambeau decided to give Herber a try at quarterback because he was a hometown boy and thus figured to be a drawing card. He paid Arnie $75 a game. Arnie didn't care. He was happy to be a member of the eighteen-player squad. But the salary has to rank as one of the great bargains of all time. In his first game with Green Bay he fired a touchdown pass to Lavern Dilweg, and the Packers whipped the Chicago Cards, 7–0. The Packers won the NFL championship in Herber's rookie season and in the year that followed, too.

Herber had a peculiar way of holding the ball. Handicapped by short fingers, he put his thumb over the laces to prevent the ball from wobbling and to assure plenty of spiraling action.

Herber's passes were noted for two qualities: distance and accuracy. At the finish of one of their championship seasons, the Packers went to Hollywood to make a movie short. One sequence called for Herber to throw the ball from the 50-yard line and break a three-foot-square piece of glass which had been suspended from the crossbar between the goalposts.

Arnie took a few warm-up tosses, then on his first attempt he took the pass from center, drifted back, and threw. It was perfect; the glass shattered. But the director had neglected to start the cameras rolling. He told Arnie he'd have to do it again. On the very next toss Herber calmly duplicated the feat. That's how accurate he was.

The arrival of Don Hutson in 1935, the premier pass receiver of all times, greatly enhanced Herber's artistry. They were an unstoppable pair. Hutson says that one reason he chose to sign with Green Bay was because of Herber. Says Hutson, "I remember Curly Lambeau yelling to me over the telephone that he had the greatest long passer in the league."

Many times Hutson had reason to agree with this estimate. "Once in a game in St. Louis," he recalls, "Herber threw me a pass for a touchdown that I thought would never come down. It just stayed up there. The next day the paper said that it had traveled 77 yards in the air."

Herber was with the Packers in an era when the quarterback was regarded as fair game. This, added to the fact that he needed time for his receivers to get downfield for his long passes, meant that he took many fierce beatings. Yet in his early years with Green Bay he never wore a helmet. Headgear slowed him down, he claimed. He was fairly indestructible, and in thirteen seasons in the NFL about the only serious injury he received was a shoulder separation, and that came in a game against the College All Stars, not a league game.

Green Bay won the Western Division title in 1936 with a 10-1-1 record, and had only the Boston Redskins to overcome for the league championship. Herber rose to the occasion. He clicked with Hutson for a touchdown in the opening minutes of play, and later he hit Mike Gantennein for a score. The final saw the Packers on top, 21–6.

During the 1937 season Herber suffered a leg injury that sharply reduced his effectiveness. A new passer, and a splendid one, Cecil Isbell, began alternating with Herber. He eventually replaced him in the Packer lineup.

Herber retired after the 1940 season, but his nonemployment was not permanent. Four years later the New York Giants talked him into coming back. This was during World War II. Herber, with characteristic modesty, admits that it was the time "when most of the good players were in military service."

Herber was thirty-four years old when he showed up at the Giant training camp in the fall of 1944. He had not thrown a football in three years, and he had so much surplus weight that newspaper writers described him as a "tub of lard." But Herber went to work with fiery diligence. He trimmed down to his playing weight of 210 and before the season was very old he had regained his passing touch.

In a game against the Philadelphia Eagles that season, the Giants were trailing, 21–7, with less than six minutes to play. Then Herber caught fire. He completed five of six passes for 114 yards and two touchdowns to gain the New Yorkers a tie.

The Giants startled the sports world that year. They had looked pitiable in training camp but in the upside-down world of wartime football, they won the Eastern Division championship. Their strong points were a splendid defense, which yielded only 75 points over the season, and a battering-ram fullback named Bill Pascal—and Herber.

Ironically for Herber, the playoff game brought the Giants face to face with the Packers. The New York press had a field day, and regaled readers with stories of Herber, the Green Bay castoff, who they said was going to wreak a terrible vengeance upon the Packers. It never happened.

On the Giants' first play from scrimmage, Pascal's leg twisted beneath him, injuring the knee. He was lost for the day. Herber saw four of his passes intercepted, and he threw only ten. His new team lost to his old, 14–7.

The year 1945 was Herber's last in professional football. It was a dismal season for the Giants, but Herber himself had one or two days of glory. One came in a game against the Philadelphia Eagles. The Giants were behind, 21–0. In the third quarter Herber exploded, passing like a man possessed. In the space of four minutes and forty-eight seconds, he fired three touchdown passes to end Frank Liebel. And in the final quarter he connected with Sam Fox for another score, the winning touchdown.

Playing only the second half, Herber completed ten of sixteen passes for 187 yards and four touchdowns. Barry Gottehrer, the historian of the New York Giants, called it ". . . one of football's most thrilling performances." In recalling his amazing outbreak, Herber says, "Hutson was great, but that day against Philadelphia, Liebel was as great an end as ever caught a pass."

When the season was over, Herber went back to Green Bay, this time for good.

Today Herber operates a soft drink franchise in Green Bay and De Pere, a city just to the south. Hunting and fishing are his principal means of exercise now.

In reviewing his career, Herber gives credit for his success to three coaches: Murph White at West High, Curly Lambeau, and Steve Owen of the Giants. He also lauds Don Hutson and John "Blood" McNally, a frequent target of Herber's early in his career. "They were the best receivers in the business," he says. "And don't forget those fellows who blocked for me. Without them I would have been a dead duck back there."

Walt Kiesling

Walt Kiesling—Big Kies was his nickname—spent his adult life-time in pro football, and although he never played on a league championship team and never coached one, he nevertheless de-serves ranking in the Hall of Fame right beside the most notable players and successful coaches.

Kiesling was a fun-loving giant of a man who saw duty as a player, assistant coach, and ultimately head coach. His career spanned thirty-four seasons until closed out by ill health. There were stopovers at Duluth, Pottsville, Chicago, with both the Bears and the Cardinals, and Green Bay. Most of his career was spent with the Pittsburgh Steelers, however. When quarterback Bobby Layne joined that team in 1958, he asked Big Kies how long he had played pro ball.

Kiesling smiled. "Until they wouldn't let me suit up any-more," he answered.

John "Blood" McNally, the legendary Green Bay halfback, and a contemporary of Kiesling's, remembers him "as the phys-ical duplicate of Babe Ruth."

Says Blood, "He was big like Ruth, and a left-hander, too. Like Ruth, he played his best when he had some belly on him." Despite his size, Kiesling had remarkable speed, and was adept at pulling from the line to lead a play.

Kiesling made his pro debut with Ole Haugsrud's Duluth Eskimos in 1926 as a 265-pound guard. Another guard on the team was Jim Manion, a mere 165 pounds. Newspapers in towns where the team played often featured a picture of Kiesling hold-ing Manion in his arms.

Kiesling's best days as a player were from 1929 to 1933 when he played guard for the Chicago Cardinals. He was the annual All League selection at that position. These were woeful days for the Cards, however, and they never finished higher than fourth in the league standings.

While Kiesling's name is absent from the NFL record manual, he helped to put Ernie Nevers' there. The day in 1929 when

Nevers scored his record six touchdowns against the Bears, Big Kies was his battering-ram blocker.

Kiesling's greatest thrill as a player came in 1934 as a member of the Chicago Bears' Monsters of the Midway team, one of pro football's most memorable powerhouses. They swept through a thirteen-game season without a defeat or tie. But in the championship game against the Giants the team stumbled, losing, 30–13, to a team that had been beaten five times that season in league competition.

Kiesling's career as a player went downhill after that. He was traded to Green Bay in 1935 and spent two seasons there. He joined the Steelers as a player-coach in 1937.

Walt Kiesling began in football as a schoolboy player at Cretin High in St. Paul. The school had no gym or locker room. To make the team, a boy had to live near enough to the school to go home, change into his uniform, and then report to the practice field.

He attended St. Thomas College in St. Paul and his long pro career began right afterward. He spent the 1926 and 1927 seasons with Ernie Nevers' Duluth Eskimos, and the next year moved on to the Pottsville Maroons.

The final two decades of Big Kies' career were as a coach of the Pittsburgh Steelers. He began as an assistant to Johnny Blood, but when Art Rooney fired Blood in 1937, Kiesling took over. He was put in charge again in 1941.

The team that he took over that year was the perennial cellar dweller in the NFL's Eastern Division. They had won a mere six games in their previous four seasons. But Kiesling turned them around. Soon they were playing winning football and attendance spiraled upward. They finished with a 7-4-1 record, the first winning season in the history of the club, and good enough to earn them second place behind the Washington Redskins.

Star of the team was Bill Dudley, a rookie from the University of Virginia, a young man with immense skill as a passer and breakaway runner. But World War II had struck, and Dudley, after just one season, went into the Air Force. In time, the whole nucleus of young players upon whom Kiesling was planning to build was called into the service. Greasy Neale came in as head coach and Walt became an assistant again.

Kiesling came back the last time as Steeler head coach in 1954 and enjoyed a brief moment of glory. The team won four of its first five games and seemed headed for a splendid season. Then suddenly everything went awry, and the club lost six of its next seven games and finished the year with a not so glittering 5-7 record.

In total, Kiesling served as Pittsburgh's head coach on four different occasions, a unique course of events to say the least. Ole Haugsrud, Kiesling's first pro coach, once clarified this record in an interview with Bill Boni, sports editor of the St. Paul *Dispatch and Pioneer Press.* "The thing about Walt was that he preferred to be an assistant," Haugsrud told Boni. "He was available whenever the Steelers needed somebody, yet he would much rather be an assistant than the boss."

Kiesling resigned his post with the Steelers in 1957 because of failing health. He died in 1962.

Dick McCann, former director of the Hall of Fame, once paid Walt Kiesling this tribute: "He didn't just watch pro football grow from the rocky sandlots. He shoved it along the way. He gave almost half a century to the game he loved."

George McAfee

The first time Bears' owner George Halas saw halfback George McAfee in action was in a training camp scrimmage in 1940. A mere 165-pounder, McAfee looked strangely out of place amidst the king-size Monsters of the Midway.

Sid Luckman, the quarterback, called a dive play.

"Oh, oh," Halas moaned to an assistant. "That kid's gonna get killed. The linebacker has smelled what's coming."

The ball was snapped. The linebacker hurtled through the opening. McAfee sprinted almost into his waiting arms, then whirled and was gone.

Halas was awed. "I think we've got something here," he said softly.

Halas was right, of course; he did have something—one of the greatest open-field runners of all time.

Consider this evidence. Red Grange once called McAfee "the

most dangerous man with a football in the game." Curly Lambeau of Green Bay cited him as "the best and most dangerous man the Packers have ever faced." Clark Shaughnessy described McAfee as "the greatest all-around back I have ever seen."

McAfee won such tributes on the basis of a relatively short career. At Duke a foot operation as a junior delayed his development, and he did not become a regular until his senior year. He played on the great Bear teams of 1940 and 1941, but then came a three-year stint with the U. S. Navy. He retired as a player after the 1950 season.

McAfee's own recollections of the Bears' training camp in 1940 dovetail with that of Halas'. "I never saw so many big men in all my life," he once recalled. "I was scared Halas would put me right in—but he didn't."

The first play that McAfee saw had Bill Osmanski carrying the ball. Harry Clark, a rookie halfback, tried to bring him down. "He was knocked cold—and he didn't make the tackle," McAfee remembers.

The play served as a valuable lesson. Says McAfee, "Whenever I ran the ball, I had that picture in my mind of Harry there on the ground, cold as a stone. I would run as fast as I could if there was any daylight."

McAfee was a star from the beginning. He won a pre-season game from the Brooklyn Dodgers by returning a punt 75 yards for the winning touchdown with 37 seconds left to play. Shortly afterward, when the team was dressing for a practice session, Sid Luckman mounted a stool, called for attention, and then made like a sideshow barker.

"Ladies and gentlemen," he began, pointing at McAfee, "you've read about it. You've seen it in the movies. But here it is in person—the one, the only, the original *Gone with the Wind.*"

The opening game of the season brought the Bears face to face with the Packers. Green Bay took an early lead on a field goal. McAfee grabbed the kickoff that followed and raced 93 yards for a touchdown. Later in the game, he passed to another rookie, Ken Kavenaugh, for a touchdown. The Bears won, 41–10, and both the season and George's career were off to an auspicious beginning.

The Bears won the Western Division crown that year, and then shocked the Redskins, 73–0, for the league championship.

McAfee's contribution was a 34-yard runback of one of Sammy Baugh's passes for touchdown No. 7 in the relentless parade.

The year 1941 was McAfee's best, despite an injury that kept him on the bench for two games. The Bears powered their way to their second straight championship, tripping the Giants, 37–9, in the playoff game. McAfee carried the ball 14 times for 81 yards and a touchdown. He played on another Bear championship team in 1946 after returning from the service.

McAfee enjoyed running back punts and kickoffs more than anything else, perhaps because he was so good at it. In his rookie year, for example, he ran back 22 punts for an amazing 851 yards. During his career, McAfee set a league record by averaging 12.78 yards on 112 punt returns. The record stands today.

In a game at Ebbets Field against Brooklyn, Jock Sutherland, the Dodgers' coach, told punter Billy Leckonby to boot the ball out of the end zone. "Don't kick it to McAfee," Jock instructed.

The kick went awry and the ball angled toward the sideline. McAfee zeroed in on it. He reached over the sideline to make the catch, just managing to keep his toes in bounds. Then he streaked 68 yards for a touchdown. Sutherland's comments were not recorded.

As this would suggest, McAfee was a game breaker. Often he would enter a close contest, execute one play for a touchdown, and then leave the game to the acclaim of the fans. He even came to be known as "one-play McAfee."

Once he joined the pros, McAfee employed a "secret weapon" to boost his speed and increase his elusiveness. In practice sessions during the week, George would wear regulation football shoes. But on the day of the game he would shed them for lightweight Oxford-type footwear. "It was almost as though I didn't have any shoes on at all," he once said.

Lightweight shoes may have helped, but McAfee also happened to have great natural speed. At Duke he was a track star and could run the 100-yard dash in 9.7. Jimmy Conzelman, the onetime coach of the Cardinals, said the reason McAfee was so slippery was that in addition to being a sprinter he had a hip shift. "That's something few really fast men ever develop," Conzelman said. "He puts the defense off balance, and fakes with his head as well as his arms and body."

McAfee played in pro football's "one-platoon era," and did

much more than merely run with the ball. He was a fine defensive player, and in 1941 and again in 1949 he intercepted six passes. He was also a splendid punter and as a rookie averaged 36.1 yards in that department. He once booted a 79-yard punt, the longest in the history of the Bears.

Actually, McAfee was a No. 1 draft choice not of the Bears, but of the Philadelphia Eagles. But Bert Bell, the Eagles' owner, had a halfback similar to McAfee in Davey O'Brien. Bell traded McAfee to the Bears for center Johnny Schiechl, tackle Milt Trost and end Les McDonald.

When George returned from the service, a pro football war—between the NFL and the All America Conference—was in full tilt. Three AAC clubs approached him, but McAfee signed with the Bears, winning a three-year contract, a rarity at Halas U.

During the early 1960's, McAfee served as an official—a head linesman—in the National Football League. In 1966, at forty-eight, he gave up this post to devote his full time to the McAfee Brothers Oil Company in Durham, North Carolina.

George Halas always regarded McAfee as something special. In 1965 Gale Sayers broke in with the Bears and set rookie scoring records with 22 touchdowns and 132 points. Often that year reporters asked Halas if he felt Sayers was better than McAfee. Halas had a stock answer. "The highest compliment you can pay a ballcarrier," he said, "is just to compare him with McAfee."

Steve Owen

Football is a game played down in the dirt, and it always will be. There's no use getting fancy about it.

This was the course that Steven Owen of the New York Giants followed. It won him renown as an All NFL tackle four times. It was the principle he followed in carving out a brilliant 22-year career as the Giant's head coach, winning the Eastern Division championship eight times and the NFL title twice. But besides the success and fame, this philosophy also caused days of anguish for Stout Steve, and eventually led to his undoing.

Jack Lavelle, Owen's chief scout in his years with the Giants, often told the story of how his boss was introduced to football.

One day Steve was riding his cow pony down a dusty road in Oklahoma when he came upon some boys playing a game he had never seen before. He watched for awhile, then asked a man who was standing nearby, "Hey, mister, what are they playing?"

"Football," the man said. "Would you like to try it?"

"Sure," said Steve. "What do I do?"

"Take the ball," the man said, "and try to run through those boys as far as the goalposts at the other end of the field."

Owen clutched the ball to his chest and started running. Some tacklers bounced off of him, while others were trampled. No one could even slow him down, and he breezed into the end zone at full gallop. Then he trotted back upfield, tossed the ball to the stranger, and said, "I did what you told me; now what?"

"Try it again," the man said, "but this time do it without your spurs."

The story is doubtlessly apocryphal, but it could be true. Steve was born in Cleo Springs in 1898 in what was then Indian Territory. His mother was a schoolmarm and his father was a Cherokee strip farmer. By the time he was twelve, Steve was a competent cowhand and a skilled rider. Even after a quarter of a century in New York, he remained as Oklahoman as a stand of sagebrush. He was natural and unaffected, and had a lazy way of speaking. Frank Graham wrote of him: "If you had never met him, you might think he had just checked his horse at the station in Enid, and expected to go back and reclaim it any day."

At sixteen, Steve weighed 220 pounds, and was 6 feet tall. After he finished high school in 1918, he enrolled in the Student Army Training Corps at Phillips University at Enid, Oklahoma. Because he was so big and solid, he was asked to play football.

In 1925, Steve traveled east with the Kansas City Cowboys for a game with the Giants. Now a bruising 240 pounds, he impressed the Giants so much that they purchased his contract from the Cowboys. The price was $500. "I had seen fat hogs go for more than they paid for me," Owen once said. "But in those days, a fat hog was a lot more valuable than a fat tackle." Owen was a standout with the team from the very beginning.

Football was a vastly different game in 1927 from what it is today. The ball was plumper and more difficult to pass, and the rules stated that one couldn't pass from closer than five yards behind the line of scrimmage. But the greatest difference was in the way the game was played. "We were a smash-and-shove gang," Owen said.

In a game against the Chicago Cardinals early in Steve's career, the Giants scored three touchdowns in the first ten minutes. The Cardinals became vengeful and set out to cripple the Giants physically. Owen took a tremendous beating from a Cardinal lineman. Late in the fourth quarter, when the Giants had the game safely tucked away, the lineman punched Steve in the mouth. The blow staggered Owen but he answered back with a prodigious left hook, getting his huge bulk behind it. The lineman fell as if poleaxed. As his teammates were carrying the lineman from the field, the referee, who had seen the fray, walked over to Steve, smiled and said, "Be nice, Steve, be nice."

"We were bone crushers in those days," Owen once said, "not fancy Dans."

Owen was popular with the players and highly regarded by Tim Mara, owner of the Giants. He was appointed co-coach during the 1931 season, collaborating with quarterback Benny Friedman. After the season Owen remained in New York and worked as a boss in a coalyard that Mara owned. Mara himself, or his son Jack, would call Steve almost every day to discuss the team. One day Mara asked Owen who he would like to see as coach.

"Guy Chamberlin," Owen said. "He was a tremendous end and he did a great job of coaching at Frankford. I think he's the best—college or professional—in the country."

Mara thanked Owen and told him he wanted to think it over. A few days later Mara called him again.

"Well, I've got my coach," he said.

"Good, who is it?"

"It's you," Mara answered.

Not only was Steve surprised, so were the Giant fans. They were expecting Mara to hire a "name."

"Owen seemed to get along with everyone, and he took his work seriously," Mara explained. "I just had confidence in him." Mara and Owen never had anything but a verbal agreement; that is, not until their later years together when the NFL came to insist upon written contracts.

In Owen's first season as head coach, the Giants finished fifth.

The next year (1933), they won the Eastern Division title, but lost to the Chicago Bears in the title game. In 1934 they again won the Eastern title, but this time they beat the Bears for the championship. This was the famous "sneakers" game. The temperature was nine degrees and the field at the Polo Grounds was frozen concrete-hard. During half time the Giants discarded their football cleats in favor of basketball shoes. They were able to get good footing as a result, and scored 27 points in the final period to overcome Chicago's lead and win, 30–13.

In 1935 the Giants won the Eastern Division title, but lost to Detroit in the championship game. The next year the club collapsed, finishing 5-6-1 for the season. Owen reacted by launching a thorough rebuilding program. He released seventeen regulars; at training camp rookies outnumbered veterans by more than two to one. The brightest prospect, fullback Ward Cuff from Marquette, Owen had scouted himself.

Owen also completely revamped the offense. He developed a platoon system, two complete squads, each one equally adept at playing both offense and defense. The idea worked well. Individual players didn't tire as quickly and were less susceptible to injury as a result. And the rivalry that developed between the A and B squads kept both of them in fighting trim.

But Owen's greatest innovation that year was the A formation. The Giants would come out of the huddle and line up:

```
            C
       ETGBGTBE
       B       B
```

Then the line would shift one way and the backfield the other. This was one alternative:

```
       E T TGC G E
              B   B
          B
          B
```

The A formation gained 365 yards for the Giants the day that Owen introduced it against Washington. But the game also marked the pro debut of one Sammy Baugh, whose passes carried the day for the Redskins. In time, however, the A worked to perfection. In 1938 and 1939, the Giants won the Eastern Division crown, and in 1938 they captured the NFL championship.

Although throughout his career Owen was often criticized for his "close-to-the-vest" style of coaching, he was not afraid to introduce new techniques. Most teams, when they win the toss, elect to receive the opening kickoff. But often the Giant teams would elect to kick off. It was Owen's theory that the opposition was often jittery and inclined to make a mistake in the early stages of a game.

Yet it must be said that Owen was no gambler. His teams were noted for their marked emphasis on the ground game, with plenty of power off tackle and around the ends. "There's no mystery to coaching," he said. "You must have the horses. The same coach, with material, can win a championship one season, then finish last the next with the same material."

The blackest moments of Owen's more than two decades with the Giants came late in 1946 when it was learned that two of his players, Frank Filchock, the team's All Pro halfback, and Merle Hapes, their fullback, had become involved with crooked gamblers. The news broke on the eve of the Giants-Bears championship playoff that year.

Hapes admitted receiving an offer of $2,500 to throw the game from a gambler named Alvin Paris, but denied he had accepted the money. Filchock admitted that he knew Paris, but denied any knowledge of the bribe. Owen reacted to the news as if he had been struck by a blind-side block. He was boiling with rage when he was called to New York's Police Headquarters where Paris was being questioned. Commissioner Arthur Wallender told Owen that Paris had refused to talk.

"Let me take that ——— into the inspector's room for two minutes," Steve said. "I'll get you that confession."

"I believe you would, Steve, I believe you would," the commissioner said. "But of course I can't do that."

NFL Commissioner Bert Bell ruled that Hapes couldn't play in the championship game but that Filchock could. The Giant back was a heroic figure, but the Bears were too powerful; they won, 24–14. Later, Filchock declared that he had lied earlier and that he, too, had been offered a bribe by Paris. For failing to report the bribe attempts to the police or club officials, Filchock and Hapes were suspended indefinitely. Filchock was reinstated in 1950, Hapes in 1954.

Filchock, by virtue of his powerful rushes and fine passing, had made the A formation click, and had almost single-handedly carried the Giants to the division title. With both Filchock and Hapes gone, the Giants fell upon evil days. They were 2-8-2 in 1947, and 4-8 in 1948. Attendance dropped drastically, and those fans that did turn out booed lustily. Hundreds of letters poured into the Giant offices, and most of them called for Owen's scalp.

But Tim Mara defended Owen. "What's happening to us isn't the coach's fault," he said. "We're not giving Owen the players to win. It's our fault, not his."

In 1948 the Giants began to come back. They acquired Charlie Conerly from the University of Mississippi, a passer who threw like Sammy Baugh and whose achievements would become almost as grandiose, Emlen Tunnell, a demon on pass defense, and end Bill Swiacki. Owen again developed a platoon system, but this time he divided the squad into offensive and defensive units.

It was during this period that Owen unveiled one of his most conspicuous achievements. Pro football of the day was dominated by the Cleveland Browns. Coached by a wizard named Paul Brown, Cleveland featured a variation of the T formation that was virtually unstoppable. Quarterback Otto Graham was especially adept at connecting on sideline passes to Dante Lavelli and Mac Speedie, while fullback Marion Motly ran trap plays up the middle to prevent the defense from spreading against the passes.

Owen scouted the Browns thoroughly, and in the first meeting of the teams, the Giants displayed what came to be known as the umbrella defense (because the arrangement of the backs resembled the shape of an open umbrella). It looked like this:

```
      E  T  G  G  T  E
            C
      B           B
         B     B
```

The ends would slide back to pick off passes, while on rushes the center would jam up the middle. The system had a stunning effect upon the Browns. Otto Graham had three passes intercepted in the first half, and missed twelve straight before he finally connected.

"Let's play a little poker with this fellow," Owen drawled between halves, and he switched from a 6-1-4 to a 5-3-3 setup. The Giants scored only one touchdown, but it was enough because the Browns didn't score any. The game marked the first time that Cleveland had ever been shut out.

Eventually, teams learned to poke holes in the umbrella. They ran on it and used short passes, and its effectiveness was diminished.

Men like Buddy Parker of Detroit, and Paul Brown of Cleveland were revolutionizing the pro offense. Spread formations became the order of the day; this would lead to the slot-T, and eventually the slotback would move to the other side of the line into a flanking position. But Steve Owen was not a part of the change. He disdained the new and fancy patterns, preferring techniques that had worked for him in the past. "You've got to get down on your belly; you've got to go nose to nose," he said. "That's football."

But pro football had become much more. One December day in 1953, during a season in which the Giants stumbled to a 3-9 record, Steve Owen stepped down as head coach.

There were no more big jobs. He coached in Canada at Toronto, Calgary and Saskatchewan, and he had a brief stopover in semipro ball as coach of the Syracuse Stormers. He returned to the Giants as scout in 1963, a year before his death.

Tom Landry, defensive coach for the Giants beginning in 1954, and who had been a defensive back under Owen, changed the 6-1-4 to a 4-3-4. Quickly this evolved into the modern three-linebacker setup. It was thus not just the Giants, but all of pro football that learned from Steve Owen.

Said George Halas shortly after Owen's death, "He taught us all plenty. He was the first to stress the importance of defense, and the first to see the advantage of settling for field goals instead of gambling for touchdowns. Every team strives today to do what Steve was doing twenty years ago."

Hugh (Shorty) Ray

Shorty Ray never carried the ball, made a tackle or coached from the sidelines, but not a soul has ever questioned his credentials for Hall of Fame membership.

Ray was technical adviser and supervisor of officials for the National Football League during the years the pro game was experiencing serious growing pains. Ray's contribution was immense. He provided the game with the streamlining it needed in order to win fan appeal.

Ray was well known in the administration of sports before he joined the pro ranks. In 1925 he organized the American Officials Association which conducted clinics to consider officiating and rules-interpretation problems. A few years later, the National Federation of State High School Athletic Associations asked Ray to write a football code. It was a masterpiece, a model for all future rulebooks. In 1938, George Halas of the Bears, like Ray a University of Illinois alumnus, persuaded him to apply his talents to the pro game.

Ray gave pro football a thorough shaking up. At the end of each season he made recommendations for new rules and urged that others be eliminated. He moved the goalposts back to the goal line. He increased the number of plays per game by twelve, simply by insisting that the ball be relayed from an official out-of-bounds instead of having a retrieving official carry it back. He even redesigned the ball, a move that helped to make the forward pass a more effective weapon.

If imitation is the sincerest form of flattery, then Ray was as much praised as any football personality ever. When the All America Conference started play in 1946, and again when the American Football League began operation in 1959, rules Ray had developed were followed almost to the letter.

Ray visited the training camps each year to explain rule changes to players and coaches. He forced his officials to become the most knowledgeable people on the field, absolute masters of rulebook information. He even gave them written tests. "At one time," Ray said, "officials couldn't score over 95 percent on a written test—even with a rulebook at their elbow. Now they can score better than 95 percent, and without the rulebook."

During a game Ray would sit in an obscure corner of the stadium, poring over his charts or making calculations on his slide rule. He took more than 300,000 stopwatch observations after becoming the league's technical director.

One fascinating item he discovered was that the faster a game is played, the more time it consumes, which isn't as contradictory as it first seems. "The faster you play, the more plays you create," he explained. "The more plays you create, the more situations you develop in which the clock can be stopped—incomplete passes, out-of-bounds runs, field goals and the like." Ray once proved to Curly Lambeau that Green Bay had beaten themselves in a game against Chicago by "playing too fast."

Ray's research also revealed that 51 percent of a team's offensive plays originate in its own territory. Only 5 percent originate between the opponent's 19-yard line and the goal line.

Ray showed that the period of action for a play was no more than 5.22 seconds, and the actual action time in a game consumes only 13 minutes, 50 seconds.

Ray stood 5 feet 6 and weighed 136, but although he was lacking in stature he was a versatile athlete. In 1906 he was the first varsity basketball captain at Illinois. He died in 1956.

Besides encouraging football efficiency, Ray was also dedicated to safety. "Football is great as long as you don't get hurt," he often said. Mark Duncan, the present supervisor of officials, once observed, "Ray's idea of a big afternoon was to see everyone leave the field without limping."

Clyde (Bulldog) Turner

When the great Sammy Baugh left his home in Texas in 1937 to join the Redskins, Washington owner George Marshall demanded that his new star dress up in full cowboy regalia—chaps, boots and a ten-gallon hat—to gain some extra publicity when he met the press. To Baugh, who had been city-raised, the idea was a bit preposterous.

In June 1940, Clyde (Bulldog) Turner arrived at Chicago's

municipal airport wearing chaps, boots and a ten-gallon hat. He had come to town to sign his contract with the Chicago Bears. George Halas had nothing to do with Turner's getup, however. Turner had been born a cowboy and had always dressed as if he were about to take part in a rodeo.

Turner was soon to prove that bulldogging steers was only one of his natural talents. Bulldogging enemy lineman and backs was another. In his thirteen-year career with the Chicago Bears he established himself as professional football's "Mr. Center." Big, fast and with superb reactions, he was to win All League honors an incredible eight times and was a bulwark for four Bear championship teams.

Turner's career in football was slow getting started. At Newman High School in Sweetwater, Texas, he tried out at guard, tackle and halfback, but could never win a starting assignment. College football seemed very remote—for two reasons. He was not big, weighing only 155. He lacked the money. Although only sixteen when he graduated from high school, he embarked on a career as a cattle trader and earned money enough in a year to enter Hardin-Simmons in Abilene, Texas. He also consumed enough double-thick steaks to boost his weight to 190 pounds.

When the team's first-string center was injured, coach Kimbrough asked Turner to try out for that position. "Right then and there," Bulldog recalls, "I knew that I had found my place." Although center was to be Turner's place all right, he was to prove amazingly versatile. After he joined the Bears he learned the assignments of every other position on each play. During practice sessions he drilled not only at center but everywhere else except quarterback. Often he filled in as either tackle or guard during games.

During Turner's junior year at Hardin-Simmons someone told Frank Korch, a scout for the Chicago Bears, to keep an eye on the big, blond youngster. Korch was impressed by Bulldog's performance in the East-West Shrine game in San Francisco in 1940 and convinced Halas to draft him. It must be said that Turner was not generally recognized as a hot prospect. During the draft meeting that year, one club owner was heard to ask, "Who is this guy Turner and where is Hardin-Simmons?" After Bulldog had been drafted by the Bears, the Detroit

Lions became curious about him. Dick Richards, the Lions' owner, did some checking and learned that Turner was highly regarded in the Southwest. Richards then tried to cozy up to the 6-foot-2, 235-pound prize. He wined and dined Turner and gave him $150 to have some urgent dental work performed, the damage having resulted from an enemy elbow or two. All Richards got for his efforts was trouble. League president Carl Storck fined the Detroit owner $5,000 for "tampering" with a player on the draft list of another team.

The Bear team that Bulldog joined was one of the most powerful pro squads ever assembled. They won the Western Division crown and overwhelmed the Washington Redskins for the championship, 73–0. Turner contributed to the rout by scoring his first pro touchdown when he intercepted a pass in the third period and galloped 24 yards for the score.

If he had not preferred to play center, Turner might well have been an All League back. In a game against Card-Pitt in 1944 the Bears were short of backfield men because of injuries. Turner was asked to substitute. To the amazement of the opposition, he consistently ground out long gains. His most notable contribution that day was a 48-yard touchdown sprint. The Bears won, 48–7.

The feat that gave Turner his greatest satisfaction came during the 1947 season. The Bears were playing the Redskins. Turner intercepted one of Sammy Baugh's tosses near the Bears' goal line and ran it back a stunning 96 yards for a touchdown. What pleased Turner was not the length of the run, although it rated as the third longest runback in NFL history at the time, but the character of it. Bulldog kept close to the sideline all the way, and faked out one tackler after another with his quick side steps and changes of speed. As Turner neared the Redskins' end zone, Sammy Baugh came angling toward the rampaging Turner. Baugh struck at the 12-yard line but scarcely slowed Turner down.

Indeed, Turner was a wizard at intercepting passes. Often he would leap high in the air to snare the ball, almost as if he had springs in his legs. In 1942, Turner's eight interceptions led the league. In the final game of the season against the Cardinals he stole one of Wilson Schwenk's aerials to beat out the Packers' Don Hutson.

Turner had his nose broken at least half-a-dozen times. Late in his career he took to wearing a face mask during games. He called it his "birdcage." He wore it, not to preserve his physiognomy, but because he regarded a broken nose as being "inconvenient" to his style of play.

Turner was a member of the Army Air Force during World War II and was assigned to Colorado Springs where he joined a service team. The club needed strength at guard and Turner was asked to switch to that position. He did—and played with such distinction that both the Associated Press and United Press named him to their All Service teams. When he returned to the Bears, Turner resumed his status as an All League center.

Once asked to name his toughest opponent, Turner cited Bill Neale, a 290-pound lineman for Green Bay. He said that Neale, besides his bulk, had an intuitive sense, the ability to "beat the gun" on every play. Clarke Hinkle, the Packers' fullback, and Mel Hein, center for the New York Giants, were also high on Turner's list. Although Turner played opposite Hein when the latter was beyond his prime, he called him "the greatest center of all time."

Turner quit as a player in 1952. He served as an assistant coach of the Bears from 1953 to 1956. In 1962, Bulldog was enticed out of retirement by Harry Wismer to become head coach of the New York Titans in the then struggling American Football League. The Titans folded at the end of the season. Afterward Turner returned to his Texas ranch where he raises cattle, sheep and horses.

At the height of his career, Turner coauthored a book entitled *Playing the Line.* It never made any best-seller lists. Little wonder. Turner "wrote the real book" every time he laced on a pair of cleats.

1967

Chuck Bednarik

The date was December 26, 1960. The scene was Philadelphia's Franklin Field, the Philadelphia Eagles vs. the Green Bay Packers for the NFL championship.

Late in the fourth quarter, the Eagles held a slim lead, 17–14. But quarterback Bart Starr had the Packers rolling. Passing from midfield, Starr hit Gary Knafelc at the Eagle 30. Knafelc was spilled immediately. It was first down. Less than a minute remained. A pass to Knafelc was good for eight yards. The clock was moving. The Packers didn't bother to huddle. The ball was snapped immediately. Starr peddled back, looking. His end-zone receivers were covered. He had no choice; he had to go to his safety valve. He looped a short swing pass to fullback Jimmy Taylor.

Taylor gathered it in and exploded for the end zone. The Eagle defenders came roaring to meet him. Dan Burroughs missed. Maxie Baugham bounced off. Now Taylor was at the 10. Chuck Bednarik roared in. He was an awesome 6 feet 3, 235 pounds. They thudded together and Bednarik applied a bear hug. His arms were like a steel collar. He squeezed, then smothered the squirming Taylor to the ground.

Bednarik watched the clock. The gun sounded. "O.K., Jimmy," he said. "You can get up now; the game is over."

For Chuck Bednarik, age thirty-six, this was the most satisfying game of his career, the climax of a truly incredible season. Bednarik had been a member of a championship team before—

in 1949, his rookie year. But he played little that season. This time it was different, acutely different.

In his first years with the Eagles, Bednarik had been a line-backer and a fearsome one. Then in 1955 he switched to offensive center. During pre-season practice in 1960, defensive coach Jerry Williams asked Bednarik to work out with the defensive unit. "It's just in case something happens," Williams said.

That something happened in a fierce game against the Browns in Cleveland, the fifth game of the season. Linebacker Bob Pellegrini was seriously injured. Coach Buck Shaw sent Bednarik in as his replacement.

Chuck went in—and stayed in. For the rest of the season, except for punt returns and kickoffs, he never came out, a rare one-platoon player in a two-platoon era. After the team had won the championship, Buck Shaw had this to say: "We got to hand it to the old pro. Bednarik's the one that held us together on offense and defense."

When he uttered these words, Shaw may have had in mind a critical November game against the Giants at Yankee Stadium. The Eagles were ahead, 17–10. In the closing minutes the Giants launched a final drive. Frank Gifford, the Giants' star halfback, took a pass from George Shaw on the Eagles' 30, then paused a split second to find an opening. The pause was a mistake. In barged Bednarik with a vicious tackle. Gifford never saw him. The ball spurted out of his hands and Chuck Weber of the Eagles recovered.

Bednarik was elated that the Eagles had the ball and, as a result, the game. He waved his arms and jumped in delight. Gifford lay still. Suddenly Bednarik dropped to his knees beside the unconscious Gifford. In came the Giant trainers to carry him from the field.

A great furor followed. Gifford was rushed to the hospital, where doctors announced he had suffered a severe concussion, narrowly escaping a fractured skull. Giant quarterback Charlie Conerly accused Bednarik of making an illegal tackle, of being "a cheap-shot artist," and there was bloodthirsty talk in the Giant dressing room.

Bednarik, a sensitive man, may have suffered more than Gifford. He deluged Frank's hospital room with flowers, telegrams, and letters. Chuck gained some solace from Giant linebacker

Sam Huff who told him, "You did nothing wrong. It was a clean tackle." Of the four hundred letters and cards Bednarik received from fans, all but two were in his favor.

Bednarik stoutly defended the tackle. "I hit him good and I hit him clean," he said. "In this game a man can get hurt."

Football was always a stormy and violent piece of business to Bednarik. Indeed, life was. He had a rough-and-tumble childhood in Bethlehem, Pennsylvania, where his father worked in a steel mill. Young Chuck's first football was a stocking stuffed with leaves. The first real ball he ever had was a premium he received in exchange for twenty-five coffee bags.

At Bethlehem High School, Chuck starred in three sports—basketball, baseball and football. He was a fullback. One day the team's regular center was clotheslined by a mathematics exam and rendered ineligible. Chuck took over in the middle of the line.

After high school, Chuck, then eighteen, entered the Air Force. Before his nineteenth birthday, he was a veteran of six bombing missions as a waist gunner on a B-24. He was discharged in the fall of 1945 and returned to Bethlehem with thirty missions to his credit, an Air Medal with four oak leaf clusters, five battle stars, and a yen to play college football.

He went to see Jack Butler, his high school coach. Butler put in a call to Coach George Munger at the University of Pennsylvania.

"What position does he play?" Munger asked.

"Center," Butler replied.

"I've got five of them, and one's the team captain," Munger said. "But send him down and I'll look at him."

Munger's centers were seventeen- and eighteen-year-olds. Chuck was twenty. When he strode in, all 6 feet 2, 215 pounds of him, Munger's eyes popped.

In no time Chuck was a Penn regular. He played both center and linebacker. "He could have played fullback or end, too," said Munger, "because he had the size, speed, and strength for both positions."

Chuck was a devastating blocker and furious tackler. A reporter on the *Daily Pennsylvanian*, the student paper, nicknamed him "the Clutch" because he made so many high, one-handed tackles. He also spilled runners in the more orthodox way, and in one game it was estimated that he made over 50 percent of all his team's tackles. He could kick the ball and did all of Penn's punting.

Twice Chuck was an All America selection and in his senior year—1948—he won the Maxwell Award given to the best college football player in America.

When Chuck graduated from Penn, another war was raging, this between the NFL and the All America Conference. Chuck got pinned down in the cross fire. At first the Brooklyn Dodgers of the AAC appeared to have landed him, but eventually the Eagles, who made him a bonus selection, got his name on the dotted line.

There must have been days when the Philadelphia quarterbacks wished that Bednarik had signed with Brooklyn. For four years he had played single-wing style, where the ball is centered to a back stationed five yards away. Chuck mashed many a quarterback's fingers getting used to the abbreviated snap of the T.

During his first year with the Eagles, Bednarik spent plenty of time on the bench. He played behind Alex Wojciechowicz, a five-year veteran. Like Bednarik, Wojciechowicz was originally a center, but he played on the right side of the line in Greasy Neale's 7-4 defense, and was the acknowledged master in the art of "chugging," delaying an end in his sprint downfield.

Bednarik broke into the Eagle lineup during a period of great change and development in pro football. The sophisticated offense initiated by Paul Brown of Cleveland, and others, demanded that the linebacker be a man of many skills. He had to be adept on the pass rush, or at plugging a hole in the line. He had to protect hook zones on pass plays, or swing wide to stop a halfback sweep. He had to be big, tall and very agile. Bednarik fitted perfectly. Along with Sam Huff of the Giants, and Joe Schmidt of the Lions, Bednarik helped to spearhead the development of modern-day defenses.

Joe Trimble, who coached the Eagles from 1952 to 1955, once said that Bednarik had "superhuman qualities" when it came to diagnosing plays. He had the gift of being able to be in the right place at the right time, as an army of enemy receivers and running backs would be willing to testify. Paul Hornung is one of them.

In the third quarter of the 1960 championship game, with the Eagles leading, 10–6, Green Bay drove deep into Philadelphia territory. Starr handed to Hornung who took off on a power sweep behind fierce blocking, but then cut away from his blockers at the 30-yard line. Bednarik was waiting. He charged into big Paul and pancaked him to the ground. The impact was such that Hornung stayed on the sidelines for most of the rest of the game.

"I knew Hornung had a habit of leaving his blockers to cut back," Bednarik said afterward. "Sometimes it got him a lot of yardage. I figured he'd do it again. And he did."

Bednarik won All Pro honors in eight of his thirteen years with the Eagles. He quit after the 1959 season, then later decided to return. It was an uncommonly wise decision. In 1960 he realized his ambition of a championship and won enduring fame as well.

Charles Bidwill

Although the St. Louis Cardinals, except for one brief period, have enjoyed little in the way of on-the-field success, in the matter of historical eminence the club has no equal. The Cardinals were founded in Chicago in 1898, twenty-two years before the National Football League, an era when backfield men crashed head on into the line, without helmets, and every play ended in an enormous pileup.

Chris O'Brien was the founder of the team. At first they were known as the Morgan A.C. They played their home games at a field near 61st and Racine streets. One day O'Brien got a chance to buy some jerseys that once belonged to the University of Chicago at a bargain price. The jerseys were "cardinal" in color so he called the team Cardinals. Eventually, the Chicago Cardinals they became.

In 1929, O'Brien sold the club to Dr. David Jones, a Chicago physician, for $25,000. Despite the fact that he hired the fabled

Ernie Nevers as player-coach, the Cards were never much more than mediocre.

One evening early in 1933, Dr. Jones was invited to attend a dinner party aboard the private yacht of Charles W. Bidwill, a wealthy Chicago lawyer who maintained an avid interest in sports. He had once owned an interest in a semipro baseball team, and later he was to acquire controlling interest in Hawthorne Park, a Chicago racetrack.

During the evening, Bidwill and Dr. Jones became involved in a casual conversation. Suddenly Bidwill asked if the Cardinals were for sale.

Dr. Jones said that they might be. It depended upon the price.

"How much are you asking?" Bidwill said.

"Fifty thousand dollars," Dr. Jones answered, an astonishing price considering that new franchises had been established for less than one-tenth that amount in recent years. Bidwill said nothing and Dr. Jones all but forgot the conversation.

A few days later the doctor received a phone call. "It's a deal," he heard Bidwill say. It took Dr. Jones a few minutes to realize what Bidwill was talking about.

Bidwill had an enthusiastic interest in pro football through his friendship with George Halas, owner of the Chicago Bears. After the 1932 season, Halas found himself hard-pressed to raise enough money to buy out a troublesome partner, and it was Bidwill who came to his rescue, lending Halas the $5,000 he needed to swing the deal and preserve the franchise.

The son of a Chicago politician, Bidwill was born and raised not far from the old Chicago Cubs ball park. Joe Tinker, of Tinker-to-Evers-to-Chance fame, was one of his boyhood heroes. Bidwill was a Bears' fan almost from the day George Halas moved the franchise from Decatur to Chicago. His interest in the Bears was so deeply rooted that he sometimes found it difficult to boost the Cards, even after he owned the club.

Once, Jimmy Conzelman, the Cardinals' coach, was leaving with the club on a road trip to New York to play the Giants. He stopped in at Bidwill's office before he left. "You're coming to New York with us, aren't you?" Conzelman asked.

"I should say not," Bidwill shot back. "The Bears and Packers are playing here that same afternoon. How could I miss that?"

The Cardinals suffered through lean times during the 1930's and early 1940's. They were thoroughly overshadowed by their crosstown rivals season after season. During one string, beginning in 1937 and extending into 1943, the Cards dropped thirteen out of fourteen contests to the Bears. (They played each other twice during the season in those days.)

The club finished last in the Western Division in 1943, and the following year almost gave up the ghost altogether. They merged with the Pittsburgh Steelers to form a club called Card-Pitt. This amalgamation helped the two clubs survive the financial rigors imposed by World War II. When the Cards resumed operations on their own again in 1945, they finished in their accustomed place in the standings—dead last.

That year, however, did have a bright spot. Although the Cardinals only won one game, that victory happened to be achieved at the expense of the Bears. After the game, Bidwill declared that his loyalty to the Bears was beginning to dissipate. "I knew it," he said, "when I saw Marshall Goldberg score that last touchdown."

Bidwill was faced with a new problem in 1946. The All America Conference put a team in Chicago called the Rockets. Now the Cards had not just one competitor, but two.

Bidwill responded to this challenge by building the best Cardinal team ever. It boasted football's "dream backfield"—Pat Harder at fullback, Paul Christman at quarterback, and halfbacks Marshall Goldberg and, in 1947, Charley Trippi.

Young Trippi, an All American from the University of Georgia, was undoubtedly the most talented player in Cardinal history. He could run, throw, pass and kick. Bidwill snatched him from the clutches of the New York Yankees of the All America Conference, signing him shortly after the Sugar Bowl game of January 1, 1947, in which Trippi starred.

The feuding between the two leagues was bitter, and Bidwill talked Trippi into withholding the announcement that he had signed, to give Dan Topping and the New York Yankees the impression that they were still in the running. Trippi told Topping he planned to come to New York to discuss terms. The Yankees alerted the press, radio and television, and rolled out the red carpet. But Trippi showed up in Topping's office a few hours before the scheduled meeting and disclosed he had signed with Bidwill.

The Cardinals whipped the Bears in the final game of the 1947 season to take the Western Division crown, and then went on to win the NFL title, edging the Philadelphia Eagles, 28–21. But Bidwill never shared in this triumph. He had died suddenly of pneumonia earlier in the year. He was fifty-one.

In Bidwill's fifteen years as president of the Cardinals, they did not have a single financially successful year. Yet Bidwill persevered; he would not permit the club to fail.

"Charley always knew the NFL would reach its present status," says the Bears' George Halas. "He had a standard answer for anyone critical of the league or of football. He'd look at the guy and snap, 'Why, you don't know what you're talking about. This is a great game.' "

The Cardinals moved to St. Louis after the 1959 season. The club is now owned and operated by Bidwill's sons. Charles (Stormy) Bidwill, Jr., is president, and William Bidwill vice-president. Both campaigned for their father's election to the Hall of Fame. Stormy Bidwill once remarked, "We feel our father should have been one of the first in there. Without people like him, there would be no NFL today."

Paul Brown

One summer's night in 1944, Mickey McBride, a short and stocky, well-to-do Cleveland businessman, walked into the sports department of the Cleveland *Plain Dealer*, a franchise to operate a team in the new All America Conference tucked away in his pocket. "Who," he asked veteran sportswriter John Dietrich, "is the best football coach in the country?"

Dietrich didn't hesitate. "Paul Brown," he answered.

A few weeks later, the thirty-six-year-old Brown signed a five-year contract as coach and general manager of McBride's yet un-named team. So began an exciting chapter in the history of professional football. Brown introduced new scouting, training and coaching techniques, and developed the forward pass into a lethal weapon. For more than a decade beginning in 1946, the

Cleveland Browns—the only team ever named after a coach—
were a football dynasty, and Paul Brown himself became the
most dominant figure in the game.

Dynasty building was not something new to Paul Brown. He
had been through it several times before.

Brown first won fame as a coach in Massillon, Ohio, which,
fittingly, was one of the first hotbeds of professional football in
America. As coach of Massillon High, Brown developed a team
that became the scourge of Ohio scholastic competition, winning six consecutive state championships. The 1940 team, which
Brown has cited as his best, scored 477 points, while Massillon
opponents got just six.

It was a case of hometown boy makes good. Brown was born
in Norwalk, Ohio, in 1908, and his family moved to Massillon
when he was twelve.

As a youngster, Brown weighed only 125 after three good
meals, yet he sought to play football at Massillon High. "He
wasn't big enough to carry the water bucket," his coach recalls.
"But he played quarterback, and the kids believed in him and
he ran them like a Napoleon."

When Brown entered Ohio State in 1926, he made the frosh
baseball and football teams, but he decided he was too small to
carve out much of a career in Big Nine (later Big Ten) football,
so he transferred to little Miami University in Oxford, Ohio.
He was quarterback on the 1929 and 1930 teams, not a notable
player but a tough competitor.

In 1930 he landed his first coaching job at Savern Academy,
the Navy's prep school in Maryland. His first year the team won
the state title.

In 1932 Brown started at Massillon and the enormous success
he achieved there won him offers from small colleges throughout the state. He turned them all down. Ohio State University
was where he wanted to coach, and in 1941 the Buckeyes signed
him.

The Brown magic worked again. In his first year at Ohio
State, the team chalked up a 6-1-1 record. The next season they
won nine of the ten games they played, and were voted the
country's No. 1 team by the Associated Press. The wartime draft
decimated the squad, but the next year, with most of his players

seventeen-year-olds, Brown still managed to win half the games on the schedule.

Brown joined the Navy in 1944 and took over the football team at the Great Lakes Naval Training Center. He made the team a winner—naturally. One of his victories in 1945 was the upset of the year, a 39–7 win over Notre Dame.

It was while Brown was football coach and athletic officer at Great Lakes that McBride signed him to coach Cleveland. He promised Brown a salary of $1,000 until the war ended, and, once the league began operation, he was to receive $20,000 a season, plus 15 percent of the profits. No coach had ever been offered so lucrative a deal, yet Brown was to prove an immense bargain.

Brown knew where to find football players and he went after them aggressively. He hired Ohio State's Lou Groza, who was to rewrite the record book for field-goal kicking, and OSU's All America tackle, Bill Willis. Also from Ohio State he signed end Dante Lavelli and halfback Eugene Fekete. Brown had scouted a big fleet halfback named Marion Motley at the University of Nevada, whom he had first seen play at McKinley High in Canton. Paul tucked Motley away on his team at Great Lakes, along with another player that Brown had taken to, a single-wing tailback by the name of Otto Graham. Graham, of course, was to become a super quarterback and the key figure in the Browns' attack.

This was the nucleus. But Brown also lured players away from the National Football League. And when the NFL's Rams exited Cleveland for Los Angeles, Paul prevailed upon several players to transfer to the Browns and stay in Cleveland.

In the early summer of 1946, Cleveland set up its training camp at Bowling Green University in northwestern Ohio. Brown went at a job like a military commander preparing for a crucial battle. From top to bottom, he ran a no-nonsense operation. There was all the standard training camp fare—calisthenics, dummy scrimmages, signal practice, special diets and bed checks. But Brown added refinements. "We'd start the year with Paul dictating on how to run," one player recalls. "He'd say, 'When you run, clench your fists a little bit, point your toes, etc.' We'd have to write all that down."

At the beginning of the training season, each player was issued a blank loose-leaf notebook. By mid-September each player's book was bulging with diagrams of defenses and offenses. Each man not only had to know his assignment on each play, but everyone else's as well. No one dozed in class. No one left a practice session without permission.

"We want the best," Brown told the players. "We'll settle for nothing less. One day when people think of pro football, I want them to think of the Cleveland Browns."

He required his players to maintain certain standards in appearance, like wearing clean T-shirts in camp, and ties and jackets when they appeared in a public place. One day a candidate for the team, a lineman with a splendid college record, knocked on the door of Brown's room. "You Brown?" the player asked. The coach stared down at the young man's soiled slacks and unshined shoes; then he scanned his unshaven chin.

"I'm sorry," Brown said icily. "There's been a mistake. See the business manager. He'll arrange your transportation home."

Brown made revolutionary changes in pro football offense. Before Brown, passing was pretty much a man-to-man piece of strategy, the quarterback firing to a single receiver. The other men who went downfield acted as decoys or merely stayed out of the way. But under the Brown system, every eligible man had a carefully rehearsed job to do, with the whole idea being to force the defense into making a mistake. There was a primary receiver, but there were secondary receivers, too, and the ball went to the man who did the best job of getting the jump on the defense.

A quick glance at the records of the All America Conference reveals the success of Brown's efforts. The first game the team ever played drew 60,135 to Cleveland Municipal Stadium. Joyously they watched the Browns take apart the Miami Seahawks, 44–0. But it was not an exceptional outing for the team; it was merely representative of the way they acted during the four years the AAC was in operation. They won 52, lost four and tied two, and took the league championship each season.

One of the rare losses that the Browns suffered was pinned on them by the San Francisco 49ers. The score was 56–28, and marked the highest point total ever accrued against the team. After the game Brown let his anger show.

"Apparently you think all you need to do to win is show up," he told the players. "Well, this attitude better change in a hurry. If necessary, we'll sell the whole team and start with men who want to play this game."

The next week the Browns steamrollered the Los Angeles Dons, 61–14.

So powerful were the Browns that they virtually eliminated competition, and league attendance began to fall as a result. Some sportswriters and league officials began to grumble about this. "Don't complain to me," Brown said. "I'm primarily a football teacher, not a professional promoter. If we win before 10,000 fans, that's swell. If we lose before 80,000, that's awful."

In 1949 the All America Conference drowned in a sea of red ink. The Browns, and the San Francisco 49ers, too, joined the National Football League. There the Browns quickly established themselves among the elite, and they ended their inaugural season in the league tied with the New York Giants at the top of the American Conference standings. They disposed of the Giants in a playoff game, and then met the Los Angeles Rams for the league crown before 30,000 fans on a bitter-cold December day in Cleveland. Otto Graham and the Rams' Bob Waterfield hooked up in a frantic passing duel, but the game was decided by Lou Groza's right foot. With twenty-eight seconds remaining, Groza booted a field goal that gave the Browns a 30–28 win. Now they were champions of the National Football League, and Paul Brown had run out of football worlds to conquer.

This was also the season that pro football adopted the unlimited substitution rule. It enabled Brown to exert even greater control over the conduct of the game. He employed a "messenger system," whereby two players would take turns bringing in plays from the sidelines.

Brown was often criticized for this practice—"He's taking the game away from the boys" was the complaint heard most often—but if the system was disadvantageous, it never reflected in the team's performance. The club won their conference title every year from 1950 through 1955, and captured the NFL championship in 1950, 1954 and 1955.

Paul came up with a new wrinkle for the 1956 season. He had his quarterback, George Ratterman, the replacement for Otto Graham who had retired the year before, wired for sound. A tiny receiving set was built into Ratterman's helmet, and

Brown, microphone in hand, transmitted instructions to him from the sidelines.

News of Brown's latest innovation spread quickly throughout the league. There were reports that some of Cleveland's opponents tried to jam Brown's communications system, or intercept his messages with their own receiving sets. Wrote Milton Gross in the New York *Post:* "Things have come to such a peculiar pass on the professional gridiron that Bert Bell can't be certain whether he's commissioner of the National Football League or a newly appointed member of the FCC." The furor ended when Bell put a ban on the use of electronic equipment in the helmets of players. All twelve owners favored the move, Bell said. Another chapter in the saga of Paul Brown had been written.

For 1957, Brown had a "gimmick" far superior to electronics. His name was Jimmy Brown. A halfback from Syracuse University, he had great speed, extraordinary reflexes, and the ability to absorb enormous physical punishment. Paul made a fullback out of him.

From the beginning, Jimmy was a stunning success. In one game during his rookie year he scored four touchdowns and registered a record 237 yards rushing. The Los Angeles Rams were the unfortunate victims. Before his retirement from the game after the 1965 season, Brown devastated football's rushing records. Paul declared that Jimmy was a "natural," that he never had to teach him anything.

Brown relied heavily on Jimmy, and often the young man was called upon to carry the ball thirty or more times a game. This policy was criticized, but Paul had a ready answer. "When you have a big gun, you shoot it," he said.

The Browns won the Eastern Conference championship in 1957; the next year they lost to the Giants in a conference play-off. Brown never again came that close to a championship—at least not in Cleveland.

The road down hill began. Other teams had learned how to cope with Brown's fancy didoes. Many of his innovations in scouting and coaching were in widespread use. There were some poor trades which hurt the Browns. Worst of all, coach Brown and halfback Brown became disenchanted with one another, and talk of team dissension and even rebellion grew rife. The club stumbled to a 7-6-1 record in 1962, their worst ever.

On a January day in 1963, Brown sat down across a desk from Art Modell, the young Cleveland owner, who had acquired the club two years before. Precisely what was said in that meeting has never been revealed, but right afterward Brown was relieved of his duties as coach and general manager.

This was not the end of the Paul Brown story, not at all. In 1967 he acquired a new franchise in the American Football League. Now he is coach and general manager of the Cincinnati Bengals, and once again he has begun the building of a dynasty.

Paul Brown has won national championships in high school and college football. His Browns were the champions of the All America Conference and the National Football League. Wherever he has gone, winning football has gone with him, and no one is betting that the trend won't continue.

Bobby Layne

In 1952, the Detroit Lions were playing the Cleveland Browns for the NFL championship. On the morning of the game most of the Lion players went to church.

"Some guys prayed they wouldn't get hurt," Bobby Layne, the Lions' quarterback, remembers. "Others prayed they would do a good job. I prayed we would win."

To Bobby Layne, winning was everything. And Layne *did* win. He was a winner in high school, in college, and he led the Lions to two world championships and three Western Division titles, and came close once or twice when he quarterbacked the Pittsburgh Steelers in the final stages of his career.

Layne was no cool technician like the Packers' Bart Starr, nor was he endowed with the splendid gifts of the Jets' Joe Namath. Layne's passes often had a crazy wobble, and in his later years his speed afoot was sabotaged by an extra roll around the middle. His extracurricular activities were well known. Yet he passed, punted, ran, kicked extra points and field goals. But most of all, he had the remarkable ability of being able to take a team, pick it up by the scruff of the neck, shake it a few times, and *make* it win.

Leadership was a key factor in the Layne scheme of things. He believed that most pro quarterbacks were about equal in ability. "The important thing," he once said, "is have the team believe in you."

But Layne was much more than a mere leader. With some players he was a stern dictator. A Pittsburgh newspaperman once called him "a hot-tempered mule-skinner who profanely berates his teammates." Layne admits to this, at least in part. "I really get hot," he once said, "when a guy misses his assignment. There's no excuse for it."

To watch Layne call a football game was to watch a Toscanini conduct. In the beginning he would pick at and probe the enemy defenses, seeking out the weak spots. Then, at the right moment, he would strike. Clark Shaughnessy once observed that Layne threw only three or four long passes a game. "But you can just bet," he said, "that two or three of them will be good for touchdowns."

The 1953 NFL championship game is a case in point. The Lions were trailing the Cleveland Browns, 16–10. Less than four minutes remained. Layne was through probing and experimenting. Now he was ready to go to work. He fired five passes. Three were on target. Swiftly he moved the team from its own 20-yard line to the Browns' 33. Then he called the key play, a pass to Jim Doran, an end who had all but been ignored through the afternoon. It clicked for a touchdown. Doak Walker came in to boot the extra point, and the Lions were the champions.

Bobby Layne was born on December 19, 1926, in what he refers to as "the little bitty ol' town" of Santa Anna, Texas. When he was six his father died, and Bobby went to live with an aunt and uncle in Fort Worth. Later they moved to Dallas.

Layne played guard at Highland Park High in Dallas, but soon was switched to the tailback spot on the team's single-wing offense. He beat out a fellow named Doak Walker for the job. After a brilliant college career, Walker was to join Layne in the Lions' backfield.

"Baseball was my game," Layne recalls. "I wasn't even sure that I wanted to play football in college."

Indeed, baseball was. Bobby received only a few scholarship offers. He chose the University of Texas because of the importance that baseball had in that school's athletic program. A pitcher, Bobby's curve was hardly a wrinkle, and his fast ball was scarcely worthy of the name. But his control was brilliant and his record was superb. He won 26 victories in the Southwest Conference, including three no-hitters. He never lost.

After his freshman year, Bobby enlisted in the Merchant Marine. Doak Walker enlisted with him. The war ended before they got to sea and they were both discharged. On their way home they stopped off in Tulane to watch Southern Methodist University play. An SMU coach convinced Walker to accept a scholarship. Layne was committed to return to the University of Texas.

The next time Bobby and Doak met it was on the football field. It was homecoming day for SMU and the Cotton Bowl was jammed. Bobby, playing tailback for the Longhorns, struck first, passing for a touchdown in the first quarter. He missed the extra point. Minutes later, Walker, the SMU tailback, boosted the Mustangs into the lead with a pass for a touchdown and the extra-point conversion.

The score remained 7–6 until the final minutes of play. Walker marched the Mustangs to the Texas four-yard line, then dropped back to fire what he hoped would be the game-clinching pass. The ball was caught—but by Layne. He sprinted out to the Texas 30.

Layne then put on a stunning display of clutch football. With time running out, he threw three passes good for 70 yards and a touchdown. Texas won, 12–7. It was the shape of things to come. Layne led the Longhorns to 28 victories in 34 games.

Bobby's career in professional football got off to an inauspicious start. He was drafted by Pittsburgh, then traded to the Chicago Bears.

The Bears already had a pair of pretty good quarterbacks in Sid Luckman and Johnny Lujack, and Layne seldom broke into the lineup. After one season, Bear owner George Halas traded him to the New York Bulldogs.

The Bulldogs were an accident looking for a place to happen. Neglected by the fans, they had abandoned Boston in 1948, and transferred to New York where they shared the Polo Grounds with the New York Giants. They had won only fourteen games in five years. Their line was sievelike. Said Layne, "I learned to throw the ball while looking up at the sky, from every position except standing up straight. But it was a valuable experience. After playing with the Bulldogs, I knew I never would be gun-shy."

The Bulldogs won only one game all season, and New Yorkers practically ignored them. In their last game of the season, attendance was announced to be 1,500, although Layne believes the figure was tremendously inflated. The club was owned by Ted Collins, the manager of singer Kate Smith, and the players joked that if Miss Smith ever got a sore throat no one would get paid.

The experience with the Bulldogs grieved Layne, and when he returned to Texas at the end of the season he made plans to retire. But fate took a hand. The Detroit Lions traded a fullback named Camp Wilson to the Bulldogs for Layne. In 1951, Buddy Parker took over as the Lions' head coach, replacing Bo McMillan, with whom Layne had feuded. Parker and Layne were to become a combination as notable as ham and eggs.

In 1952 the Lions roared through the exhibition season without a single loss. But then they stumbled, losing to the 49ers and barely beating the Rams. Their first game at home that season was a rematch with San Francisco, and they lost, 28–0. Parker used three quarterbacks in an effort to spark the team.

Layne was livid with rage after the game. He told Parker that he was the team's quarterback, and their only quarterback. He vowed he would get the team moving or cripple them in the attempt.

Against Los Angeles the next week, Layne refused to take any plays from the sidelines. He called the entire game, passed with skill and daring, ran often and well, and tongue-lashed his teammates whenever he felt it necessary. When the smoke had cleared, the Lions had won. More important, a bright era had dawned in Detroit football.

The Lions lost only one more game through the rest of the season, and ended with a 9-3 record that won them a tie with Los Angeles at the top of the Eastern Division. In the playoff they beat the Rams, 31–21.

The next week they won the NFL championship, turning back the Browns, The next week they won the NFL championship, turning back the Browns, 17–7. Layne ran for one touchdown, Walker for another, and Pat Harder kicked two extra points and a field goal. It was Detroit's first championship in seventeen years.

In 1953, with a 10-2 record, the Lions won the Western Division again, and repeated their victory over the Browns for the NFL title. Detroit was division champion again in 1954, but in the playoff game they met a vengeful Cleveland team who whipped them, 56–10.

The next year Layne was struck by misfortune. He was holding the reins of a horse for his son, Bobby, Jr., when the animal suddenly bolted. Layne suffered a shoulder separation as a result, and it took a full year for the injury to heal. He continued to play, but he was so far below par that the Lions plummeted to last place in the division standings.

The next season, Ed Meadows, a defensive end for the Bears, smashed into Bobby from the blind side. Layne went down and didn't get up. He suffered a concussion.

But the mishap had little bearing on Layne's play that year. He booted twelve field goals and 33 extra points, and he tallied five touchdowns to lead the league in scoring with 99 points. The team did a complete turnabout, winning nine and losing three.

In 1957, with George Wilson the Lion coach, Layne was two-platooned with Tobin Rote, a policy that irked Bobby, and that is putting it mildly. "Neither of us could do anything," Bobby said. "It was miserable."

One afternoon that season in a game against the Bears, Layne was buried in a pileup. When they unraveled the players, Layne was at the bottom, his leg broken in three places. Soon afterward the Lions traded him to the Pittsburgh Steelers.

Layne liked the bright lights, a fact he never denied. "I don't try to hide; I never sneak in a joint," he once said. Newspapers made the most of his off-the-field antics, but Layne felt they vastly exaggerated his social activities. Once he was accused of drunken driving and he decided to fight the charge.

The Lion players turned out *en masse* for the trial, and when a "not guilty" verdict was brought in, they stamped and cheered as if someone had just scored a winning touchdown. The testimony revealed that the arresting officer had confused Layne's Texas drawl with the garbled speech of one who is intoxicated.

After the trial, the Lions had a "not guilty party." Friday

Macklem, the team's equipment manager, made up a sign that said: AH ALL AIN'T DRUNK. AH'M FROM TEXAS.

Bobby was just as carefree on the field as he was off. Throughout his career, he played with a minimum of protective equipment. He wore no hip pads, no thigh pads, and only the flimsiest pair of shoulder pads, about as strong as those a youngster would wear for a sandlot game. He was one of the few men in the league never to wear a faceguard. He claimed it impaired his vision.

When Layne arrived upon the scene at Pittsburgh, the Steelers had already lost their first two games. He played in the third game and they won, but they dropped the next two to make them 1-4 for the season. Everyone counted them out. But Layne convinced the team they could win, and they came surprisingly close to taking the conference championship. They won five consecutive games and finished with a 7-4-1 record. No Pittsburgh team in sixteen years had done as well.

Not long after he joined the Steelers, Layne set a league career record for passing, topping Sammy Baugh, who had accrued 22,085 yards in sixteen years of NFL play. Told about it, Layne shrugged.

"I'm not interested in records," he said. "They're just a reminder I'm getting old."

It was while Layne was at Pittsburgh that he unveiled his tricky "What's the matter" play. The Steelers, trailing the Giants by two touchdowns, had driven deep into New York territory. Layne was calling signals. Suddenly halfback Tom Tracy shouted out, "Wait a minute!"

Layne, waiting the snap from center, stood up and said, "What's the matter?" On the word "matter" the center snapped the ball directly to fullback John Henry Johnson, who streaked into the end zone without a hand touching him.

But the play was *too* deceptive. It not only caught the Giants napping, but also the officials. They called an offside penalty against the Steelers and disallowed the touchdown. Layne never used that "What's the matter" strategy again.

In 1959 the Steelers sagged to fourth place in the conference standings, but Layne provided Pittsburgh fans with many a thrill. He threw twenty touchdown passes that year. In 1961 Pittsburgh supporters, distressed by the team's frequent losses, began to boo Bobby. He was thirty-five; he knew he could not do what he did at twenty-five. The next year he retired. His final appearance was in the Playoff Bowl.

Layne's playing career stretched fifteen seasons. Afterward, he coached Steeler quarterbacks, and later did the same for the St. Louis Cardinals. He also has scouted for the Dallas Cowboys.

Layne now lives in Lubbock and tends his various West Texas business enterprises from there. From time to time rumors circulate that Layne is about to become a head coach with a professional or college team, but he has misgivings about such a career.

"Maybe sometimes a situation will come along that's just right," he says. "But I doubt it. Being a head coach is too much like being a quarterback—you get too much credit if you win, and too much criticism if you lose."

In 1967, when Layne was inducted into the Pro Football Hall of Fame, Sam Blair of the Dallas *News* interviewed Bobby.

"What was your biggest thrill during your fifteen years in pro ball?" he asked.

Layne thought a minute. "Just winning was a big thrill," he said. "One win was about as good as another for me."

His old friend Doak Walker best summed up Layne's career. "Bobby never lost a game," he once said. "The clock ran out on him a couple of times, that's all."

Bobby Layne Career Passing Record

Year	Attempts	Completions	Pct.	Yards	Touchdowns	Interceptions
1948	52	16	30.7	232	3	2
1949	299	156	52.1	1,796	9	18
1950	336*	152	45.2	2,323*	16	18
1951	332*	152*	45.7	2,403*	26*	23*
1952	287	139	48.4	1,999	16	21
1953	273	125	45.7	2,088	16	21
1954	246	135	54.8	1,818	14	12
1955	270	143	53.2	1,830	11	17
1956	244	129	52.8	1,909	9	17
1957	179	87	48.6	1,169	6	12
1958	294	145	49.3	2,510	14	12
1959	297	142	47.8	1,986	20	21*
1960	209	103	49.2	1,814	13	17
1961	149	75	50.3	1,158	11	16
1962	233	116	49.7	1,686	7	17
Total	3,700	1,814	49.0	26,721	194	243

* *Outstanding Performance.*

Dan Reeves

Sport fans on the West Coast, in general, and the city of Los Angeles, in particular, hungered for a big league representation for many decades before 1946, the year that Dan Reeves, owner of the Los Angeles Rams, pioneered the parade of franchises to California.

While Reeves' Rams were the first modern-day team to represent Los Angeles, they were not *the* first. That honor rests with the Los Angeles Buccaneers, a group of ex-collegians, who were members of the National Football League for just one year— 1926. Barred by local universities from using their stadiums, the Buccaneers played all their games on the road, not a small factor in their failure. Even so, they managed to compile a 6-3-1 record in their one year of existence. After the demise of the Buccaneers, interest in noncollegiate football was centered on semi-pro teams, principally the Hollywood Bears and the Los Angeles Bulldogs.

Reeves found getting established in California extremely difficult. He may not have faced starvation and hostile Indians like the pioneers of a century before, but the problems were almost as rugged. The story begins in Cleveland in 1941. That year Reeves, then twenty-nine, heir to a grocery chain fortune, and a partner purchased the hapless Cleveland Rams. "Hapless," says the dictionary, means "unfortunate; unlucky; luckless." That was the Cleveland Rams, all right. Founded in 1937, the club had a record of 28 losses, 14 wins, and two ties, no player personnel to speak of, and a penchant for losing money.

Reeves' interest in pro football developed over a long period. A native New Yorker, he had been a schoolmate of Jack Mara, son of the president of the New York Giants. Reeves' older brother Ed was the owner of a 25 percent interest in the Washington Redskins. Before Dan's acquisition of the Rams, he attempted to buy an interest in the Pittsburgh Steelers, and later in the Philadelphia Eagles.

To Reeves, southern California was the promised land, however. In 1935, he saw the University of Southern California play in the Coliseum and became completely captivated by the glamour of West Coast football. Several years after he gained control of the Rams, Reeves admitted that his basic plan was to obtain a pro football team he could eventually move to Los Angeles.

In his first year as an owner, Reeves saw the Rams finish with a 2-9-0 record. He realized that the club required a complete overhaul before any other city would consider having it, but World War II intervened before he could begin his rebuilding program. Reeves went into the Army Air Force. During the war years the club continued on its dismal way, and was even forced to suspend operations in 1943.

Amazingly, the Rams did a complete turnabout in 1945. Coach Adam Walsh installed the T and to power it he relied upon the skills of a lanky, rubber-armed quarterback named Bob Waterfield. Just before the Rams' opening game of the season, Reeves, a captain, was placed on inactive status by the Air Force, and he watched his club whip the Chicago Cardinals, 21–0. They kept right on winning. Late in November, they turned back the Lions for their eighth victory against a single loss and clinched the NFL title.

The Rams returned to Cleveland for their next game, and despite the fact that they now reigned as conquering heroes, their contest with the Boston Yanks drew only 17,000 fans. Reeves became concerned when city officials jacked up the rent on Cleveland Stadium for the title playoff to $10,000, a 300 percent increase. If Reeves was entertaining any doubts about leaving town, they were eliminated now. The Rams first settled the matter of the league championship by downing the Redskins, 15–14, and then Reeves turned his attention to the business of switching the club. It is not likely he realized what a task it would be.

Reeves proposed the transfer from Cleveland to Los Angeles at the NFL owners' meeting in January 1946, figuring he had the necessary eight (of ten) votes. But a number of clubs, principally the Bears and Redskins, went sour on the idea of traveling 2,000 to 3,000 miles to Los Angeles for road games, and branded Reeves' plan as "economic insanity." Reeves was voted down, 6–4.

Reeves got up and started cramming papers into his briefcase. "You call this the 'National League,' " he declared. "Well, consider the Cleveland Rams out of it." And he stormed out of the meeting room.

George Marshall of the Washington Redskins and George Halas of the Chicago Bears went after him. Reeves kept insisting he was getting out. Once the other owners became convinced he had no intention of backing down, the opposition collapsed. Los Angeles it would be.

The picture was very bright at first. Los Angeles gave the Rams a thumping welcome, and Reeves was able to work out a favorable lease arrangement with the Coliseum. The team was bursting with talent, and owned the Coach of the Year in Adam Walsh and the Player of the Year in Bob Waterfield. Nevertheless, the club could not regain its winning ways and slumped to a second-place finish. Adam Walsh was fired at the end of the season. Bob Snyder, who succeeded Walsh, did not last much more than a year. Clark Shaughnessy was elevated to the head coach's post after the first game of the 1948 season.

To make matters worse, there were the All America Conference Dons. Supported by the racetrack millions of Ben Lindheimer, the Dons battled the Rams for four full years. Reeves' money, instead of merely trickling away as it had in Cleveland, now departed in a great torrent. It is estimated that the hostilities with the Dons cost the club more than $700,000.

Shaughnessy had the Rams moving smartly by the end of the 1948 season. In 1949, 1950 and 1951, the team won the Western Division championship, and in 1951 also captured the NFL title, turning back the Cleveland Browns, a team many people considered to be invincible.

The Ram teams of these years have been judged to be as sensational as any pro football has produced before or since. Besides Waterfield, they featured Elroy (Crazylegs) Hirsch, Tom Fears, Deacon Don Towler, Norm van Brocklin, Glenn Davis and Paul (Tank) Younger. They played a wide-open brand of football, featuring hard running and plenty of passing, and they broke records by the helmetful. In 1950 the club scored more points in one season (466), scored more touchdowns (64) and gained more yards passing (3,709) than any team ever before. These records still stand.

Los Angeles became an unqualified success at the gate, too.

They were the top drawing team in the NFL by 1951, and they set a league attendance record of 746,598 in 1958.

On-the-field success eluded the Rams after their championship win in 1951. Coach Shaughnessy had left in 1949 to be followed by Joe Stydahar, who was followed by Hampton Pool, who was followed by Sid Gillman. Under Gillman, the Rams, in 1955, won another division title. But the next season they finished dead last and, except for 1958, when they finished second, losing became an accepted practice.

Attendance slipped during the Rams' losing years, but there was still solid evidence of deep loyalty. In 1959, Barron Hilton fielded a team named the Los Angeles Chargers in the American Football League. Although the club won the AFL's Western Division title, they were outdrawn by the Rams at the rate of five to one. After the season, Hilton took the Chargers and fled to San Diego.

In 1962 the Rams were in desperate straits. They tumbled to last place in the Western Conference with a 1-12-1 showing. Worse, Reeves and his partners were feuding. That year Reeves bought out his unhappy associates. It cost him $7.1 million and, at the time, he was judged to have been fleeced. Today, however, it is claimed that the stock Reeves purchased is worth about twice what he paid for it.

Once in full control again, Reeves began an aggressive rebuilding program. "Only two things are necessary to build a championship team," he once said. "First you have to have the best players. Then you have to get the coach, one who can get the most out of the players." Reeves took care of both. A key factor in the club's revival was the signing of George Allen as head coach. In 1966, his first season with the Rams, Allen steered the club to an 8-6-0 finish, their first winning season in eight years. The year 1967 was even better. The Rams won the Coast Division crown, but lost the Western Conference title to all-powerful Green Bay.

Besides the fact that Reeves started pro football on the West Coast, the sport has many reasons to be grateful to him. He crashed down a formidable barrier when he signed Negro halfback Kenny Washington of UCLA in 1946, a full year before Branch Rickey brought Jackie Robinson to the Brooklyn Dodgers.

It was Reeves' early experiments with television that led to pro football's present policies concerning that medium. The Rams televised their home games in 1950. "That convinced us," Reeves said, "that home TV was disastrous to the economics of the game. We came up with the plan of 'road TV.' This gave our fans half the schedule free—and at the same time exposed pro football to millions of new fans." Reeves' recommendations led to the development of the NFL's "blackout" policy, often cited as *the* reason for pro football's enormous popularity.

It was Reeves who brought real efficiency to pro scouting. He was the first to employ a year-round staff of paid talent scouts who covered the length and breadth of the country.

Reeves' Rams got company of big league stature in California in 1950. That year the San Francisco 49ers, a holdover from the AAC, became an NFL entry. Baseball moved west in 1958 when the Dodgers set up shop in Los Angeles and the Giants in San Francisco. Later, basketball and ice hockey made the trek. On the West Coast today there almost seems to be a major league franchise for every mile of freeway, and there is a lot of freeway. Sports fans will remember that the man who started the great march west was Daniel F. Reeves.

Ken Strong

Grantland Rice was rhapsodic.

It was November 25, 1928, and he had just watched New York University crush Carnegie Tech with a storming attack, which he described as being "led by a runaway buffalo, using the speed of a deer.

"He ran all over a big, powerful team," Rice wrote, "smashed its line, ran its ends, kicked fifty and fifty-five yards, threw passes and tackled all over the lot. He was the best running back I have seen in years, and that includes Red Grange."

Rice's ecstatic praise was heaped upon the broad shoulders of Elmer Kenneth Strong, a 6-foot-1, 201-pound halfback for the Violets. Strong went on to become one of the all-time greats of the New York Giants in the power football days of the 1930's.

Strong was an All American at NYU during his senior year and, more important, the leading college scorer in the country.

Naturally, the Giants wanted this local hero, and they sent Coach Leroy Andrews to sign him. Andrews fumbled the ball, however. Giant owner Tim Mara told Andrews to offer strong $4,000, but Andrews, believing he could get Strong's name on a contract for less, offered Ken only $3,000, a sum Strong quickly rejected. Instead of becoming a Giant, Strong signed with the Stapleton Stapes, a club on Staten Island which was owned by Dan Blaine and coached by Doug Wycoff, a onetime star with the Giants. The Stapes were members of the NFL from 1929 to 1932.

Actually, Strong was more enthusiastic about a career in baseball than in football. He was signed by the New York Yankees, and in the 1931 season hit .343 and blasted fourteen home runs for their farm team in Toronto. The Detroit Tigers purchased him for $40,000 and five players. But Strong's career in baseball came to an abrupt end. While chasing a fly ball during a game in Buffalo he injured his wrist. After the season the wrist was operated on and the doctor who performed the surgery took out the wrong bone. Ken couldn't bend his hand backward as a result, and was no longer able to make long throws from the outfield. He had no choice but to give pro football another try.

This was 1932 and the Stapleton team had folded. Strong, bereft of all his bargaining power, went to see Tim Mara. "Why should I take a chance on you?" Mara asked, still smarting from Strong's decision to sign with Stapleton in 1929. "Who knows if you can still play with that bad wrist?" At length they came to terms, Strong receiving the same money that he had turned down a few years before.

Strong was just what the Giants needed. He ran with great speed and hammering power. He threw passes or received them, and blocked like Nagurski. He could kick 45-yard field goals and punt 70 yards.

Led by Strong and Harry Newman, the NFL's leading passer of the day, the Giants won the Eastern Division crown, but lost to the Bears in the championship game, the first playoff in league history. The next year—1934—the two teams were division titlists again.

The playoff game that year was the fabled "sneakers" game. The scene was New York's Polo Grounds. On the day of the game, temperatures plunged to an arctic-like eight degrees, and the field was as hard as a basketball court. At half time the Giant players donned basketball shoes, and suddenly and dramatically reversed the course of the game to win, 30–13.

The sneakers worked better for Strong than anyone else. He was the driving force in the Giants' victory. Despite a leg injury that kept him sidelined through most of the first half, he scored two touchdowns on long runs, and booted a field goal and three extra points. After his second touchdown, hundreds of joyous fans ran out on the field to clap him on the back. Commented the New York *Post:* "The only time Ken Strong was stopped was by the crowd after the game."

Despite his brilliant season and the fact that he was an All Pro selection, Strong had to hire a lawyer to win himself a salary increase for the next season. The boost he received got him as high as $6,000.

More and more, Strong was winning renown as a kicker. In a game against the Bears, though hampered by a muddy field and a wet ball, he kicked a field goal. The Giants were off side. Strong had to try again. He calmly booted the ball cleanly through the uprights a second time. This time both teams were off side. A third time Strong swung his foot. This time it was good. The Giants won, 3–0.

In 1935 the National Football League instituted the draft. If a college player refused to sign with the team that had selected him, he was not free to negotiate with another club. This policy had a deflationary effect upon all salaries of the day, Ken Strong's in particular. The Giants set a figure of $150 a game as the amount they would pay Strong, an amount that represented a substantial cut.

A friend suggested that Strong jump to the new American Football League, then being put together by Jack McBride, a former Giant star, and a promoter par excellence. Strong did. He received a $5,000 salary from the American League's New York Yankees. He was wise enough to have the money put in escrow. The league folded after one full year and four games of a second season, and Strong was one of the few people associated with it who escaped financial damage.

The National Football League regarded Strong's abandonment of the Giants as an act of extreme disloyalty, and he was suspended for five years. In 1938 the Giants asked Strong to join their Jersey City farm in the American Conference, a pro football minor league with clubs in northern New Jersey cities. The Giants promised that if Strong helped get the farm club successfully launched, he could return to the parent club the next season. Strong had a splendid year, and the next season he was welcomed back to Mara Tech.

No kicker ever had a more powerful leg drive than Strong. When he was with the Stapleton team, he had just gotten off a punt when the Giants' Bill Owen hurtled over the line to block it with his chest. It sounded like a thunderclap. The day after the game Owen, stripped to the waist, looked at himself in a mirror and could see the outline of a football blazoned on his chest in varying shades of black and blue. And looking closely he could see a trademark and the words: A. G. SPALDING COMPANY. OFFICIAL LEAGUE FOOTBALL.

In 1943, after Strong had been in retirement for two years, the Giants enticed him to return to the team. He was thirty-seven then. It must be said that this was wartime, and the Giants, like all teams, had been struck by a manpower shortage. Strong was used for kickoffs and place-kicks exclusively. He wore no shoulder pads and seldom took off his wristwatch when he went in to kick.

Through the war years, games were close but the talent seldom sparkled. In an exhibition game against the Bears in 1944, Strong kicked off. Bulldog Turner, leading Chicago's downfield blocking, headed for Strong. Just before he threw his huge body at Ken, Turner suddenly stopped. "Hell," he said, "I can't hit you. You're too damn old." And he walked away.

Strong's son, Ken, Jr., once remarked that he had never seen his father do anything but kick. Strong sought to correct this impression. The Giants were playing the Redskins at Griffith Stadium and late in the fourth quarter were leading, 31–0.

When the Giants huddled, Strong asked quarterback Tuffy Leemans to let him carry the ball. Leemans saw no harm in this. But on the play there was a mix-up in the backfield, and Strong was smothered by Redskin tacklers. Dizzy, his body racked with pain, he staggered into the huddle. "Want to try again?" asked Leemans. "No," Strong managed to gasp.

On the last play of the game, Ken carried a second time. Sammy Baugh and the other Redskin veterans, aware of what was afoot, agreed to let Strong have his taste of glory. But as he angled for the goal line, a Washington rookie rocketed into him like a guided missile, adding to the damage.

Though battered and in acute pain, Strong took solace in the fact that his son had seen him carry the ball at last. When he met his wife after the game, he was surprised to see her standing alone. "Where's Ken?" he asked.

"Oh, I forgot to tell you," she said. "He had a cold and I made him stay home."

Strong never carried the ball again, not for his son, not for anyone.

In 1947, Strong retired for good. In his nine seasons with the club he scored 351 points, which stood as a team record for many years. He also held the club records for the longest field goal (47 yards), most extra points (147), most consecutive extra points (67), and most points scored in one season (72). In his four years with the Staten Island Stapes he scored 175 points.

In the late 1950's, Strong was an assistant coach for the Giants, specializing in the schooling of place-kickers and punters. Don Chandler was one of the stars he helped to develop.

There is an intrinsic quality in the leg of a great kicker. It has little to do with the muscles or size of the leg. It is almost an intangible quality. Sometimes it's called "snap" or "pop." Whatever it is, Ken Strong had it in abundance.

Joe Stydahar

In their meeting in February 1936, the owners of the National Football League adopted a method of selecting college players called the draft, the purpose of which was to foster a well-balanced league. Playing talent was pooled, and the team that finished last in the league standings was allowed to have first choice. The next-to-last team chose second, and so on.

When it came to George Halas' turn to pick, he stood and announced loudly and clearly, "Joe Stydahar." The selection startled the assembled owners and coaches; some had never even heard of "Jumbo Joe." But it proved a very happy choice for Chicago. The professional football player draft has continued to this day and seldom, if ever, have the Bears acted with the discernment they displayed in 1936.

A fearless, 6-foot-4, 240-pound tackle who had incredible power and remarkable speed, Stydahar was to bulwark the Bear line from 1936 through 1942. This was the era of the legendary Monsters of the Midway, an image that Stydahar epitomized. World War II interrupted his career, but he returned to the Bears for the 1946 and 1947 seasons. During his tenure with Chicago, Stydahar was a member of five Western Division championship teams and three NFL championship teams.

The end of his career as a player signaled the beginning of his career as a coach, and again he achieved distinction. As head man of the Los Angeles Rams, he steered the club to two Western Division titles and a world championship.

Stydahar played a rough and rugged brand of football, and as a coach he wanted his players to do the same. In 1950, his first season as the Rams' head coach, the team was handed a 49–14 thrashing by the Philadelphia Eagles. After the game, Stydahar boiled with rage.

"No wonder you guys get kicked around," he roared. "Every guy on the team has still got all his teeth."

Stydahar preferred a lineman with a toothless grin rather than an All America rating. "When you charge, you have to keep your head up," he once said. "Sure, you lose a lot of teeth that way, but you make a lot of tackles."

Stydahar's own teeth, at least the front ones, were contributed to the Bears' cause one afternoon in Detroit. He blocked one point, almost blocked another, and was showing up in the Detroit backfield so often he was beginning to be regarded as a member of the Lion team. The blocker assigned to restrain Stydahar became desperate. Once more Joe charged in. The lineman missed his block, but delivered a stony elbow to Joe's mouth. He knocked out two teeth completely and broke off two others. Despite the excruciating pain, Joe stayed in the game and played thirty-eight stormy minutes more.

Once, in a game against Brooklyn, Stydahar crashed into Bruiser Kinard, the Dodgers' great tackle. The collision was so violent that a deep gash was opened in the Bruiser's arm. He had to leave the game to have it stitched. The officials could not believe a mere collision could cause such an injury.

"They thought Joe must have been carrying a weapon," said Bill Osmanski, the Bears' fullback. "They searched everyone. They even looked in Joe's mouth to see if he could have bitten Kinard.

"That was a waste of time," Osmanski observed. "Joe couldn't bite anyone. Not without teeth."

Joe Stydahar was born on March 3, 1912, in Taylor, Pennsylvania, one of a family of five brothers and five sisters. When he was four, the family moved to Shinnston, West Virginia, where Joe's father went to work in the coal mines.

In high school, Joe, a curly-haired 220-pounder, excelled in every sport he tried. He won varsity status in baseball as a third baseman, played center on the basketball team, and in football won All State honors twice, once as a tackle, once as a fullback.

Jock Sutherland, the famous University of Pittsburgh coach, recruited Joe for the Panther team, but after a month on the Pitt campus Joe was beset by homesickness and returned to West Virginia. He enrolled at West Virginia University at Morgantown, a scant 35 miles from home. His career there was sensational. As a sophomore Joe played the entire season without a substitution. As a junior he blocked punts that led to touchdowns against Temple, Washington and Lee, West Virginia, Wesleyan and Duquesne. Following his senior year he won every honor worth winning—All Eastern, Little All America and All America. He played in the East-West game and the College All Star game.

George Halas was tipped off about Stydahar by Bill Karr, a back for the Bears and a West Virginia alumnus. "Being drafted by the Bears was the turning point for me," Stydahar once said. "George Halas was like a second father to me. I really didn't know anything about playing football until I played for him."

Stydahar was a member of the All League team from 1937 through 1940. After the 1942 season, he entered the U. S. Navy, became a lieutenant, and was put in charge of a gun crew aboard the USS *Monterey,* a carrier stationed in the Pacific.

While in the service, Stydahar refused to play any football. "I just don't have the heart to play against some of these kids," he said. "They're just too damned small."

When Joe came out of the service in 1945, he went to see

Halas about rejoining the Bears. Halas asked Joe what he thought he was worth.

Joe shrugged. "I'm just about washed up as a player," he said. "Write in whatever you think is right and I'll sign."

Halas put down $8,000. "That was twice as much as I had ever been paid before," Stydahar said, "but Halas was that kind of a guy."

Stydahar retired as a player at the end of the 1947 season, a year in which the Bears won the NFL championship, and took a job as assistant coach to Clark Shaughnessy at Los Angeles. While he was there, Gene Ronzani, a backfield star with the Bears in the gaudy days of the 1930's, became head coach of the Packers, and he asked Joe to leave the Rams and come to Green Bay to be his right-hand man. Joe went to see Los Angeles owner Dan Reeves to obtain his release. Reeves told him he wanted time to think over his request and to come back in a day or two for an answer.

Two days later Joe walked into Reeves' office expecting to be granted his release, and prepared to say his good-byes. But Reeves had a surprise in store. "Joe," he said, "you are the new head coach of the Rams."

The day that Coach Shaughnessy learned that he had been fired and that Stydahar, his assistant, was taking over, he made a remark that he was to regret the rest of his coaching days.

"Stydahar, coach of the Rams?" he said. "Why, I could take a high school team and beat him."

What made the statement all the more unfortunate was the brilliant manner in which Stydahar conducted operations. He brought the Rams to a Western Division title in 1950, his first year at the helm, and missed beating the Cleveland Browns in the playoff game by the margin of a last-minute field goal.

While with the Rams, Stydahar had the extremely delicate problem of handling two quarterbacks, both of them superstars —Bob Waterfield and Norm van Brocklin. Stydahar never played one man against the other, but instead used each in specialized situations. As a result, there was no bitter competition. It ended up with Bob cheering on Van, and vice versa. The NFL statistics for 1951 reveal how well Joe's system worked. Waterfield led the league in passing, and Van Brocklin was only a percentage point behind him.

During the 1950 season, the Rams established a new NFL record with 3,709 yards gained passing. Against the Brooklyn Dodgers the next year, the team set a game mark for yards gained passing—554 yards. Both records still stand.

Despite the club's aerial brilliance, the Rams were no cinch to coach. They would be unstoppable one week, but rank push-overs the next. "Never a dull day with L.A." became the team's slogan. Cleveland beat them twice. Washington and Detroit also whipped them. Stydahar's jet-black hair became flecked with gray. He couldn't sleep; he had to diet.

The four losses notwithstanding, the Rams managed to cop the Western Division title. Then, following their erratic pattern, they went out and convincingly whipped the highly favored Cleveland Browns, 24–14, for the NFL title. The game snapped the Browns' five-year string of championship seasons.

After the championship was won, Stydahar was admitted to the Scripps Clinic in La Jolla, California. A doctor said that he was suffering from "marked mental tension."

The Rams suffered a surprising loss to the Browns in the opening game of the 1952 season. Shortly afterward, and for reasons never fully explained, a rift developed between Stydahar and owner Reeves, and Joe quit the club. In later years both men admitted that they had acted rashly, that the break should have been allowed to heal.

Stydahar spent 1953 and 1954 as head coach of the quite hap-less Chicago Cardinals. Later he returned to the Bears as a defensive coach. In announcing Joe's return, Halas said, "We're confident he can help us. Nobody ever ran very far against Joe."

Stydahar is one man who has an intimate knowledge of cham-pionship football in two different eras. "Is today's football superior to that of the 1930's?" he was once asked.

"It's better football now," Stydahar declared. "I don't care what the old guys say. It's not because the guys are bigger or faster. It's just better. I know. I was there."

Emlen Tunnell

The story has become a legend. On a hot, sunny day in 1948, Emlen Tunnell strolled into the offices of the New York Giants, unknown and uninvited.

"A Mr. Tunnell is here to see you, Mr. Mara," the switchboard operator said. "He says he's a football player."

"Tunnell? Who's he?" the Giant owner asked. "Oh well, show him in. What can we lose?"

Tunnell, so the story goes, asked for a tryout, got it, and won himself a contract.

All this is only partly true. Tunnell did visit the Giant offices in 1948. But Tim Mara and Ray Walsh, the Giants' general manager, knew that he was coming. Further, Tunnell was not a football player unknown, not by any stretch of the imagination. He had been a standout halfback at the University of Iowa for two years. Many professional teams were aware of his skills, but he had not been drafted or even contacted because he still had a year of college eligibility left.

After the meeting with Tunnell, Mara, wanting to handle the situation properly, checked with coach Eddie Anderson at Iowa. "You might as well sign him," Anderson said. "I don't think we can keep him in the classroom any longer."

A week later, Jack and Wellington Mara went to Tunnell's hometown of Philadelphia to sign their 6-foot-1, 190-pound prospect. The trio met at the old Broad Street station on a hot August afternoon. The Giants gave Tunnell a salary of $5,000, plus $500 for signing and another $500 when he reached camp.

Emlen Tunnell would have been a great bargain at almost any price. He became a key strut in Steve Owen's famed umbrella defense, and ultimately one of the most celebrated halfbacks in the history of the National League. He spent eleven years with the Giants and three with the Green Bay Packers. Records he set still stand. They include most pass interceptions, 79; most yards gained on interceptions, 1,282; most punt returns, 258, and most yardage gained returning punts, 2,209. As strong as a keg of nails, he played in 158 consecutive games. Only a handful of players have been so durable.

There is one interesting footnote to Tunnell's prowess as a punt return specialist. In his rookie year with the team he made several "fair catches." When a defensive man signals "fair catch," the opposing team is not allowed to tackle him, while the man catching the ball is not allowed to run. Giant fans, unaware that Tunnell was acting under Steve Owen's orders, booed him heartily for what they felt was excessive caution. This hurt. "I made up my mind," Tunnell said, "I'd never field a punt without trying to advance it."

He did what he said. In 1953, Tunnell established a new record with 38 punt returns. (Alvin Hammond of Baltimore, with 41 returns, broke the record in 1965.) Tunnell once returned eight punts in a single game.

For years Tunnell was the most feared runback agent in the league. In 1952, Emlen accounted for 924 yards gained on defense. That year the NFL rushing leader was Deacon Dan Towler of the Los Angeles Rams. Towler's total was a mere 890 yards.

Bobby Layne, who achieved greatness with the Detroit Lions, remembers Tunnell as "a real cutie." Says Layne, "Tunnell was a genius for setting up the offense for a mistake."

Layne quarterbacked the New York Bulldogs during his sophomore season in the NFL, and Tunnell made an unforgettable impression on him. The Bulldogs had a fine receiver in Bill Chipley, and during a game against the Giants, Chipley came back to the huddle and told Layne that he could beat Tunnell.

"I thought we had found New York's Achilles' heel," says Layne. "Whenever I sent Chipley down as a decoy, Tunnell acted as if he wasn't even on the field."

The Bulldogs got a drive started in the second quarter and worked the ball just past midfield. It was third and seven. With the team badly in need of a lift, Layne wanted first down desperately.

"This is it!" he told Chipley in the huddle. "We'll run the same play, but this time we'll teach Em a lesson."

Chipley sprinted downfield, ignored by Tunnell. Layne dropped back, faked a pass to his right, then turned left and fired. "The moment I threw," Layne says, "I knew I made a mistake. Tunnell was suddenly in front of Chipley, and made an easy interception which he ran for a touchdown."

It is something of a miracle that Tunnell ever played football at all. A poor kid from Garrett Hill, Pennsylvania, a Philadelphia suburb, Tunnell's athletic skills won him a scholarship to Toledo College. During his freshman year he suffered a broken neck, and was told he'd never play football again. The Army and Navy rejected him as a physical risk, but the Coast Guard took him in. He survived two torpedo attacks on his ship during World War II. His football playing in the Coast Guard eventually led him to the University of Iowa.

Tunnell often played tailback in the old single wing at Iowa. But Coach Anderson wanted to limit Tunnell to playing only on defense. Tunnell, however, much preferred offense. This clash of opinions was a contributing factor in Tunnell's departure from Iowa.

Tunnell was the first Negro to play for the Giants. One-third of the New York roster was made up of Southern boys, and the Giant management was apprehensive that Tunnell might encounter an adjustment problem. But there was not even a hint of one. "After a few days in camp," said Giant coach Steve Owen, "Emlen was going to the movies with the rest of the gang. He was as popular as any man on the team."

While Tunnell was a social success from the start, on the playing field it was different. Owen was undecided whether to use him on offense or defense. But the matter was settled when the Giants obtained Charlie Conerly of Mississippi. Conerly quickly won his spurs as the Giants' tailback and Tunnell was assigned to defensive chores, a decision that was not altogether pleasing to him.

The slick play of pro football's quarterbacks made life hellish for Tunnell during his rookie year. One afternoon Sammy Baugh of the Washington Redskins, taking advantage of Tunnell's lack of experience, completed five touchdown passes against the Giants. The Redskins won, 41–10.

After the game, Owen called Tunnell into his office. "Isn't Baugh the best passer you ever saw?" he asked.

"Yes, sir, he is," answered Tunnell, aware that he had played poorly.

"Well, I hope you got a good look," said Owen. "It's going to cost you a $100 fine. And the next time you want to watch, buy a ticket."

By the end of the season, however, Tunnell was playing defense like a Hall of Fame candidate. What's more, he was beginning to enjoy it. In a game against Green Bay late in the season, he intercepted four passes, running one of them back 55 yards for a touchdown, and he tackled with the ferocity and finality of a Jim Thorpe. On one play he hit the Packers' "Indian Jack" Jacobs so hard that he knocked him right out of the game. The tackle took place near the Green Bay bench. "All they could do," said Steve Owen, "was roll Jacobs under the bench and then throw a blanket over him. He was stiffened."

As the season progressed, Tunnell became more and more attracted toward playing defense. "There's something about knifing in and bringing down a guy with a sharp tackle that provides more satisfaction than a long run behind good blocking," he said. "Tackling is football; running is track."

In 1950, Steve Owen introduced his famed umbrella defense, the forerunner of present-day defensive formations. Instead of the standard defense, with the center and the four defensive backs dropped back behind the line (a 6-4-1 setup), Owen also had two ends drop back to cover on pass plays. This made for a 4-1-6 setup, with the "6" so placed as to resemble the shape of an open umbrella.

The top of the umbrella was Tunnell and three new Giants—Otto Schnellbacher, Harmon Rowe and Tom Landry. "We learned to play as one man, as one mind," Tunnell once said.

The umbrella defense was presented for the first time when the Giants met the Cleveland Browns, who were headed for the league championship. It worked to perfection. New York shut out the Browns, 6–0. After that game, Tunnell was sure he never wanted to play on offense again.

Twice in his years with the Giants, Tunnell played on championship teams. In 1956 he was a member of the Giant squad that won the NFL title by overwhelming the Chicago Bears, 47–7. In 1958 he was on the team that won the Eastern Conference crown, but lost to the Baltimore Colts, 23–17, in the famous "sudden death" overtime game. Johnny Unitas' passes to Ray Berry spearheaded the Baltimore win. "Unitas and Berry—I still see them in my sleep," Tunnell says.

When Tom Landry took over as New York's defensive coach, Tunnell found out that he didn't fit into the new scheme of things. Tunnell was a daring performer, always shooting for the big play. His blinding speed plus a sixth sense that enabled him to be at the right place at the right time often produced spectacular results. But such freewheeling was not suited to the more formal style of play that Landry favored.

Tunnell quit the Giants early in 1959. Not long afterward, Vince Lombardi, who had left his post as New York offensive coach to become head coach of the Packers, asked Tunnell to join him in Green Bay. There Tunnell played on Western Conference championship teams in 1960 and 1961, and the 1961 team won the NFL title.

Early in 1961, Tunnell came to the realization that his playing days were numbered. When running wind sprints, a favorite trick of Tunnell's was to jump up and touch the crossbar when he ran between the goalposts. The crossbar is ten feet above the ground, but Tunnell had been a jumping center in basketball in high school, so the feat was not too difficult. This time he couldn't reach the crossbar, however. He realized his legs had lost their spring.

When the season was over, Tunnell retired. "I could make tackles until I'm fifty," Tunnell said. "Your body goes but your heart doesn't."

But though Tunnell didn't know it, his second career was just beginning. The Packers and Giants hired him as a talent scout and game scout. He proved invaluable in uncovering Negro talent at smaller colleges. Once he got a tip on a halfback at Philander Smith College. He went to take a look. As a result the Packers landed a premier running back named Elijah Pitts.

In 1963, Tunnell became a full-time scout for the Giants exclusively. But the best was yet to come. Two years later he was made a Giant defensive coach under head coach Allie Sherman. He thus became the first full-time Negro coach in the National Football League.

Early in 1967, Director Dick McCann called Tunnell to tell him that he had been elected to membership in the Pro Football

Hall of Fame. Tunnell was surprised that the honor had come so soon, and he thanked McCann.

"Don't thank me," McCann said. "You did it yourself."

As one of the all-time defensive greats, and the first of his race to become an NFL coach, Emlen Tunnell has written a vibrant chapter in pro football history.

1968

Cliff Battles

In 1931, George Preston Marshall was involved in a vigorous talent search to stock a new pro football franchise he had acquired for the city of Boston and which was to begin play the following year. West Virginia Wesleyan was one of the college teams he had been keeping close tabs on. ("I was always partial to West Virginia teams," he once said.) Wesleyan had a sorry season, losing by big scores to Navy, Georgetown, and a few others. But this didn't dim Marshall's enthusiasm for a 6-foot-1, 195-pound halfback named Cliff Battles. He could blast through the line with a fullback's power, and once in the open field could rip out great chunks of yardage with his speed and deceptiveness. After the season Marshall dispatched his business manager to Wesleyan to negotiate with Battles.

"Sign him," Marshall ordered, "or just keep going south."

Battles, a superb athlete, had also won letters in basketball, baseball, tennis and track. He graduated at the top of his class, made Phi Beta Kappa, and probably would have won a Rhodes Scholarship. But he signed with Marshall instead.

Battles wasted little time in establishing himself as one of the most talented of Marshall's players. He did not play much during his rookie year, but the next year, 1933, he led the league in rushing and captured All Pro honors. He also won All Pro recognition in 1936 and 1937, in which he again was NFL rushing leader.

In 1936, Battles' long gallops were a vital factor in helping Boston to win the Eastern Division championship, which they took by defeating New York in the mud and the rain at the Polo Grounds. Battles contributed an 80-yard touchdown run in the Redskins' 14–0 win.

While the Redskins were champions of the East, they were unhappy ones. Attendance at their home games had been pitiable, and Marshall lost heavily. In disgust and anger, he made plans to move the franchise to Washington, and he switched the title game with Green Bay to the Polo Grounds instead of playing it at Boston's Fenway Park.

The playoff game was a sad one for Battles. Green Bay's deadly Arnie Herber-to-Don Hutson combination struck early in the first period to put the Packers in the lead. Soon after the ensuing kickoff, Battles injured his leg and had to be carried from the field. He watched from the sidelines as the Redskins lost, 21–6.

Cliff's last season as a professional was 1937 and he put on a sensational curtain act. He set an NFL rushing record of 874 yards and became the first man ever to repeat as a rushing leader.

Throughout the season the Redskins dueled the Giants for first place in the division standings. On the final day the two teams met in the payoff game. The week before the contest, Steve Owen, the Giants' coach, made a tactical error. "The Redskins may have won the opener from us," he told the press, "but our boys have really improved. I don't think the Redskins are in the same league with us now."

If that statement did not put the Redskins on the warpath, Owen's All Pro selections did. He failed to include a single Washington player on his team—not Sammy Baugh, the Redskins' sensational rookie quarterback, not Turk Edwards, their demon tackle, not Wayne Millner, their snake-hipped end, not Battles. No one.

Even though the game was being played at New York's Polo Grounds, Marshall had whipped Washington into a frenzy. Special trains, with coaches bearing the names "Sammy Baugh," "Wayne Millner," and "Cliff Battles," brought ten thousand Redskin fans to New York on the morning of the game. They marched up Broadway behind the 55-piece Redskin band that Marshall had garbed in buckskins and long Indian headdresses.

There were 58,285 fans in the stands at game time, the second largest pro football crowd up to that time. They watched Battles in what was his greatest day as a professional. Almost single-handedly he sank the Giants.

The game got off to a dismal start when Battles fumbled, but the Giants were not able to exploit the opportunity, giving up the ball on the Redskins' 17-yard line. Now Battles set to work. Time after time he ripped big holes in the Giant line. Baugh threw two passes to keep the defense honest, and the Redskins drove 83 yards, Battles capping the march with a two-yard plunge into the end zone.

Later the Redskins took over possession of the ball on their own 20. Baugh sent a decoy wide to the right and handed off to Battles who took off down the left sideline. Giant halfback Ward Cuff made a desperate dive at the five-yard line to stop him. Cliff asked for the ball again; Baugh obliged. Battles picked up four yards off right tackle. On the next play he scored.

Baugh passed for the Redskins' third touchdown which gave the team a 21–0 lead at half time. The Giants came back after the intermission to score twice and put themselves within hailing distance. Then the Redskins exploded, scoring four touchdowns in the final twenty-one minutes of play. Battles chipped in with a 76-yard run following an intercepted pass during this outbreak. He was brought down one yard shy of the goal. Washington scored soon after. It was a complete rout, the Redskins winning, 49–14. Battles had gained 165 yards.

In the Washington dressing room after the game, Battles criticized Owen for his remarks a few days earlier. "You can blame what happened on Owen," he said. "He made a typical Bill Terry remark, and we made him pay for it. Maybe next year he'll put a Redskin or two on his All Star team."

The Redskins faced the Chicago Bears for the NFL title. On the opening play from scrimmage, with Washington in possession on their own nine-yard line, Baugh dropped back as if he were going to punt, but crossed up the Bears with a feathery pass to Battles in the flat. Cliff gathered in the ball and sprinted 42 yards. A few plays later he went ten yards on a reverse for the game's first touchdown. After that, Baugh and end Wayne Millner dominated play. The Redskins won, 28–21.

This was Battles' last game. He had played six years for Marshall. His salary each year had been $3,000. Now, as the best running back in pro football, he wanted a substantial raise.

Marshall turned him down. Battles promptly left the pros to take a job as an assistant coach to Lou Little at Columbia.

In 1955, Battles was named to the college football Hall of Fame. He was the first player from a small college to be so honored.

Although Battles played only one season for the Redskins in Washington, that city's fans have never forgotten him. There is a legend that a guide was lecturing a group of visitors in one of the capital buildings, when he pointed to a statue and said, "That's former president William Howard Taft of Ohio—Ohio, that's the home of that great halfback, Cliff Battles."

Cliff Battles Career Rushing Record

Year	Carries	Yards Gained	Average Gain	Touchdowns
1932	148	576	3.9	3
1933	146	737	5.0	4
1934	93	511	5.0	6
1935	67	230	3.4	2
1936	176	614	3.5	6
1937	216	874	4.0	6
Total	846	3,542	4.2	27

Art Donnova

Someone once asked Bob Maisel, sports editor of the Baltimore *Sun,* to name his favorite people in sports. "Casey Stengel is first," Maisel answered, "and right behind him is Art Donovan."

Baltimore sports fans would disagree. Their undisputed No. 1 choice was Donovan, a sweet and good-natured gentleman off the field, but a rugged tiger on.

Round-faced Art Donovan, at 6 feet 3, 265 pounds a mountainous hunk of man, was Baltimore's All League tackle during the club's days of glory in the late 1950's. He was everything a good lineman should be—and then some. He had gargantuan strength in his tremendous forearms and could handle offensive linemen as if he were playing with rag dolls. When he tackled a runner, you knew it was a Donovan tackle by the resounding thud that reverberated through the stadium. He had excellent intuitive powers, too, and was often leaning in the direction the play would go before the ball was snapped. There was no one better at "reading the keys" or closing off the middle.

Besides being one of the best linemen in the business, Donovan was also one of the best-liked. An easy-smiling Irishman, he was universally admired by players, sportswriters and fans. "I doubt anyone will ever have to worry about Donovan," said his coach after Art retired. "He'll do all right financially. In fact, he's got so many friends in this town he'll probably wind up mayor someday."

Art took to Baltimore with the same ardor Baltimore took to him. He married a Baltimore girl and after his retirement settled down there. Donovan was born in New York City—in the Bronx. His family had a rich sports background. His father was the famous Arthur Donovan, the noted boxing referee, who handled more championship bouts than any other man in ring history. His grandfather was Mike Donovan, the former middleweight champion who once gave instructions in boxing to Teddy Roosevelt.

Art was a star lineman at Mount St. Michaels High School in New York. After graduation he went on to Notre Dame, but he stayed only one year. This was 1943 and World War II was in full swing. Art enlisted in the Marine Corps. When he was discharged in 1946, he decided to attend a school closer to home and his choice was Boston College. He was a varsity tackle there for three years, but received little attention. He played on a squad that was to send fourteen players into pro football, including tackle Ernie Stautner, who went on to a glittering career with the Pittsburgh Steelers. Donovan was usually referred to as "the other tackle." He was so overshadowed by Stautner and the others that the highest honor he received as a collegian was being named to an All New England team one year.

Attracted by his size, the Baltimore Colts drafted him in 1950. "The big guys down there will kill you," his father warned him. "You'd better not go." But Arthur went. These were mean days for the Colts, and he believed for a time that the team didn't want him because of a scarcity of uniforms. Although he did make the team, there must have been days he was sorry he did.

The Colts of 1950 set records for losing by big scores and Baltimore fans stayed away in droves. After dropping eleven games, the club dropped right out of the league. It was the first of several disillusioning years for young Mr. Donovan, as he became a sort of gridiron gypsy.

With the Colts defunct, Donovan was redrafted, this time by the Cleveland Browns. Even though he played splendid football in exhibition games, Donovan failed to make the last squad cut, and was traded to the New York Yanks. The Yanks starved to death, too. Donovan's next stop was another loser—the Dallas Texans. The Dallas club was overwhelmed by competition from college games in the area. It folded in 1952, a year in which Donovan suffered a broken leg.

In 1953 Commissioner Bert Bell returned the franchise to Baltimore, with Carroll Rosenbloom the owner. It marked the beginning of a bright new day for both the Colts and Donovan.

Not long after the franchise switch somebody asked Bobby Williams, then with the Chicago Bears, what he knew of the playing talent the Colts had fallen heir to.

"I know they got one helluva ballplayer," Williams said, "a fellow named Donovan. One of our best linemen came back to the huddle last year with blood streaming down his face, and said, 'I just met my match. I gave that guy my best shot, and he just grins and beats hell out of me. He never got mad; he just enjoys tearing you apart.' "

Williams' appraisal was accurate, and soon other people began to notice. In 1954 Donovan was named All League tackle, thus gaining attention that had been denied him in four previous years as a pro and throughout his college career.

Experience had made the difference. "Some fellows don't pick up that extra something until they've been around for awhile," he once said. "I was like that. I just kept growing and 'sawing-wood.' " Donovan said he owed "an awful lot" to two people, Howie Smith, his coach at Mount St. Michaels, and Weeb Ewbank, the Baltimore coach (who later was head coach of the New York Jets). "Weeb is just the greatest," Donovan declared.

The feeling was mutual. "Art is a pro's pro," Ewbank once said. "He's got that one thing every great athlete must have—pride. We grade the performance of every player after every game. Art always asks, 'What's my grade?' He's never satisfied.

He's always trying to improve." Donovan was also named All Pro in 1955, 1956 and 1957.

Almost every fall Donovan battled a weight problem. During one of his early years with the Colts, he hopped onto a drugstore scale and the dial spun so crazily he was unable to get an accurate reading. A freight scale revealed he had reached a beefy 309 pounds. When the Colt management found out about it, they put a clause in his contract calling for a $50 fine for every pound he weighed in excess of 265 when the training season was under way. Art showed up in tip-top shape, well under the designated figure.

Hot dogs were Donovan's great weakness. He preferred them to steaks, and once he is reported to have eaten 28 franks at one sitting. One of Donovan's favorite characters was Chubby Griggs, a teammate during his days with the hapless Dallas team. Griggs once concealed himself under a sideline cape in the dressing room at half time and consumed four hot dogs.

Although he was always a serious-minded competitor, Donovan could see the humor in every situation. Bob Maisel once told about the day the San Francisco 49ers ran a "sucker" play against the Colts, with halfback J. D. Smith winding up with the ball. Everything went according to plan, except that Donovan wasn't faked out. He met Smith right at the line of scrimmage and flattened him. Donovan got up, tugging at his pants in typical fashion, and grinning down at the ballcarrier. J. D. was livid. "Why you baggy-drawered, blankety-blank so-and-so," he howled.

Donovan didn't utter a word, just turned his back and walked over to teammate Gino Marchetti, and with a very hurt tone in his voice said, "Can you imagine that guy calling me baggy-drawered?"

In 1958 and 1959 the Colts won the NFL championship, and Donovan played a major part in the team's success.

The year 1961 was Donovan's last. He was thirty-six, a rather advanced age for an NFL tackle. His teammates needled him good-naturedly. Dick Szymanski told him he was the only player in the league who was "thirty-six going on forty-six," and on another occasion Szymanski informed the team that Donovan was the only man in the league who had a personally autographed picture from Walter Camp.

It was not the needling, but Donovan's own pride that forced his retirement. In 1962, a few weeks after the training season had begun, Donovan, convinced that he could no longer do the job, suddenly announced he was calling it quits.

Later in the year Baltimore fans gave Donovan a "day." Memorial Stadium was jammed to the rafters. Donovan, who had been prevailed upon to wear his uniform for the day, accepted the accolades and gifts with these words: "Up in heaven there is a lady who is happy that the City of Baltimore was so good to her son—a kid from the Bronx." Then he turned and walked slowly from the field. There were more than a few wet eyes. Those who were there say it was one of the most moving receptions ever tendered an athlete.

Elroy (Crazylegs) Hirsch

They called him "Crazylegs" and the name was perfect.

Lean and likable, Elroy Hirsch of the Los Angeles Rams, regarded as pro football's most spectacular receiver of the 1950's, had the speed of a sprinter and the elusiveness of a cake of soap in the bathtub. He could fake, vary his speed, change direction, and, in general, outmaneuver enemy tacklers with a degree of skill that the National Football League has seldom seen. "You've heard about the fellow who zigged when he should have zagged," Ram quarterback Norm van Brocklin once remarked. "Well, Roy also has a 'zog' and a couple of varieties of 'zug.'"

Hirsch had another highly developed skill—catching long passes. Bob Waterfield and Van Brocklin, who alternated as Ram quarterbacks, would aim to overthrow him by a few yards. Roy would explode downfield under a full head of steam, and he always seemed to be able to put on an extra burst of speed if he needed it. The catch itself was another feature of his genius. He did not turn his body, but played the ball like a center fielder, taking it over his head, his arms stretched out in front of him, his long, steely fingers making the grab.

Hirsch was one of the principal reasons that the Rams won the NFL title in 1951. It was a banner year for him. He led the league in passes caught (with 66), and in points scored (with 102).

One of his touchdowns was a 91-yard run against the Chicago Bears. Also that year he and Waterfield or he and Van Brocklin put together touchdown plays that covered 72, 76, 79 and 81 yards, along with another dozen of varying lengths.

Many of Hirsch's attainments are today prominently displayed in the NFL record manual. In 1951, Roy gained an astonishing 1,495 yards, an all-time record. In the 1950–1951 seasons, he caught touchdowns in eleven consecutive games to establish another league mark. The seventeen touchdown passes he caught in one season (1951) are also a record, one that he shares with the great Don Hutson. One September afternoon in 1951, Hirsch grabbed four touchdown passes against the New York Yanks. "He must have a second set of eyes in back of his ears," said New York coach Jimmy Phelan, "or maybe the answer's radar."

Success did not come easily to Hirsch. Up until the time he joined the Rams, his career was filled with perilous swerves and bad moves. He was born in Wausau, Wisconsin, and played his first football as a halfback during his junior year at Wausau High. Hirsch scored 102 points during his senior year to lead the Wisconsin Valley Conference and stir up interest among college coaches. He also lettered in baseball and basketball.

In 1942, Roy enrolled at the University of Wisconsin and skyrocketed to stardom during his sophomore year. He broke loose on a 35-yard touchdown gallop to earn the Badgers a tie with heavily favored Notre Dame. He was even better against Ohio State, the nation's No. 1 ranked team, as he tossed a pass for one touchdown and scored another himself in Wisconsin's 17–7 upset win.

With the United States involved in World War II, Hirsch entered the Marine Corps as an officer candidate, and ended up at Michigan playing football for Fritz Crisler. During his first year at Ann Arbor, Hirsch injured a nerve in his shoulder and was sidelined for two games. Even so, he missed taking the Big Ten scoring title by a margin of only four points. He earned letters in four sports at Michigan—football, of course, track, basketball, and baseball.

Roy's last year of football before joining the pros was with the El Toro Marines. There he was coached by Dick Hanley, for whom he came to have high regard.

Roy was the outstanding performer in the College All Star game in Chicago in 1946. Late in the first quarter he took a pitchout from quarterback Otto Graham, and his elastic limbs carried him 68 yards for a score. In the third quarter he grabbed one of Graham's passes for another touchdown, the play covering 35 yards. The Los Angeles Rams happened to be the victims, 16–0.

Two pro teams held draft rights to Hirsch, the Rams and the Chicago Rockets of the All America Conference. Each offered him the same amount to sign—about $7,000. Roy debated whether to go with the well-established Rams or take a flier with the fledgling Rockets. His friendship with Dick Hanley, who was now the Rockets' coach, was the deciding factor, and he signed with the AAC club. It was a grave mistake.

Hirsch has characterized the three years he spent with the Rockets as "frightful." Hanley left soon after Roy joined the team. Four other coaches came and went as well. The team was woefully undermanned and torn with dissension. In Hirsch's three years with the Rockets, they won only seven games.

Hirsch took more than his share of punishment. He tore muscles in his back and damaged his right knee so severely there were times that he believed he would never run again. The worst came in 1948. In a game against the Browns at Cleveland, Hirsch suffered a fractured skull. He spent weeks in a Chicago hospital, and when he was well enough to try running again, he discovered that his coordination was gone. But he undertook a stern training program of gym exercise and little by little his timing and reaction improved. By the summer of 1949, he felt he could play pro ball again. His contract with the Rockets had run out. The Rams, who still had NFL rights to him, made him an offer and Hirsch quickly accepted.

Hirsch was fitted with a custom-made helmet. It was molded from light, extra-strong plastic, the type used in the manufacture of jet aircraft fuel tanks. Extra padding protected the area around his right ear where he was injured.

The days of glory did not come fast. Hirsch played little during his first year with Los Angeles. He was still rated as a halfback, and often he was flanked wide and used as a decoy on passes. Occasionally he caught one. His statistics for 1949 show 22 receptions and four touchdowns.

The turning point in Hirsch's career came in 1950. Dan Reeves, the Rams' owner, fired coach Clark Shaughnessy, and installed Joe Stydahar as head man. Shaughnessy had rejected end coach Red Hickey's suggestion that Hirsch be switched to end. Stydahar didn't. When right end Bob Boyd was injured during an exhibition game, Hirsch took over his position. His first game was ghastly. The defenses wholly bewildered him and he dropped two passes that settled right in his hands.

Hickey worked diligently with Hirsch throughout the year. The schooling paid dividends. For the season, Hirsch showed 42 receptions for 687 yards and seven touchdowns. Playing the end position on the other side of the line from Hirsch was Tom Fears, the league's leading pass receiver in 1950. But the following year it was Hirsch's turn. He topped Fears' marks and those of almost every other player who ever played end. The record of 1,495 yards gained that Hirsch established that year has never been equaled.

His long experience as a halfback was an important feature in Hirsch's success. Once he had the ball in his possession, he could run with a halfback's elusiveness. He seldom tipped off the defense as to what route he was going to take. Coach Stydahar said that Hirsch had an edge on his contemporaries because he knew how to run with a football under his arm. "There are plenty of players," Stydahar explained, "who can run faster than Hirsch in a straightaway race. But when they carry a football, they lose balance; they slow down. But give Hirsch a football and he speeds up. Don't ask me how. He just does."

A key game during the Rams' championship year of 1951 was a mid-season duel with the Bears. The Rams' record was 4–2 and a loss to Chicago would have put a damper on their title hopes. The Bears scored two quick touchdowns to take a 14–0 lead. On the kickoff following the second score, Los Angeles returned the ball only to their nine-yard line. On first down Waterfield faked a hand-off beautifully, then cocked his arm to throw. Hirsch had taken off with the snap. When Waterfield fired, Roy was close to midfield and still going full throttle, the Chicago defenders now well behind him. Waterfield's pass sailed over Hirsch's head as usual. Roy, without turning, gathered it in and sprinted for the end zone. The play covered 91 yards.

The touchdown inspired the Rams; now they knew that the

game could be won. Five more times they scored that afternoon. The final was Rams 42, Bears 17. The team went on to nail down the Western Conference crown, and then upset the Cleveland Browns for the NFL title.

Hirsch retired as a player following the 1957 season. He stayed on with the Rams in an executive capacity; first, as general manager of the club, and later as assistant to president Dan Reeves.

Elroy (Crazylegs) Hirsch Career Pass Receiving Record

ALL AMERICA CONFERENCE

Year	Passes Received	Yards	Average	Touchdowns
1946	27	347	12.9	3
1947	10	282	28.2	3
1948	7	101	14.4	1
Total	44	730	16.6	7

NATIONAL FOOTBALL LEAGUE

Year	Passes Received	Yards	Average	Touchdowns
1949	22	326	14.8	4
1950	42	687	16.4	7
1951	66*	1,495*	22.7*	17*
1952	25	590	23.6	4
1953	61	941	15.4	4
1954	35	720	20.6	3
1955	25	460	18.4	2
1956	35	603	17.2	6
1957	32	477	14.9	6
Total	343	6,299	18.4	53

* *Outstanding Performance.*

Wayne Millner

Wayne Millner of the Washington Redskins was the last of professional football's outstanding two-way ends. When he wasn't catching Sammy Baugh's passes, he was blocking for him.

Millner, an All American at Notre Dame in 1935, was known for his catlike reflexes and sure hands. He was also renowned as a "money player," at his best when the stakes were the highest and the pressure the greatest.

The 1937 NFL championship game against the Bears, played at the end of Millner's sophomore season with the Redskins, is a case in point. In the third quarter he took a pass from Sammy Baugh and galloped 53 yards for a touchdown that tied the game at 14–14. In the fourth period the Bears moved to a 21–14 advantage, but Millner grabbed another one of Baugh's tosses and scored a second time. This play covered 78 yards. The winning touchdown came late in the game on a Baugh pass to Ed Justice. Millner was used as a decoy. In total, Wayne took down eleven passes that day, a playoff record at the time.

In the 1945 championship game against the Cleveland Rams, Millner was part of a freak play that led to a change in the playing rules. In the first period he got loose for what seemed a sure touchdown reception. Baugh, throwing from the Redskins' end zone, let fire. But the ball never reached Wayne. It struck the crossbar, rebounded into the end zone, and was scored as a safety against Washington. Those two points proved to be the winning margin in the Rams' 15–14 triumph. The next year the rules were changed; forward passes were made incomplete upon striking either teams' goalposts.

Millner's career record shows 124 receptions for 1,578 yards and thirteen touchdowns. The statistics, however, tell nothing of Millner's great value as a blocker.

His teammate Cliff Battles, the Redskins' splendid broken-field runner of the 1930's, testified as to Millner's talent when it came to blocking. Said Battles, "I always knew if I could get out into the open, Wayne would be there to throw a block for me. He would swing over from the weak side after making his initial block and hit a defensive back. Wayne's blocks determined whether or not I would get away for a long run."

Millner was in the Redskin lineup in 1940 when the team was massacred by the Chicago Bears, 73–0, in the championship playoff. The Bears were as perfect that day as a team can be. A few weeks after the game, a Chicago newspaperman asked Wayne what he thought the outcome might have been if Charlie Malone hadn't dropped one of Baugh's passes in the end zone early in the game. "Hell," said Millner, "the score would have been 73–6."

Wayne was born in 1913 in Roxbury, Massachusetts. He was an All State fullback when attending high school in Salem, Massachusetts. He first won national recognition at Notre Dame, where he was a varsity star at end for three seasons. In 1935 he caught the winning touchdown pass in Notre Dame's conquest of Ohio State, 18–13, one of the most memorable college games of all time.

After the 1941 season, Wayne spent the next three and one-half years in the U. S. Navy. He was discharged in time to take part in the Redskins' championship game in 1945. That was his last season as a player.

Wayne then became an assistant coach at Catholic University in Washington, D.C., and later an assistant at the University of Maryland. In professional football he coached for the Baltimore Colts and Philadelphia Eagles. He served as head coach of the Philadelphia team during part of the 1951 season. In 1952, with the Eagles losing and the pressure mounting, Wayne resigned. Today Millner lives in Arlington, Virginia, and is the public relations director for an automobile agency.

Had Millner played with another team, he might have gotten many more headlines. But at Washington his standout performances were often overshadowed by those of the great Sammy Baugh. And there was another problem. So often did he deliver under pressure that the press and the fans came to take his clutch performances for granted.

Wayne Millner Career Pass Receiving Record

Year	Passes Received	Yards	Average	Touchdowns
1936	18	211	10.7	–
1937	14	216	15.4	3
1938	18	232	12.9	1
1939	19	294	15.5	4
1940	22	233	10.6	3
1941	20	262	13.1	–
1945	13	130	10.0	2
Total	124	1,578	12.9	13

Marion Motley

Coach Paul Brown's instructions to Marion Motley, his quick-starting, pile-driving fullback, were clear and concise. "Just run right at them and over them," Brown said. Motley did—and with such unqualified success he became an essential element in the Cleveland Browns' many years of greatness which began in 1946.

A basic piece of Brown's strategy was the trap play. Quarterback Otto Graham would take the snap, spin, and then drop back as if to pass. From his post at fullback, Motley would take Graham's hand-off, and with his tremendous speed and great bulk (he weighed 235) blast through the hole created by the "trapped" defensive linemen. Once in the secondary, Motley was not supposed to get fancy, but simply roar ahead. In one of Motley's first games with the Browns, Elroy Hirsch, then a safetyman for the Chicago Rockets, met Motley head on. Hirsch never knew what hit him. Motley trampled him into the ground and took off on a long touchdown run.

Motley played his high school football at Canton's McKinley High School. He played guard during his junior year, but also some halfback and end. As a senior he played halfback almost exclusively and was one of the leading runners in the state. During Motley's three years of varsity football at McKinley High, the Bulldogs lost only three games, these to archrival Massillon High. The coach at Massillon was a fellow by the name of Paul Brown. After Motley enrolled at the University of Nevada, Brown kept a watchful eye on him.

There was plenty to watch. Motley, the team captain, smashed the university's running records, winning All America honors galore.

During World War II, Brown became head coach of the Great Lakes Naval Training Center team. He managed to snare Motley as one of his stars. The big fullback's bursts up the middle were a key feature in Great Lakes' 39–7 upset of heavily favored Notre Dame in 1945. Although power was Motley's stock in trade, he was also noted for his explosive speed. At Great Lakes he could outleg Grover Klemmer, then the world's record holder on the 440-yard dash, at distances of up to 75 yards. When Paul Brown started putting the Cleveland Browns together in 1946, Motley was one of the first players he signed to a contract.

Once they were together in the Browns' backfield, Motley and Graham complemented one another perfectly. The threat of Motley's lightning takeoffs prevented the defense from concentrating too heavily on Otto, while Graham's masterly passing worked to loosen up the defenses for Marion. The Browns won 47 games, lost four, and tied three in the four years that the AAC was in existence. They never failed to win the league championship.

In 1950 the Browns entered the National Football League. There they found the competition a bit stiffer. The team dropped two of its first six games in NFL play, but a late-in-the-season surge carried them to the Eastern Conference crown and the NFL title. During the team's brief slump, Brown paid tribute to Motley. "He was the one," the coach declared, "who carried us along and kept us winning when our passing was spotty."

The Browns took the Eastern Conference crown in 1952, and the conference title again and the NFL championship in 1953, Motley's last season with the club. Injuries slowed him that year and a bad knee kept him on the bench throughout 1954. He retired after a comeback attempt with the Pittsburgh Steelers in 1955.

Motley led the Browns in rushing in six of his eight years. He carried the ball 826 times and gained 4,712 yards, an average of 5.70 yards per carry. Yet Motley feels he could have done even better. "The trap was a fantastic play, but I was seldom sent outside," he once told Chuck Heaton of the Cleveland *Plain Dealer* and a Hall of Fame selector. "I remember that I once asked Paul Brown to give me a flip play so I could get the ball with the opposition scattered, but he said the play wasn't designed for me.

"There's no telling how much yardage I might have made if I ran as much as some backs do now."

Three years after Motley retired as a player, Jimmy Brown's magnificent career began. Brown eventually eclipsed most of the records that Marion had set. However, one record Motley established still remains on the books. On October 29, 1950, he averaged 17.09 yards per carry (11 carries; 188 total yards) in a game against the Pittsburgh Steelers. The figure remains a league high.

Motley refuses to be drawn into any discussion comparing his skills and accomplishments with those of Jimmy Brown. He points out, however, that he was an efficient blocker. Indeed, he was an almost infallible bodyguard to Otto Graham. Seldom did a pass rush get to the Browns' quarterback. Blocking was always a controversial aspect of Jimmy Brown's career.

During the late 1960's, Motley again teamed up with Graham. He served the Graham-coached Washington Redskins as a part-time scout. Marion was also a full-time participant in the Neighborhood Youth Corps in Cleveland.

Besides his prowess as a running or blocking back, Motley's career is significant for one other reason—a social reason, not an athletic one. Although the All America Conference had no written rule stating that Negro players should be excluded from rosters, there were none listed on any of the team rosters in 1946 when the players began reporting to training camp; that is, except for the roster of the Cleveland Browns. The Browns had Motley and also Bill Willis, an All American from Ohio State. These two were the only Negro players in the All America Conference during its first season, and they opened the way for the hundreds of others of their race who were to achieve preeminence in the sport.

Marion Motley Career Rushing Record

ALL AMERICA CONFERENCE				
Year	Carries	Yards Gained	Average Gain	Touchdowns
1946	73	601	8.23	6
1947	146	889	6.09	10
1948	157	964	6.14	7
1949	113	570	5.04	8
Total	489	3,024	6.37	31

NATIONAL FOOTBALL LEAGUE

Year	Carries	Yards Gained	Average Gain	Touchdowns
1950	140	810	5.80	4
1951	61	273	4.48	1
1952	104	444	4.27	3
1953	32	161	5.00	0
Total	337	1,688	4.88	8

Charley Trippi

Charley Trippi, a 6-foot, 190-pound halfback, toiled for eight years in the backfield of the Chicago (now St. Louis) Cardinals, but undoubtedly he nailed down his Hall of Fame selection during 1947, his rookie season, when he led the Big Red to the Western Division title and a blazing win in the NFL title play-off.

The championship game was played in icy Comiskey Park; the Philadelphia Eagles were the opposition. Trippi opened the scoring in the first period by darting off tackle on a quick opener and breaking loose for 44 yards and a touchdown. In the third period he returned a punt 75 yards for a second score. Elmer Angsman also scored twice for the Cards, as they captured their first—and only—league championship, 28–21.

Trippi was no less than spectacular that day, a fact the NFL record manual affirms. He carried the ball fourteen times and gained 206 yards to establish a title game high. On his two punt returns, he gained 102 yards, another record.

Jim Thorpe once called Trippi the finest player he had ever seen. He may have watched him perform in the 1947 title game. Or it may have been that Big Jim was influenced by Trippi's style of play. Trippi, like Thorpe, could do it all—run, pass, kick and receive.

Trippi was born in Pittston, Pennsylvania, in 1923. He tried out for tackle when he went to high school but his coach switched him to the backfield when he saw how versatile he was.

Since Charley weighed only 160 pounds when he graduated, colleges did not exactly clamor for his services. He had to go looking. Beginning in Maryland, he worked his way down the Eastern seaboard. He had about run out of states when Georgia agreed to take him. There he was to carve out a career of legendary proportions.

As a sophomore tailback in Georgia's single wing, Trippi made such a vivid impression on coach Wally Butts that he switched his All America tailback, Frankie Sinkwich, to fullback to make room for Charley in the starting lineup. Coach Butts never claimed much credit for Trippi's development. "He doesn't need to be shown much," Butts once said. "Just give him the football and he'll do the rest. Our main trouble is trying to find someone fast enough to block for him."

Trippi played in the 1942 Rose Bowl as a sophomore. Then came three years with the all-star Third Air Force team in Tampa, Florida. He returned to Georgia in the middle of the 1945 season, and he probably wished he hadn't. The Bulldogs suffered a 35–0 rout at the hands of LSU in Trippi's first game. But both he and the Bulldogs recovered neatly and ended the season in winning form. The next year Trippi steered Georgia to its first and only undefeated season and to a conquest of North Carolina in the Sugar Bowl. Trippi played in an unprecedented five All Star games, two as a collegian, two while in the Air Corps, and once as a member of the Cardinals.

Charley graduated from Georgia in 1947, a propitious time. The NFL was locked in a fierce struggle with the All America Conference, and triple-threat backs like Mr. Trippi were in the driver's seat when it came to contract negotiations. Both Dan Topping's AAC New York Yankees and Charlie Bidwill's Chicago Cardinals sought him. Trippi signed with the Cards, and it was a wise move. The AAC folded two years later.

Trippi was the final building block in the Cards' "dream backfield" assembled by Bidwell. It may have been a dream to Bidwill, but it was a nightmare to the rest of the National Football League. Trippi and Marshall Goldberg of Pittsburgh were the halfbacks; Pat Harder of Wisconsin was at fullback, and Paul Christman from Missouri was at quarterback. They were a rugged and hard-hitting foursome, each man well seasoned in blocking and tackling. They roared to a 9-3 record, good enough to win the Western Division title, and then came the victory over Philadelphia in the championship game.

The Cards continued their winning ways in 1948; in fact, they devastated the opposition. They turned back Green Bay, 42–7, Detroit, 56–20, and New York, 63–35, and lost only one game. Again they won the Western Division crown. But bad fortune struck the team on the day of the championship game against the Eagles. The field was covered with snow and a fierce wind whipped the players. Trippi was held to a mere 26 yards in nine carries. The game turned on a break—a last-period fumble—and Philadelphia won, 7–0.

The Cardinals went downhill after that. Seldom were they in contention, and there were even some last-place finishes.

Trippi rolled up a helmetful of records in his years with the Cards. He rushed for a total of 3,506 yards with 687 carries, good for a 5.1-yard average; he caught 130 passes for 1,321 yards; he completed 205 of 434 passes for 2,547 yards; he punted 196 times for a 40.4-yard average; he returned 63 punts for 864 yards, and 66 kickoffs for 1,457 yards; he scored 37 touchdowns. Jimmy Conzelman, his coach, said of him, "Trippi is the greatest player I coached in seventeen years."

Trippi also played professional baseball. He starred with the Atlanta Crackers of the Southern Association, batting .334. Later he coached baseball for two years at the University of Georgia.

Trippi's career in pro football came to an end in 1955 following a violent collision with John Henry Johnson of the San Francisco 49ers. Charley was unconscious for hours, and surgery was necessary. Later plastic surgery was required.

After his retirement as a player, Trippi was an assistant coach at Georgia and with the Cardinals. He gave up coaching in 1966 to devote full time to his real estate business in Athens, Georgia.

Trippi is also a member of the Georgia State Hall of Fame and the National Collegiate Hall of Fame. In 1968, when he was told that he had been named to the Pro Football Hall of Fame, Trippi took the news with mixed emotions. While he deeply appreciated the honor, it did not bring him unbounded joy. "There's nothing left to look forward to," he said, "and the realization hit me when I heard the news. There's nothing more that I can get out of football, a game that's given me so much."

Charley Trippi Career Passing Records

Year	Attempts	Completions	Pct.	Yards	Touchdowns	Interceptions
1947	2	1	50.0	49	0	1
1948	8	4	50.0	118	1	0
1949	2	0	00.0	0	0	0
1950	3	1	33.3	19	0	0
1951	191	88	46.1	1,191	8	13
1952	181	84	46.4	890	5	13
1953	34	20	58.8	195	2	1
1954	13	7	53.8	85	0	3
Total	434	205	47.2	2,547	16	31

Charley Trippi Career Rushing Records

Year	Carries	Yards	Average Gain	Touchdowns
1947	83	401	4.8	2
1948	128	690	5.4*	6
1949	112	553	4.9	2
1950	99	426	4.3	3
1951	78	501	6.4	4
1952	72	350	4.9	4
1953	97	433	4.5	0
1954	18	152	8.4	1
Total	687	3,506	5.1	22

Outstanding Performance.

Alex Wojciechowicz

Earl (Greasy) Neale, who coached the Philadelphia Eagles from 1941 to 1950, is generally credited as the man who first developed a strategy that could throttle down the effectiveness of the T formation. Neale's defense was based on a 7–4 alignment, with the linebackers stationed a step or two behind the line of scrimmage and under instructions to "chug" the ends, delay their downfield progress by whatever means necessary.

One of Neale's linebackers was a 240-pound bundle of dynamite named Alexander Wojciechowicz. He was acknowledged as the unrivaled master in the art of chugging. One observer described Wojie as "one thousand elbows put together without a plan." And Allie Sherman, then an assistant coach for the Eagles, commented that Wojie's technique "involved hands and feet and arms and maybe even fingernails, plus some conversation."

When Wojciechowicz joined Neale's Eagles in 1945, he was no youngster; he was thirty-one. He had completed eight years with the Detroit Lions, where, playing center, he had established himself as one of the most awesome blockers and tacklers in NFL history.

Wojciechowicz first came to national attention as a two-time All American at Fordham University, a member of one of college football's most magnificent defensive lines, the "Seven Blocks of Granite," or as sportswriter Tim Cohane once called them, "the Seven Samsons." Wojie, the center, played shoulder-to-shoulder with a guard named Vince Lombardi. During Wojie's days at Fordham, the Rams were a national powerhouse and a perennial participant in post-season bowl games.

Wojie was born in South River, New Jersey, in 1915. He was All State in football and baseball at South River High before entering Fordham.

The Detroit Lions made Wojie their No. 1 draft choice in 1938. It was the start of a career that was to last as many years as there are letters in his name—thirteen. Unfortunately for Wojciechowicz, the Lions were on a downhill slide when he joined the club. They struck bottom in 1942, failing to win a single game. Other years were only slightly better.

Fewer than a dozen men had the ability plus the durability to survive in the NFL as long as Wojie. And there was no platooning in Wojie's days with the Lions; he was a sixty-minute-a-game performer. In 1942 he was operated on for the removal of bone chips from his shoulder. Even that didn't sideline him for long. He returned to action soon afterward, even though his upper body was wrapped in so much bandage and tape he looked like a mummy.

Greasy Neale acquired Wojie from the Lions on waivers in 1946. He decided to use him only on defense and as a linebacker.

Wojie, along with Joe Muha, quickly became a key operative in the novel defense that Neale installed. It helped Philadelphia win a division title in 1947, and both the division title and national championship in 1948 and 1949. Wojie retired in 1950.

Today Wojciechowicz lives in Fairhaven, New Jersey. He is employed by the State of New Jersey Real Estate Department. He served, with Steve Van Buren, as co-coach of the Newark team in the Atlantic Coast Football League.

During his college days at Fordham, Wojciechowicz once consulted coach Jim Crowley about changing his name. He wanted to shorten it to Wojack.

"Don't do that," Crowley advised. "Keep your name as it is and you'll always be remembered."

Crowley's advice wasn't particularly well founded. Wojie never needed a distinctive name; no one who ever saw him play will forget him.